ALLIED SMALL ARMS OF WORLD WAR ONE

John Walter

The Crowood Press

First published in 2000 by
The Crowood Press Ltd
Ramsbury, Marlborough
Wiltshire SN8 2HR

British Library Cataloguing-in-Publication Data
A catalogue record for this book is available from the
British Library.

ISBN 1 86126 123 3

Acknowledgements

I must thank the many people who, over the years,
have encouraged my interest in the weapons of the
First World War. I am particularly keen to thank Ian
Hogg, who supplied many photographs and then
completed this book when circumstances forced me to
relinquish control. I am also grateful for the support of
Herbert Woodend, custodian of the Pattern Room
Collection now held in the King's Meadow factory of
Royal Ordnance plc in Nottingham; David Penn,
Keeper of Exhibits, Imperial War Museum, London;
Christian Cranmer of Firepower International,
South Godstone, Surrey; and Bernie Rolff in Germany.

To ARW and ADW with love.

John Walter
Hove, 2000

Designed and typeset by Focus Publishing,
The Courtyard, 26 London Road,
Sevenoaks, Kent TN13 1AP

Printed and bound in Great Britain by Antony Rowe,
Chippenham

Contents

Introduction

My personal fascination with World War One arises from the participation of both grandfathers in the war in the trenches. My paternal grandfather, Clarence Walter (1883–1956), was a professional soldier, a veteran of the Boer War who rejoined the Colours in 1914 as a serjeant major to gain a battlefield commission and the Military Cross for gallantry in 1917 at 'Third Ypres'(Passchendaele). My maternal grandfather, John Douglas (1883–1938), was altogether different: by profession a schoolmaster, and by all accounts a very gentle man, he was conscripted into the Royal Artillery and passed at least part of the war in the trenches poring over a correspondence course in psychology!

As a boy, I remember seeing a photograph of my paternal grandfather with his bothers and a cousin, together with a newspaper clipping drawing attention to the fact that all five had survived World War One. My grandfather had been seriously wounded in 1917, crawling agonizingly 'towards the lines' (only to be captured by the Germans), and one of his brothers had been slightly wounded, but the

Pre-war confidence pervades this view of four British soldiers and their dog. The rifles are early-model SMLE, with charger-guides on the bolt heads. Author's collection.

others had escaped more or less unscathed. However, even then I knew that the overall casualty figures had been terrible, and that the survival of my family intact meant that, to balance the scales, other families could have lost all their sons. I still cannot comprehend how the slaughter was allowed to continue for so long, or indeed, how so many high-ranking officers could be so stupid (or perhaps, so hidebound by tradition) to send waves of men at walking pace into the mouths of well sited Maxim machine-guns.

Consequently, I also find it difficult to support attempts to let today's children 'Experience Grandpa's Life in the Trenches': are they really to endure the maelstrom of mud, blood and body parts, gas gangrene and trench foot? The recollections of those who were there lay bare the horror of it all so much more eloquently: the books compiled by Lyn MacDonald, for example, reflect emotions ranging from jingoistic optimism to the blackest despair imaginable.

Some time ago I found a handwritten draft of a war poem – I call it 'Passchendaele'– among unbound copies of *The War Illustrated* rescued from a house-clearance. I have no idea who wrote it, or when, but it fits my own view of World War One perfectly.

Sunrise calls to mind
so much that was won and lost, those troubled years afar.
And how fearless, jaunty strides to war became
a heartless journey of despair.

Lifting shadows etch
the furtive, snaking trench-trace, where once in nightmare dreams
And pervading search of reason, good sense fell
to bullet, bomb and witless scheme.

Furrows cut so straight
deck fields of death, where a whistle's icy blast sent stout hearts
to fall so soon and swift, to a rifle-crack
or machine-gun bark.

Wild flowers now mark
the criss-cross paths of No Man's Land, gaunt wire-barbed scars seared
russet-hue by earth and blood, where autumn rain
so soon turned mud to poisoned mere.

Dew-ponds cloak the ground
deep-holed in the flash of explosive mine and shell,
For gas to linger, searing lungs, burning eyes,
and turning lives to blinded hell.

Ash and beech, now strong,
crown ridges where once men sought brief mastery
amongst blasted stumps, until blown in turn to dust
by counter-thrust and battery.

Birds wheel in blue skies
where steel-eyed aeronauts, winged chariots gay and bright,
once soared high in victory, or at length fell
fiery, the charnel-field to blight.

A hawthorn thicket
shrouds the hollow where red-crossed men in bloodied aprons fought
so hard to save shell-sliced flesh and shattered bone
while all around life ebbed to naught.

If disbelieving
that such untold horror could ever lie serenely,
Look a hill away. Where wood-cross sentinels address your doubts so silently
As if on parade.
Asking only eternal recollection of the pain
and loss in their thousand-fold sacrifice,
that betrays war's gain

John Walter, Hove, 2000

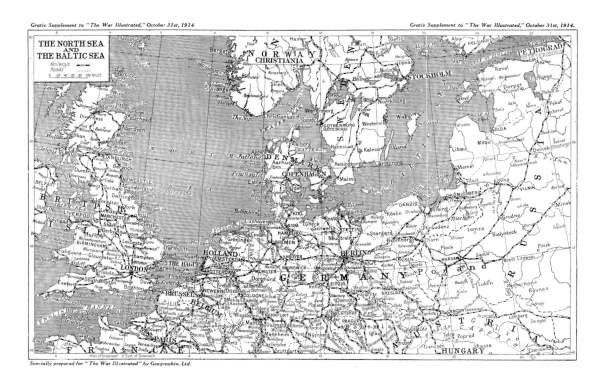

The 'War Map of Western Europe', from a supplement given away with The War Illustrated *on 31 October 1914.*

CONTENT

Although the tripartite format of this book follows that of its companion, *Central Powers' Small Arms of World War One* (1999), a few changes have been made to keep the text to much the same length. Most significantly, the detailed descriptions of construction and operation have been omitted, owing to the far greater diversity of Allied weapons. Additional information may be readily obtained from some of the books listed in the Bibliography.

WORLD WAR ONE

The complexity of fighting that spread over more than four years cannot easily be reduced to a one-page summary, and readers are directed to works such as Liddell Hart's classic *History of the First World War* (Cassell & Co., 1970) or John Keegan's *The First World War* (Hutchinson, 1998) for more comprehensive coverage. Other studies, such as Richard Holmes' eminently readable *The Western Front* (1999), are listed in the Bibliography.

The catalyst of war was the assassination in Sarajevo of the heir to the Austro-Hungarian empire and his wife, Archduke Franz Ferdinand and Sophie von Hohenberg. Their attacker – a Bosnian patriot named Gavrilo Princip – was part of a group seeking to return to Slavic dominance the province of Bosnia-Herzogovina, which had been annexed by Austria-Hungary in 1908. His simple act of defiance was to change the map of Europe for all time.

Austria-Hungary declared war on Serbia on 28

July 1914, and others, tied either by ethnic bonds or treaties of friendship, had soon joined the fray; thus Germany declared war on Russia on 1 August, then on France on 3 August. Britain began war with Germany on 4 August, goaded by the invasion of Belgium – but interestingly, did not officially commence hostilities with Austria-Hungary until eight days later.

Fighting along the frontier between France and Belgium reputedly cost the French 250,000 dead. It has been said that one in ten of the entire French officer-class fell in this opening phase of the war, though losses of such magnitude were never admitted officially. In the east, the battle of Gumbinnen, a minor German defeat at the hands of the Russians, was followed by the first great set-piece confrontation of the war: Tannenberg (26–30 August 1914), which reversed initial Russian progress. The battles of the Masurian Lakes, unreasonably costly to both sides, subsequently ejected the Tsar's men from East Prussia.

The opening phases of the war in the west found the French attempting to stem the German tide, aided by the remnants of the Belgian army and the small British Expeditionary Force (BEF). The British suffered heavily at the battles of Le Cateau and Mons – even though the professionalism of the 'Old Contemptibles' left an indelible impression on their enemies – and were forced into precipitate retreat. By the first days of September, the French government had even withdrawn from Paris to Bordeaux, fearing the worst, although battles fought along the Marne and Aisne rivers stopped the immediate German threat to the French capital city.

A 'Race to the Sea', with each army endeavouring to outflank its rival, allowed the Germans to seize Ostend, but not the other Channel ports so vital to Anglo-French communications: Calais, Boulogne and Dunkirk. The Yser-Lys defensive line had been secured by flooding the low-lying countryside between Nieuport and Dixmunde, so most of the major engagements in the autumn of 1914 took place around Ypres. There, fighting from 18 October to 11 November cost the British

50,000 men, including a large contingent of surviving Old Contemptibles, for nothing in return but stalemate. Casualties mounted on both sides, with few territorial gains, yet the Ypres salient – so often threatened but never breached – became an immutable symbol of Allied resistance to set alongside the Angel of Mons and the 'Leaning Virgin' on the spire of the Albert basilica.

A German victory at the battle of Lodz (18–25 November 1914) forced the Russians to withdraw, preferring to confront the weaker Austro-Hungarian forces in Galicia. Austrians and Russians fought each other to a standstill at Cracow (16 November–2 December), and the Eastern Front also gradually stagnated. At sea, a minor British triumph at the battle of Heligoland Bight (28 August) was followed firstly by

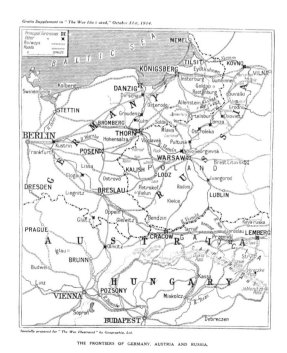

THE FRONTIERS OF GERMANY, AUSTRIA AND RUSSIA.

'The Frontiers of Germany, Austria and Prussia', from a supplement given away with the The War Illustrated *on 31 October 1914.*

Cheerful British soldiers pose with German war trophies, principally helmets and a selection of bayonets. This particular postcard is marked 'New Cross S.E. [London], 11. 15. PM, 24 Sep 16'. Author's collection.

Coronel, a maritime disaster off the Chilean coast on 1 November, and then by retribution in the form of the battle of the Falkland Islands (8 December 1914), where the Royal Navy destroyed Admiral von Spee's Kreuzergeschwader once and for all.

The New Year began as its predecessor had ended, with the participants grid-locked in northern France and a comparable lack of progress in the east. The Germans began a submarine blockade of Britain on 18 February, hoping to wreck the British economy by stifling maritime trade, but the sinking of the Cunard steamship *Lusitania* (7 May) attracted far more attention, with the loss of nearly 1,200 lives and an unexpected opportunity to make anti-German propaganda.

On land, the battles of Neuve Chapelle (March), 'Second Ypres'(April–May) and Loos (September–October) did little than swell the ever-escalating casualty rate; the fighting around Ypres alone cost the British Army nearly 60,000 men. Sir John French was replaced as commander-in-chief of the British forces by General Sir Douglas Haig, and the slaughter continued apace. For instance, an Allied attack on the Dardanelles was begun on 19 February 1915, in the hope of preventing combined Germano-Turkish forces from blockading the Black Sea supply route from the Mediterranean to Russia. But the attack was unsuccessful, and the landing of men at Gallipoli (25 April 1915 onwards) was a disaster. Moreover, although more than 120,000 combatants were withdrawn in January 1916 with unparalleled precision, the earlier slaughter of thousands of ANZAC troops created a long-lasting rift between Britain and Australia.

On 23 May 1915, the Italians declared war on their one-time ally Austria-Hungary, hoping to gain additional territory in the Alps and extend

Latin domination along the eastern coast of the Adriatic Sea. Most of the fighting was costly and ineffective, until insignificant Italian gains from eleven battles along the Isonzo river were lost after a twelfth battle (better known as 'Caporetto') that began on 24 October 1917. Within a few weeks, German and Austrian forces had pushed the Italians back as far as the Piave river.

The year 1916 was remarkable chiefly for the prodigious slaughter endured by both sides; this was centred on Verdun, where, according to General Von Falkenhayn, German ambition was simply to 'bleed France dry'. The intensity of the fighting that began on 21 February rarely subsided for three hundred days, but Verdun held out – though the casualties (350,000–400,000 apiece) traumatized the French army and so disillusioned the Germans that they lost their last real chance of decisive victory.

The ill-fated British attacks on the Somme, where more men fell on 1 July 1916 than in Wellington's entire Peninsular Campaign, paled by comparison with Verdun. Yet it was said that the rumble of the artillery barrage preceding the Somme attacks could be heard in far-off London, and the first tanks had been used in the British sector on 15 September. The battle subsequently became better known for carnage: casualties have been estimated as 203,000 Frenchmen, 420,000 Britons and about 437,500 Germans.

The Brusilov offensive of June–October 1916 gave the Russians unexpected respite from a series of setbacks on the Eastern Front, military and political, large and small. Unfortunately, reinforced by German forces, the Austro-Hungarians gradually forced the Russians back the way they had come. Territory-hungry Romania declared war on the Central Powers in 1916, inspired by Brusilov's successes, but was speedily overrun; German and Austro-Hungarian forces took the capital, Bucharest, on 6 December and had soon reached the Black Sea coast.

The principal maritime action of World War One, the battle of Jutland, fought throughout the night and morning of 31 May/1 June, was inconclusive; the British suffered the greater losses, but gained an important strategic victory that all but bottled up the German High Seas Fleet in Jade Bay for the remainder of the war. German submarines, however, were beginning to take a deadly toll of British and Allied merchantmen.

A policy of unrestricted submarine warfare was announced on 17 January 1917 – but just as the U-boat campaign posed a real threat to the ability of Britain to feed the British people; just as ships were being sunk faster than shipyards could replace them; and just as a major victory beckoned, the Germans rashly sank American ships. Incensed, the USA broke off diplomatic relations with Germany on 3 February 1917, and declared war on 6 April. The introduction in May 1917 of a convoy system, escorting packs of mechantmen with speedy warships, had an immediate beneficial effect. Losses slowed, and the British economy steadied perceptibly.

On land, set-piece battles still claimed Allied lives by the thousand, during 'Second Aisne' (April–May 1917), Arras (April–May), Messines (June), and 'Third Ypres' or Passchendaele (July–November). Fighting on the Aisne left the French army teetering on the brink of mutiny, while the British lost 159,000 men at Arras and more than 400,000 in Passchendaele.

It is now hard to comprehend the magnitude of such slaughter, and how, indeed, public opinion ever allowed the war to continue. Bravery and fortitude undoubtedly added many a regimental battle honour, but the use of immense mines to blow Messines Ridge skywards – the explosions were heard clearly in London – and the advent of mustard gas, used for the first time by the Germans in Passchendaele, were far less savoury.

Serious political implications lay in a mutiny of Russian troops on 10 March 1917, which precipitated the abdication of Tsar Nikolai II. Although the so-called 'Kerensky Offensive' (July 1917) made short-term territorial gains, thereby restoring morale, the arrival of German reinforcements had soon thrust the Russians back, with losses that had become too great for the rank-and-file to bear. Descent into anarchy brought the October Revolution, heralded with a single blank shot from the cruiser *Avrora* and the storming of the Winter Palace in Petrograd. Fighting on the Eastern Front spluttered to a halt, and an agreement concluded on 3 March 1918 between Bolshevik Russia and Germany – the Treaty of Brest-Litovsk – finally brought it to an end.

The collapse of Russia released more than enough troops to allow the German High Command to attack on the Western Front, the spring offensive encompassing thrusts from Operation Michael (March–April 1918) to Operation Marne-Rheims (July 1918). The last great challenge to Allied supremacy in the West mustered enough strength to threaten Paris, shelling the city with a unique long-range gun, and to menace the Channel ports until a crucial lack of reserve manpower and shortages of ordnance material forced them back. Thereafter, Allied offensives pressed the Germans armies into defensive positions, particularly after the battle of Amiens (August 1918) – where the British fielded more than four hundred tanks – and by the thrusts of the American Expeditionary Force. Not only did the US Army gain its first battle honours on European soil at places such as Belleau Wood, it also expelled German troops who had been defending the Saint-Mihiel salient since the first year of war.

With spirits finally broken, many German soldiers deserted as the summer of 1918 ran its course; mutiny among the sailors of the High Seas Fleet, berthed in Kiel harbour, then led to insurrection in the 'Free Towns' of Bremen and Hamburg, and this spread nationwide. Kaiser Wilhelm II abdicated on 9 November, fleeing to neutral Holland, and an Armistice finally took hold on the battle-ravaged Western Front at 11am on 11 November 1918.

Europe would never be the same again. Huge numbers had been mustered under arms, and the losses had been terrible. Figures published by the Ministry of Information in July 1919 noted that the British armed forces, which had totalled 733,514 on 1 August 1914 (including just 253,045 'regulars'), had been enlarged so greatly that a suspiciously precise 8,689,467 British, Empire and Dominion men had served by the time the Armistice had been signed. More than 5 million of them had at some time been on the Western Front, peaking at 2.046 million at any one time. The costs had also been high. The 1919 figures returned deaths as 724,407, wounded as 2,064,451, and missing as 270,117, but subsequent analysis raised the fatality total to nearer a million by including 'missing, presumed dead'. The other Allies suffered, too. Although losses are still difficult to gauge accurately, is seems that French dead reached 1.39 million, compared with 1.2 million Austro-Hungarians, 1.7 million Russians and 1.85 million Germans.

SMALL ARMS IN WORLD WAR ONE

And what of the weaponry with which millions had fought and died? The ordnance history of each country differed in detail, but the underlying problems were often common. No pundit had expected the war to last as long as a year when fighting had started in 1914; had four-year projections been offered, derision would have been the understandable response. Yet the economies of many major powers, superficially strong but customarily underpinned with inefficiency and compromise, were now asked to supply unimaginably large quantities of weapons and ammunition in support of vast armies.

The British shipbuilding industry, for example, was asked to build merchantmen faster than the German submarines could sink them; and the munitions industry, comparatively feeble prior to 1914, was asked to replace shells which were being expended in their millions.

Even the simplest military firearm was a complex manufacturing proposition. A 'Rifle, Short, Magazine, Lee-Enfield, Mark III', for example, contained more than a hundred parts. Though some were simple, such as screws and

British soldiers celebrate the Armistice, 11 November 1918. Author's collection.

pins that were bought in from specialist suppliers, others such as the body were complicated machined forgings. Tolerances had to be held to surprisingly fine margins to ensure not just that the gun worked, but also that, at least theoretically, its parts would interchange with those of another rifle. And if this was true of an infantry rifle, it was true also of a machine-gun – and of a tank.

The major gunmakers all strove to accelerate production, doubling and redoubling output by expedients such as the introduction of shift work, allowing (in some cases) around-the-clock output. In Britain, the introduction of British Summer Time gave an additional daylight hour to extend the working day.

The need for munitions was particularly keen. An artillery barrage laid for eight days prior to the Battle of the Somme consumed 1.733 million shells; yet the comparable barrage preceding the Battle of Messines in July 1917 expended 3.258 million. The one-day bombardment preceding the attack on the Hindenburg Line on 27 September 1918 consumed 943,837 shells – who counted them? – weighing in excess of 40,000 tons – greater than all the shells expended in the South African War of 1899–1902.

It was asking much of pre-war industry to adapt to such unprecedented demand, and periodic 'shell shortages' were highlighted in the popular press. An idea of the huge demands made on manufacturing capacity can be seen in Ministry of Munitions statistics published after the end of the war. From 1 August 1914 until 11 November 1918, the output of large-calibre guns had reached 25,430 (new) and 9,170 'repairs'; no fewer than 239,850 machine-guns had been made, a majority being .303 Lewis guns emanating from BSA; rifle production reached 3,954,200; and more than 162 million artillery shells had been supplied. A munitions-industry workforce estimated at 50,000 men in 1914 had risen by the autumn of 1918 to 3.2 million, including 900,000 women.

Comparing the July–September quarter of 1915 with the same period of 1918 reveals that the production of machine-guns rose from 1,719 to 33,507; rifles from 176,239 to 287,755; and small-arms ammunition from 368.5 to 746 million.

Attempts were made to produce simpler weapons, though this was customarily resisted by military authorities and was to be seen to better effect in World War Two. When the Birmingham Small Arms Co. Ltd decided to omit the cut-off of the SMLE Mark III in order to speed up production, the War Office responded in the frostiest terms possible and forced the component to be immediately reinstated.

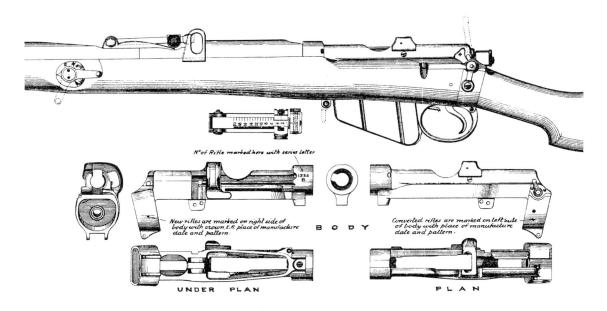

Drawings of the .303 SMLE Mk III rifle, from Instructions to Armourers, *1912. The shape of the 'Body' gives a good idea of the complexity of individual components, and the difficulties encountered in manufacturing them in quantity.*

An obvious way to accelerate production was to recruit new manufacturers. Britain, France and the USA – like Germany – all attempted to do this, with mixed results. The 'Peddled Rifle Scheme', an attempt to assemble SMLE rifles from sub-contracted parts, was a failure; so, too, in many ways, was the German Stern-Gewehr project. One British handbook lists more than 16,000 agencies recruited to make ordnance material, ranging from bomb fuses and shell components to fieldguns, aircraft and armoured vehicles.

Problems of logistics, especially that of ensuring that components made by companies separated by hundreds of miles were compatible with each other, must often have seemed insuperable. Yet the production of weapons did keep pace with demand, and very few men went into battle without regulation equipment.

When World War One began, short-term problems were often solved by combing storerooms, gun-dealers' inventories and even museums for obsolete weapons which could then be pressed into second-line service. Consequently, Belgian Albini-Braendlin, British Snider, French Gras or Russian Berdan rifles could be found in the hands of lines-of-communication or garrison units. Even front-line units sometimes had to make do with second-line equipment until fresh supplies of more appropriate quality were made available; and although this did not customarily affect small arms, some British Territorials went into action in 1914 with cumbersome charger-loading Lee-Enfield rifles instead of the SMLE. The Royal Navy used Arisaka and then Ross rifles, freeing their Lee-Enfields for land service; single-shot Remington rifles were purchased from France; lever-action .44-40 Winchesters came from the USA; and more than 800 Mauser pistols were retrieved from the shipboard armouries of two battleships being built in Britain for Chile when war began!

The maxim that 'more progress is made in a year of war than in a decade of peace' applied to the Allies as greatly as it did to the Central Powers. Consequently, great technological strides

A soldier armed with an SMLE and P/1907 sword bayonet peers anxiously 'Over the Top'; a British Official photograph taken on the Western Front in 1917. Author's collection.

were made in 1914–18: the introduction of light automatic weapons, for example, or the refinement of gas-shell manufacture. The modification of machine-guns to fire through the arc of an aero-engine propeller was another leap of faith, which, after losing more than a few pilots their airscrews, made a vital contribution to the war in the air. Yet the principal weapons of the Allied soldiers – their rifles – remained much the same in 1918 as they had been four years earlier. This was because research had largely been abandoned in favour of accelerated production of tried and tested designs such as the SMLE, the Springfield and the Berthier, lest the introduction of new ideas (and the consequent mass-manufacture teething troubles) left soldiers at the mercy of the enemy.

The British did succeed in introducing a new rifle, the Pattern 1914, but only because it was made in quantity just prior to the entry of the USA into the war; and ironically, the supposedly redun-dant SMLE was retained in British service long after the fighting had ceased. The French managed to get an automatic rifle (the RSC or Mle 1917) into service in some numbers in 1918, but guns of this type were regarded as 'ammunition wasters' by the French high command, and were customarily relegated to marksmen. The Italians had the unique double-barrelled 9mm Villar Perosa, but mistakenly saw it more as an ultra-portable light machine-gun than a machine pistol.

Promising ideas failed to make the transition from drawing-board to production, either because trials showed them to lack the qualities claimed for them, or simply because all available manu-facturing capacity had already been allocated. Others originated, often unofficially, to answer specific problems such as the desire to shoot over trench parapets without exposing the firer, or to place shots accurately at long range. These created overbank rifles, periscope and telescope sights, and a host of strange-looking wirecutters.

Flamethrowers and chemical weapons also made their appearance. The first 'gas-shells', filled with lachrymatory compound, were apparently fired on 27 October 1914 near Neuve Chapelle, but had so little effect that their existence was unknown until German military records were examined in 1919. Chlorine gas was used by the Germans on 22 April, near Ypres; and the British had replied in kind during the battle of Loos as the hue of war grew ever darker. The Germans made the first use of phosgene gas-shells on 22/23 June 1916, during the fighting for Verdun. Although most of these chemical weapons proved to be inef-fectual, indeed more dangerous to the users than to their opponents, malignant seeds had been sown: war would never be quite the same again.

PART ONE: ORDNANCE HISTORY

1   Western Europe

BELGIUM

Rifles

The earliest metallic-cartridge breech-loaders to be used in Belgian service were designed by Augusto Albini, an Italian navy officer, but they were perfected with the assistance of Francis Braendlin, who had been associated with Albini in patents granted in Britain in 1866–7. The gun was tested throughout Europe, but adopted only in Belgium.

The Albini breech embodied the familiar hinged and lifting block used by many inventors to convert muzzle-loaders simply by cutting away a portion of the breech. The essence of Albini's patent was the use of a bolt attached to the hammer body to lock the breech at the instant of ignition. Rotating the hammer to half cock withdrew the bolt and allowed the breech-block handle to be lifted, hinging the block forward and extracting the spent case that was then tipped from the feedway. Once the gun had been reloaded, the breech-block was closed and the hammer was thumbed back to full cock. Pressing the trigger allowed the hammer to fly forwards to strike the firing pin, forcing the locking bolt into the back of the breech-block as it did so.

After testing differing rifles, including the Remington Rolling Block, the Belgians selected

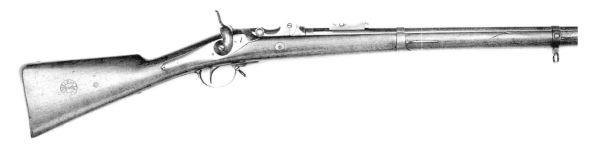

A typical Albini-Braendlin M1853/67 rifle, converted from an old rifle-musket, showing the breech mechanism. The knob mid-way between the hammer and the lateral breech-block pivot is lifted to open the breech. Courtesy of Wallis & Wallis, Lewes, Sussex.

A full-length view of a newly-made M1873 Albini-Braendlin rifle. Courtesy of the MoD Pattern Room Collection, Royal Ordnance plc, Nottingham.

the Albini-Braendlin breech because of the ease with which existing rifle-muskets could be converted. Chambered for a rimmed 11mm cartridge, many of the earliest were converted from an assortment of obsolete guns, including flintlock muskets acquired from France. A typical M1853/67 conversion was 53in long, weighed about 10lb, and had a 34.75in barrel, rifled with four grooves turning to the right. Muzzle velocity was about 1,365ft/sec with 1867-pattern ammunition.

However, problems with the first Albini-Braendlin breech were serious enough to prevent the Belgians re-equipping immediately. The Terssen system was adopted as a temporary measure, but was not perpetuated once Albini-Braendlin and Comblain weapons were available in quantity. Credited to the commandant of the Manufacture d'Armes de l'État in Liège, the Terssen mechanism relied on a longitudinal locking bolt in the breech-block entering a recess in the rear face of the receiver. Rotating the operating handle withdrew the bolt into the block, after which the breech could be pivoted upwards.

Terssen conversions had a more effective extractor than the Albini-Braendlin type (rectified on the 1873-model Albini), but were apparently much more prone to jamming. They chambered the 11×50mm rimmed cartridge shared with the Albini and Comblain rifles.

Favoured by the Garde Civique, the Comblain rifle also served in Belgium in large numbers. Created by Liège gunmaker Hubert-Joseph Comblain, it was compact and surprisingly durable; the basic action consisted of a sturdy receiver with the breech lever – that doubled as the trigger guard – pivoted at the front edge. Pulling the lever lowered the breech-block (which contained the hammer, trigger and main spring) to disengage the locking shoulders, then moved the block radially. The hammer was cocked as the breech opened.

First introduced in 1871 to replace the Albini and Terssen weapons, the Comblain is easily recognized by its massive slab-sided receiver, the recurved trigger-guard, and a unique vertical housing immediately behind the trigger. It used the same 11×50mm rimmed cartridge as its predecessors. Infantry rifles, short rifles or 'musketoons' (*Mousquetons*) and cavalry carbines were produced in 1871–83; some were still serving the Garde Civique in 1914.

A typical Belgian M1871 Comblain musketoon. Drawing by John Walter.

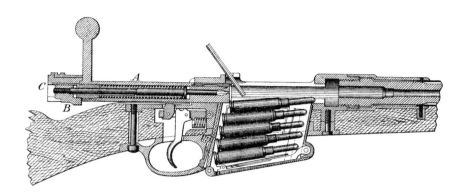

The action of a typical 1889-pattern Belgian Mauser rifle, shown in the act of closing. Note how the charger (from which the cartridges have just been stripped) is automatically expelled as the bolt closes.

Small-Calibre Magazine Rifles

The Belgian military authorities began testing an assortment of magazine rifles in the 1880s, and in 1888, once the French had adopted the 8mm Lebel, tests with small-calibre guns commenced in earnest. A 7.65mm-calibre Mauser was selected, a licence was obtained to manufacture the rifle in Belgium, and the company known as the Fabrique Nationale d'Armes de Guerre of Herstal-lèz-Liège was created to tender for the first large-scale order. A contract for the production of 150,000 M1889 rifles was duly signed in Berlin on 26 November.

The new weapon was not only a step forwards for the Belgians, it was also a milestone in the development of the infantry rifle. The M1889 was the first Mauser to feed from a box magazine beneath the stock, and the first to be loaded from a charger; it also introduced a new one-piece bolt with front locking lugs. Other noteworthy features included a cylindrical jacket enclosing the barrel almost to the muzzle, giving a unique outline, and a rounded projection at the front of the protruding single-column box magazine that anchored the pivot for the cartridge platform.

The barrel jacket was supposed to dissipate the heat from the comparatively thin barrel, at the same time protecting the soldier's hands from burning. Eventually, however, moisture entering between barrel and jacket led to excessive rusting; and although many features of the M1889 were to become standard Mauser practice, the barrel jacket was not among them.

The 7.65 × 53mm rimless Belgian cartridge – subsequently adopted by the armies of Argentina, Turkey, Bolivia, Colombia, Peru and Paraguay – was loaded with the flat-base roundnose bullet typical of the period, obtaining a velocity of about 2,035ft/sec in the 780mm (30.7in) barrel of the standard M1889 infantry rifle. In addition to the basic rifle, Fabrique Nationale – or 'FN' as the company came to be universally known – produced the usual engineer and cavalry carbines; something in the order of 200,000 weapons were produced to satisfy Belgian Army contracts. It had been intended that once these were completed the company would be closed down; however, word of its efficiency in producing rifles had spread, and the Russian government appeared with a large contract to refurbish rifles. This was too good to be turned down, and FN took on the contract; others followed, and the company has continued to flourish to the present day.

The success of the infantry rifle persuaded the Belgian authorities to introduce a series of short-barrelled guns for cadets, cavalrymen, the artillery, and gendarmerie units. These can be identified by their compact dimensions, the design of the nosecaps, and the position of the swivels. Some accepted bayonets, others did not. Details will be found in Part Two.

Automatic Weapons

In common with many other European nations, at the turn of the century the Belgians adopted the Maxim gun, chambering it for the standard 7.65 × 53mm rimmed cartridge. Not enough guns were needed to justify the expense of a production line, and so the earliest were bought from Deutsche Waffen- & Munitionsfabriken ('DWM') of Berlin. The 'M1900' was simply DWM's 'definitive' export model; thereafter, many other German-made Maxims bought by other European armies prior to 1914 were described simply as 'similar to the Belgian M1900'. DWM then revised the standard design, producing the German army MG. 08 that ultimately became the 'stock' M1909. Guns of this type were bought by Belgium as the 7.65mm M1910. The Belgian guns were conventional Maxims with the downward-breaking toggle mechanism, the earlier pattern with a phosphor-bronze water jacket, the later one with plain steel.

A light machine-gun designed by Adolphe Berthier – promoted by Anciens Établissements Pieper of Herstal – was also acquired in small numbers. About 1,100mm long, weighing 6.9kg, and chambered for the 7.65 × 53mm rimmed cartridge, the Fusil Mitrailleur Berthier Modèle 1910 had a top-mounted twenty-round box magazine, a tubular metal butt, a pistol grip, and

a slender barrel jacket with widely spaced annular fins. The oddest feature of the gun – other than the spindly bipod attached to the muzzle crown – was its water reservoir: this required pressure on an india-rubber bulb to circulate coolant. The gun apparently worked well enough, but it needed a two-man crew, and it is assumed that the advent of the Lewis Gun brought the military career of the Belgian Berthier to an end.

The Liège area, the gunsmithing centre of Belgium, naturally inspired designers to explore new projects. These included a variety of semi-automatic rifles, among them designs credited to Fabrique Nationale's design bureau (Bureau d'Études). It has been claimed that one of these recoil-operated rifles would have been adopted by the Belgian army as the 'Fusil Automatique d'Infanterie, Modèle F.N. 1914' had not World War I intervened. The locking system relied on the heads of lateral flaps engaging recesses in the receiver immediately behind the chamber.

Handguns

In 1898 the Belgians were seeking a replacement for the Nagant-type officers' service revolver, and so convened a committee at the Manufacture d'Armes de l'État (the state arms factory in Liège) to test handguns: these included Nagant

In addition to military adoption, the 1900-pattern FN-Browning pistol was a great commercial success – as this finely engraved version demonstrates. **Courtesy of FN Herstal SA.**

and Pieper gas-seal revolvers, large and small Brownings, and also Bergman, Borchardt, Mannlicher and Krnka-Roth automatic pistols.

All were rejected excepting the two Brownings, the Borchardt-Luger and the Mannlicher. The Département de Guerre then scheduled a second series of trials, and the small Browning won these on account of its simplicity, its light recoil and low cost – although its Belgian origins were no disadvantage. Adopted for officers on 3 July 1900, its use was subsequently extended to the gendarmerie, some cavalrymen, sections of the artillery, and the officers of the Garde Civique.

Known after the introduction of the M1903 as the 'Old Model', the original FN-Browning chambered the 7.65mm Browning cartridge and can be identified by longitudinal flutes in the front of the slide that separate the barrel from the return-spring housing. Experience soon showed that, while the gun was efficient, the cartridge was scarcely in the man-stopping category. But John Browning soon produced an improved pistol, easier to make and better to handle, and the 9mm Browning Long cartridge. This was weaker than the 9mm Parabellum, introduced in the same era, but it had been designed specifically to maximize the power of a blowback mechanism.

The 1903-pattern FN-Browning was the ultimate in simplicity: a fixed-barrel blowback with an internal hammer and grip safety. It was adopted by the Belgian Army as soon as it appeared, it competed successfully in Sweden (where it became the Pistol M/1907), was sold in quantity to Russia and Turkey, and was avidly pirated in Spain.

GREAT BRITAIN

Rifles

The first British breech-loader, like most of the successes of its era, was selected as the most cost-effective method of converting cap-lock rifle-muskets. The committee that selected the Snider conversion was aware of its shortcomings, but it gave the British Army an effective breech-loading rifle while a more deliberate choice was being made. Gun design had begun to advance so rapidly in the 1860s that over-hasty commitment to new and untried designs could be regretted within months. But the .577 Snider, a lifting-block design accompanied by its metal-and-paper cartridge, if it achieved nothing else, at least accustomed the British Army army to breech-loading with a weapon robust enough to withstand the rigours of colonial campaigns.

Most Sniders were conversions of Enfield P/53 rifle-muskets, P/58 naval and P/60 Serjeant's short rifles, P/56 cavalry carbines or P/61 artillery carbines, though a few thousand had been P/55 engineer carbines with Lancaster's oval-bore rifling. Once as many as possible of the existing guns had been altered, production commenced anew; indeed, it continued into the 1880s largely because of a reluctance to arm colonial troops with anything more effectual. The last Snider to be approved was a short-barrelled Yeomanry Carbine Mk I, sealed in July 1880 and made in the Royal Small Arms Factory in Sparkbrook, Birmingham, until 1884.

The approval of the Snider conversion allowed the British authorities to begin trials with the guns that would be newly made. The Henry dropping-block rifle almost managed to satisfy the War Office criteria after trials had been held in the spring of 1867, but its cartridge was too poor; and the Burton No. 2, which also had much to commend it, had performed badly at long range. Eventually, only three submissions remained: from Swiss-born Friedrich Martini, Scotsman Alexander Henry, and Englishman Westley Richards. The Richards rifle was the first to go, leaving the Martini and the Henry to wrestle for the prize.

The Martini breech mechanism had been patented in Britain in July 1868, based on a hollow box-like receiver containing a sturdy block with a transverse pivot through the rear upper tip. Pushing the operating lever downwards dropped the front of the breech-block to reveal the

The butt and breech of a commercial-pattern .577-calibre Snider military rifle, made in the 1870s for the 'Army & Navy Co-Operative Stores Ltd, London'. The breech-block opens laterally to the right. Courtesy of Weller & Dufty Ltd, Birmingham.

A full-length view of the .577-calibre Snider Pattern II** rifle, converted from the P/53 Enfield rifle-musket. Courtesy of the MoD Pattern Room Collection, Royal Ordnance plc, Nottingham.

chamber, extracting the cartridge as it did so. If the movement was swift enough, the spent case flew clear of the gun and a new round could be pushed into the chamber manually. Returning the breech lever raised the front of the block and cocked the internal striker.

An improved Martini made in 1868 in the Royal Small Arms Factory, Enfield Lock, showed little superiority over the Henry. However, as the Martini breech mechanism was simpler and more compact than its rival, it was married with Henry's rifled barrel and a 'Trials Rifle' was sealed on 1 October 1869. About 200 rifles were made in the Enfield factory, chambered for a rimmed .450 cartridge; they were 51in overall, weighed 9.34lb, and had a 35in barrel with seven-groove composite rifling. A cocking indicator pivoted on the right side of the action and a safety catch protruded from the trigger guard ahead of the trigger lever. A short-wrist butt and an unusually long action body were also most distinctive.

Just as the first long-chamber trials rifles were being issued, William Eley successfully adapted the compact .577 Snider cartridge case to hold a .450 bullet whilst simultaneously duplicating the powder capacity of the straight Martini-Henry round. Tests soon showed the advantages of the new necked cartridge, and, in February 1871, the rifle committee reported that the short-chamber gun should be adopted for service immediately.

The Mark I Martini-Henry rifles were made in the Royal Small Arms Factory in 1871–6. Chambered for a .450 rimmed cartridge giving a muzzle velocity of about 1,315ft/sec, they were about 49in overall (the short-butt version) and weighed 8.75lb empty. The 33.2in barrel, rifled with seven grooves turning to the left, could mount either a bushed P/53 or a P/1876 socket bayonet.

The Martini-Henry rifle had its problems, however: in particular, the wrapped-case cartridges had a distressing tendency to uncoil on firing. Combat experience, especially in the

A Mk I .450 Martini-Henry rifle. The breech-block tips to expose the chamber when the lever behind the trigger guard is pulled downward. Courtesy of the MoD Pattern Room Collection, Royal Ordnance plc, Nottingham.

Men of the Duke of Cornwall's Light Infantry in Egypt, 1882. Drawn by Frederic Villiers (1852–1922) for the Illustrated London News. Courtesy of Philip Haythornthwaite.

hotter parts of Africa, showed that cases too often jammed in the chamber, and then the extractor either tore off the separate case head or pulled straight through the rim, leaving the luckless soldier holding a jammed rifle with potentially fatal consequences; in fact, so great did the problems become in Egypt and the Sudan that a government enquiry was mounted. Solutions were eventually found in the form of solid-case ammunition (which had already been developed for the Gatling and Gardner machine-guns), and by lengthening the operating lever to make extraction more positive. However, radial-block breeches of Martini type never extract spent cases as efficiently as a properly designed turn-bolt breech.

The faults of the Martini-Henry were not great enough to dissemble its strength and durability, nor sufficient to prevent the authorities wanting to recoup on the investment in time and money that had characterized its development. Consequently, the Martini breech formed the basis for a variety of improved .450-calibre rifles and a series of short-barrelled cavalry and artillery carbines. Many of these survived to be re-chambered for .303 ammunition, and then to receive barrels with Enfield rifling instead of the original Metford pattern. The 'Rifles, .303, Martini-Enfield, Mk I* and II*' – the last to be approved in Britain – dated from February 1903.

By 1914, most guns of this class had been withdrawn into store, though survivors were recalled for training and home-defence purposes.

The Enfield-Martini

This gun linked the .450 Martini-Henry and the first .303 magazine rifles. It was a conventional Martini-action rifle firing a rimmed .402 cartridge developing a muzzle velocity of about 1,570ft/sec; it was 49in overall, and weighed 9.17lb empty. Its 33.2in barrel had nine-groove ratchet rifling. The goal was to flatten the trajectory by reducing the calibre and increasing velocity. In fact, apart from the reduction in calibre, there was little difference between the .402-calibre guns and the earlier .45 Martini-Henrys, though the Enfield-Martini was provided with a clip-like 'quick-loader', attached to the receiver, which allowed cartridges to be reached quicker than if they were in a waist-belt pouch.

The 'Rifle, Enfield-Martini, .402-inch (Mark I), with cleaning rod' was sealed on 17 April 1886 to guide manufacture of a thousand guns for troop trials; however, the quick-loader was universally unpopular, and extraction troubles became evident as soon as the first guns had been issued. The 'Pattern No. 2' rifle, substituted for the original in May 1887, discarded the aberrant cutaway fore-end of the original design in favour of the standard Martini-Henry design. The unpopular safety bolt was superseded by a small cocking indicator, and the quick-loader was abandoned. However, although production continued until 1888, few guns were ever issued; most were

impressing the authorities sufficiently for a '.402 Improved Lee' to be built in the Enfield factory.

However, development of an 8mm smokeless cartridge in France persuaded the British to abandon the ineffectual .402 calibre, experimental work revealing that a .298 jacketed bullet offered flatter trajectory, better accuracy and greater penetration. Ballistic calculations and further tests

A .303 Martini-Metford Cavalry Carbine Mk II. Courtesy of Ian Hogg.

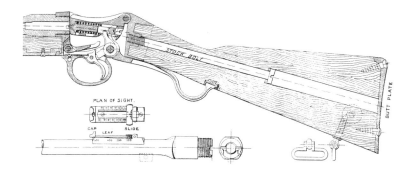

A cutaway drawing of the .303 Martini-Metford Artillery Carbines Mks II and III, and the Martini-Enfield Artillery Carbines Mks I, I*, II, II* and III. From Instructions to Armourers, *1912.*

subsequently converted from .402 to .450 and issued as 'Martini-Henry Rifles Mk IV'.

Magazine Rifles

The Lee action first appeared in Britain at the end of March 1880, when three 1879-pattern rifles and two carbines chambering the .45 drawn-case Gatling cartridge were amongst a selection of guns tried by the Small Arms Committee. A report made on 21 March 1881 noted that, despite niggling extraction problems, the .45 Lee had performed best of the submissions. By April 1883, a new Lee rifle chambering the .45–70 US Army cartridge was being tested at Enfield,

suggested that .303 would be the optimum calibre, and approximately five hundred .303 rifles and carbines, the former predominating, were made in the Royal Small Arms Factory in 1888. The action was locked by a single lug on the bolt body engaging a recess in the receiver as the bolt handle was turned down, and by the rear of the bolt guide rib abutting the receiver bridge.

The first guns chambered a straight-case cartridge, and had distinctive butts with a continuous comb and a straight wrist. A bolt-head release catch lay on the right side of the receiver and a long ejector was let into the left side of the bolt-way. The design of the box magazine, the cut-off

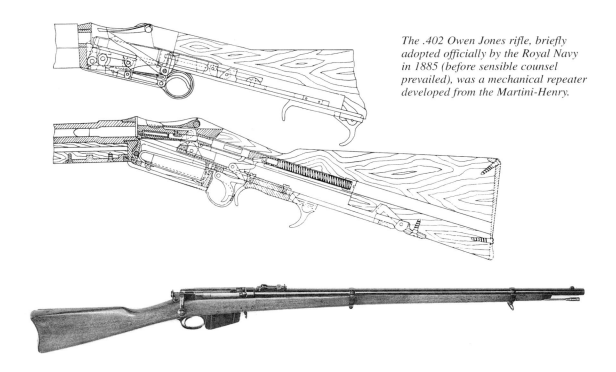

The .402 Owen Jones rifle, briefly adopted officially by the Royal Navy in 1885 (before sensible counsel prevailed), was a mechanical repeater developed from the Martini-Henry.

Several hundred .433 1885-pattern Remington-Lee rifles were acquired in the mid 1880s for trials that led ultimately to the development of the Lee-Metford. Courtesy of the MoD Pattern Room Collection, Royal Ordnance plc, Nottingham.

and the long-range dial sight was credited to Joseph Speed of the Enfield factory. A Martini-style upper band accepted a special sword bayonet.

Experiments with rimmed, rimless and semi-rim necked cartridge cases continued throughout the autumn of 1888. Changes were made to the rifle, such that it gained Rigby's patented nose-cap, Lewes-pattern sights, and an eight-round single-row magazine instead of the original seven-round type. The ejector was simplified, a safety catch appeared on the left side of the receiver, and a hand guard was added behind the backsight. The result was the 'Lee-Metford' (initially known simply as the 'Magazine Rifle Mk I'), the design of the barrel and rifling being due to William Metford.

The introduction of smokeless propellant by the French in 1886 set the chemists of the world searching for suitable alternatives; thus Cordite was

introduced to British service in 1892, the first .303 cartridges being approved in March. But experience showed that the intense heat of Cordite – it was approximately 45 per cent nitroglycerine – soon attacked the deep seven-groove Metford rifling, originally developed to counter the inevitable fouling caused by using black powder as a propellant. Technicians in the Royal Small Arms Factory therefore developed new five-groove rifling with different contours and shallower angles to resist erosion more effectively. The guns that used the new-pattern rifling became known as 'Lee-Enfields', and many Lee-Metford rifles were upgraded simply by exchanging barrels.

Although the introduction of the Lee-Metford and Lee-Enfield satisfied the needs of the infantrymen, a bewildering variety of single-shot rifles and carbines remained in service. There had always been differences between the carbines

The .402 Lee-Burton rifle, with a hopper magazine on the right side of the receiver, was an unsuccessful competitor of the Remington-Lee. Courtesy of the MoD Pattern Room Collection, Royal Ordnance plc, Nottingham.

issued to the cavalry and the artillery, as the former was carried in a saddle scabbard and the latter was invariably accompanied by a hefty sword bayonet. About 60,000 Lee-Metford and Lee-Enfield cavalry carbines had been made between 1894 and 1902, with short, six-round magazines faired into the stock, but these were not deemed successful enough. Information sent back from the fighting in South Africa suggested that a short rifle would provide an ideal compromise, and development work began immediately in the Enfield factory. The Lee bolt system was retained, but the barrel was shortened by 5in. Trials showed that the prototypes fitted most requirements: long enough to retain the accuracy desired in an infantry rifle, short enough to be carried on a cavalryman's saddle, and sufficiently handy to be slung over the shoulders of gunners and sappers as they pursued their trades. Whatever the theoretical drawbacks of the bolt may have been, the 'SMLE' or 'Rifle, Short, Magazine, Lee-Enfield' was a truly innovative weapon.

The SMLE Mk 1 was introduced to service in 1903, to a mixed reception; the gun trade was particularly hostile. Like every other rifle before or since, the short Lee-Enfield experienced many teething troubles, and trade journals such as *Arms & Explosives* described how magazines were held in place with bootlaces. Yet the worst of the problems had soon been remedied, and the rank-and-

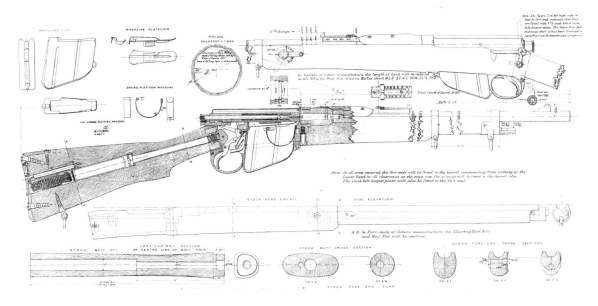

Drawings of the Mk II Lee-Metford rifle, from Instructions to Armourers, *1912.*

*A private of the King's Own Regiment in marching
order, c. 1896. The rifle appears to be a Lee-Metford
with the orginal single-row magazine.*
Courtesy of Ian Hogg.

*The Lee-Enfield was the principal weapon of the
British line infantryman during the Second South
African ('Boer') war of 1899–1902.*

file were well satisfied with their new rifles. Not so
the civilian experts, who derided the SMLE as use-
less, inaccurate and an abomination; this 'expert'
opinion eventually drove the War Office to develop the .276 Pattern 1913 rifle, described below.
The acid test of war, however, proved conclusive-
ly that the SMLE was the finest combat rifle of its
day. It was destined to remain in service, with
nothing but minor modifications, for fifty years;
indeed, Lee-Enfields are still to be found in service
in India and Pakistan.

The principal theoretical objection to the Lee
action was actually the feature which made it a
supreme weapon in combat: the rear-locking bolt.

Front-locking bolts are stronger and generally
promote better accuracy, particularly if they lock
directly into the barrel to give the cartridge rigid
support. Placing the lugs at the rear gives a 'free'
length of bolt behind the cartridge which com-
presses in the instant before the strain is taken up
by the lugs.

In theory, this degrades accuracy. It is important
if target shooting is being undertaken at a range of
2,000yd (1,800m), but the differences are academ-
ic when the task is to shoot rapidly at a quickly
moving figure 500yd (450m) away. What is more
to the point is that the front-lug bolt has to be
inserted into the chamber before it can be rotated

Grenadier Guards at the battle of Biddulphberg, during the Second South African War. From a sketch by Richard Caton Woodville (1856–1927) published in With the Flag to Pretoria *(1900).*

to lock, and it must be fully rotated to unlock before it can be withdrawn. A rear-lug bolt, on the other hand, can have its locking abutment so shaped that the turning movement to lock can commence before the bolt is fully home, the fact that it turns against a cam face adding to the leverage to force a stubborn cartridge home. Similarly, the opening and withdrawal stroke can begin almost as soon as the bolt begins to rotate. All this means speed, and a Lee-Enfield can be fired much faster than any other pre-1945 bolt action. A trained soldier could easily manage thirty aimed rounds per minute, and instructors at the Small Arms School could manage fifty shots as their party piece.

A New Rifle

In 1910, increasingly worried that the German Gewehr 98 and the US M1903 Springfield developed a greater muzzle velocity than the short Lee-Enfield, and with the criticisms of the self-styled experts ringing in their ears, the Small Arms Committee was asked to list features to be incorporated in an entirely new rifle. As much of the SMLE was to be retained as possible, but a Mauser-pattern action was desirable, and an aperture backsight was to be substituted for the open notch. The first experiments were undertaken with a converted M1903 'Enfield-Springfield', but a much modified rifle and an experimental .276 cartridge were recommended for field trials early in 1912.

More than 1,000 Pattern 1913 rifles were made by the Royal Small Arms Factory, Enfield. They were locked by two lugs on the bolt head rotating into their seats in the receiver as the bolt handle turned down, and by the bolt-handle base entering its seat behind the bridge. A typical gun was 46.2in long, weighed 8.56lb empty, and had a 26in barrel with conventional Enfield-type five-

The Thorneycroft, an ultra-short design, is often mistakenly associated with the commander of an irregular force active in the Second South African War. It was patented in 1901 by James Thorneycroft, an 'ironmaster' of Mauchline, Ayrshire, and is not the catalyst for the SMLE that is sometimes claimed. The magazine lay in the butt-wrist behind the bolt handle. Courtesy of Ian Hogg.

A typical British 'Redcoat' of the South African War period displays a full-length .303 Lee-Enfield rifle. That he wears the Queen's and King's South Africa Medals shows the image to post-date the death of Queen Victoria in 1901.

groove rifling. The internal five-round box magazine could be loaded with a charger; the magazine platform held the action open when the last round had been fired and ejected; the leaf-type backsight was graduated to 1,900yd (1,740m); and an auxiliary long-range sight lay on the left side of the distinctively British-style one-piece stock. Initially four diagonal grasping grooves appeared on each side of the fore-end immediately ahead of the breech, but these proved to be unpopular.

Based on the .280 Ross round that had proved highly successful in competition shooting, the '.276 Cartridge, Ball, Mk I' developed a muzzle velocity of 2,785ft/sec. The P/1913 sword bayonet was essentially similar to the P/1907, except the muzzle ring was set farther from the back of the hilt.

The rifles underwent trials successfully, generally proving to be accurate and robust, although they did show a tendency to misfire. Problems were also experienced with the charger guides. However, though only poor magazine feed caused real worry with the rifle, the excessive recoil and the noise, blast and flash of the cartridge all affected the average soldier's shooting. Optimistically, in 1914 the British authorities tentatively recommended that the .276 rifle should replace the .303 Lee-Enfield, although at the same time they did acknowledge that the cartridge needed refinement.

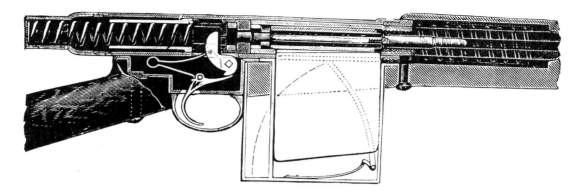

The Griffiths & Woodgate rifle was one of the first attempts to interest the British Army in auto-loading designs. From W.W. Greener's The Gun and Its Development *(1910 edition).*

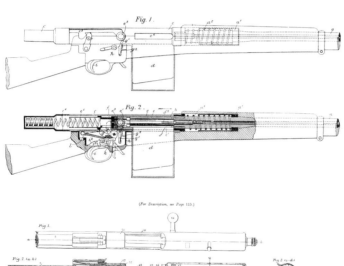

The Griffiths & Woodgate rifle, from British Patent 16,730/92, granted on 19 September 1892.

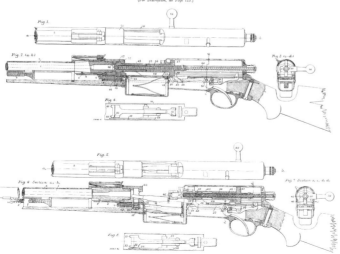

The Rexer automatic rifle was tested by the British at Bisley in 1904. However, though performing better than the rival Hallé design, it was deemed unacceptable. The recoil-operated action was locked by rotating the bolt. From Engineering, *22 July 1904.*

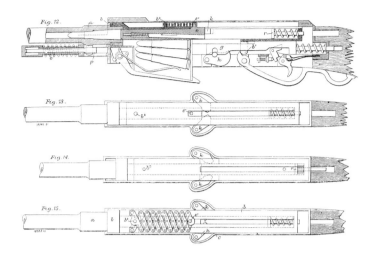

The Hallé automatic rifle, a competitor of the Rexer pictured previously, was another recoil-operated weapon. Embodying a unique 'lazy tongs' return-spring mechanism, the design was not successful. From Engineering, *22 July 1904.*

Early Machine-Guns

Like most armies, the British had been attracted to the Gatling gun almost as soon as the American Civil War had ground to its end. A Colt-made gun was tested as early as 1867, but was rejected after failing to compare with a 9pr field-gun. Trials were subsequently undertaken with a variety of weapons at Shoeburyness in 1870, and in October the Gatling was recommended for adoption. However, the first .45- and .65-calibre Gatlings made by the British licensee, Sir W.G. Armstrong & Company, did not appear until the beginning of 1874. The 'Gun, Gatling, .45 Mk I', the 'Trail, Mk I' and the 'Limber, Mk I' were successful enough to persuade the British authorities that the machine-gun had a future, but they still had their problems; most significantly, although some Armstrong-Gatlings seem to have been fitted with Accles Positive Feed, the giant spring-powered drums proved to be cumbersome and unreliable.

The fixed-barrel Gardner and Nordenfelt guns were more successful in Britain than the rotating-barrel Gatling had been. Patented in the USA in 1874, the Gardner gun relied on crank-driven reciprocating breech-blocks. First offered to the Committee on Machine-Guns in 1875, the Nordenfelt was the brainchild of a Swedish engineer, Heldge Palmcrantz; it was operated by a radial lever protruding from the right rear side of the receiver. But although the 'Gun, Nordenfelt, 0.45-inch, 3-Barrel, Martini-Henry Chamber (Mk I)' was approved for naval service in July 1880, controversy over the varying merits of the Gardner and the Nordenfelt designs raged for years. In 1883, the machine-gun committee recommended the adoption of a two-barrel, .45-calibre Gardner gun for general service, and a similar five-barrel pattern for special service. It is interesting that according to contemporaneous information, the navy was supposed to have 565 Nordenfelt, 350 Gardner and 142 Gatling guns by the spring of 1884!

A few Gardner guns were made in 1886–7 for the experimental .402 'Enfield-Martini' cartridge, but were subsequently converted for regulation .45 ammunition. By this time, however, interest was being shown in the Maxim, and in fact the era of the mechanically operated machine-gun was almost at an end. Even so, instruction on guns of this type was still being undertaken by the staff of the School of Musketry in 1894, and *Instructions to Armourers* (1912 edition) suggests that a few guns were still being held in reserve. But it is unlikely that any of them fired a shot in anger during World War One.

A four-barrel .450 Nordenfelt Gun in Royal Navy service. From Engineering, *19 January 1883.*

The Maxim Gun

The Maxim Gun Company had been formed in 1884 to exploit the patents granted to an American, Hiram S. Maxim. A factory had been established at Crayford in Kent in 1885, and early .45-calibre guns had been successfully demonstrated to the Machine Gun Committee in November 1885. The committee, suitably impressed with the Maxim, then programmed an arduous test for 1886. To succeed, the gun – which was to weigh less than 100lb (45kg) – would have to fire not less than 400 shots in the first minute; 1,000 rounds would have to be fired in four minutes. But even the prototype Maxims were very efficient, passing their trials with ease. After completing the prescribed course, the inventor had joined two ammunition belts together and fired 666 rounds in a minute. There were no jams.

Encouraged, the War Office immediately bought three .45 calibre Maxim guns for extended trials. However, though the issue of one gun per infantry battalion for instructional purposes had been approved in 1890 (increased to two in 1891), the programme was still woefully incomplete when the Second South African War began in 1899. There were two basic Maxims in British service, the .45 Mark I and the

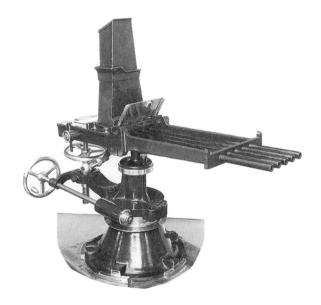

A typical five-barrel .450-calibre British Nordenfelt Gun, on a pedestal mount. Fed from the hopper on top of the breech, the barrels were fired by a reciprocating lever protruding beneath the right side of the frame. Courtesy of the MoD Pattern Room Collection, Royal Ordnance plc, Nottingham.

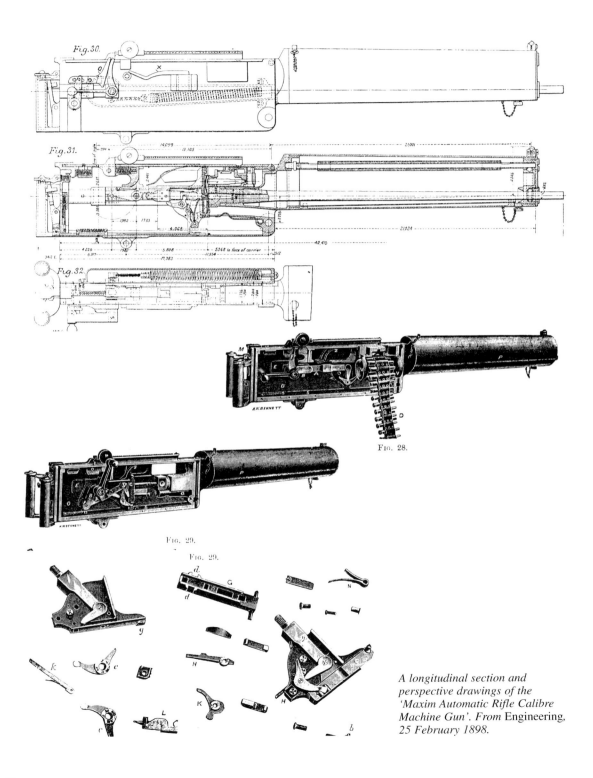

FIG. 28.

FIG. 29.

FIG. 29.

A longitudinal section and perspective drawings of the 'Maxim Automatic Rifle Calibre Machine Gun'. From Engineering, *25 February 1898.*

'.303 Mark I Magazine Rifle Chamber'; large-calibre guns were subsequently rechambered under the designation '.303 Converted, Mark I'.

The failure of the machine-guns during the Second South African War was due partly to inept tactics – they were still often seen as light artillery – and partly because their cumbersome field carriages were vulnerable to the Boer artillery and 1pr Maxim pom-poms. British interest remained minimal when the twentieth century began, though Maxims were embraced in Germany with great enthusiasm. And although both Hotchkiss and Maxim guns had shown their potential during the Russo-Japanese War of 1904–5, the War Department did very little; when World War One began in August 1914, British purchases from Vickers, Sons & Maxim and its successor, Vickers Ltd, had amounted to just 100 guns in the preceding ten years.

The Vickers Gun
The Maxim gun was sturdy and reliable, but, like many weapons of its day, it was surprisingly

A .303 Maxim Gun on a naval-service wheeled carriage, pictured at HMS Excellent, the Royal Navy gunnery school. From a photograph by Gregory & Co., Strand, London, published in *The Navy and Army Illustrated*, 17 January 1896.

Maxim Guns in South Africa, c. 1900.

Cleaning a .303 Mk I Maxim Gun on manoeuvres. This picture is difficult to date – the men are not regulars – though one of the ammunition boxes is dated '1901'. Author's collection.

heavy. Over-caution and a poor appreciation of the strength of materials forced most of the earliest machine-gun manufacturers to design components that were far too large for their purpose. Consequently Vickers, Sons & Maxim, sensing that a lucrative export market was being threatened by *Deutsche Waffen- und Munitions-fabriken*, embarked on redesign.

Replacing the massive phosphor-bronze water jacket with a sheet-steel version, thinning the receiver walls and lightening many individual parts allowed Vickers, Sons & Maxim to announce a lightweight machine-gun in the autumn of 1906. This retained the original downward-breaking lock and the deep slab-side receiver, but inverting the mechanism brought another great step forward. The guns exhibited in London in April 1911, for example, accompanied by the 'Mark E' (wheeled) and 'Mark F' tripods, weighed merely 36lb with full water jackets, as compared with 68.75lb for the .303 service-pattern Maxim. The improved machine-gun was formally approved in November 1912 as the

'Gun, Machine, .303, Vickers, Mark I'. Unfortunately, adoption occurred just as emphasis was being put on the development of a new .276 rifle, and procurement of .303 Vickers guns was reduced to the barest minimum necessary to bring infantry battalions up to their peacetime establishment.

There was little point placing a .303 machine-gun in series production if a .276 rifle was to be approved in the near future. This logic cannot be faulted, but it was at the root of the machine-gun shortage that confronted the army in 1914–15.

A standard Vickers-armed machine-gun company comprised 100 men, each of its four sections being armed with four guns under the command of a subaltern, a sergeant, and a corporal entrusted with the gun limbers and belt-filling equipment. Each gun team consisted of 'No. 1', the gunner, who carried the tripod; 'No. 2', who carried the gun and was responsible not only for mounting the weapon but also for the smooth feed of cartridge belts during firing; 'No. 3' and 'No. 4', responsible for supplies, ammunition, water and spare parts; 'No. 5', the 'runner', responsible for communicating with the section or company commander; and 'No. 6', usually a range-taker. Thorough training ensured that each man could replace any of his team-mates who became casualties.

Revolvers

Although production of the Mark III Adams was sufficient for guns to be sold commercially and despatched to colonial agencies, by 1878 there was a shortage of handguns in the British Army. For once, however, problems had been foreseen, and 500 assorted Colt, Tranter and Webley revolvers had been ordered in time for the Zulu War of 1879.

The Colts are believed to have been the so-called double-action Model 1878, though confirmation is still lacking. The 'Pistol, Revolver, Breech-Loading, Tranter, .450-inch, inter-

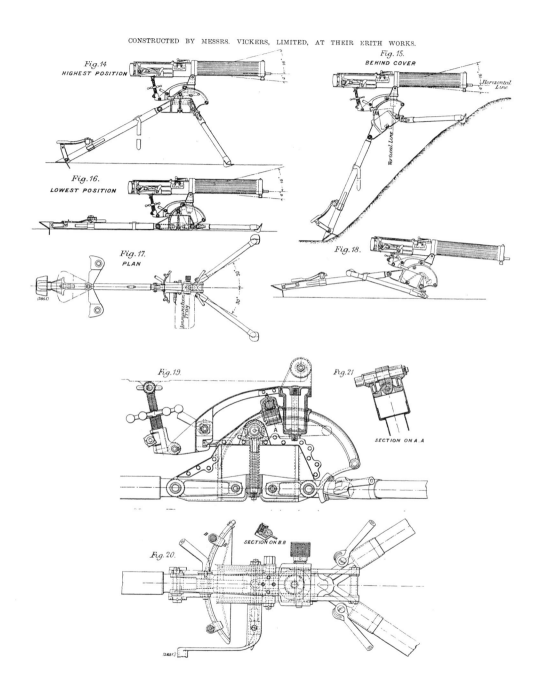

CONSTRUCTED BY MESSRS. VICKERS, LIMITED, AT THEIR ERITH WORKS.

Fig.14
HIGHEST POSITION

Fig. 15.
BEHIND COVER

Fig. 16.
LOWEST POSITION

Fig. 17.
PLAN

Fig. 18.

Fig.19.

Fig. 21
SECTION ON A.A

SECTION ON B B

Fig. 20.

Drawings of export-pattern Vickers Guns (note the tangent-type back sights), from Engineering, *28 April 1911.*

This distinctive two-trigger concealed-hammer .450 revolver – made by Kynoch to the 1885–6 patents of Henry Schlund – is typical of the weapons purchased by the British officers corps. Courtesy of Ian Hogg.

changeable (Mark I)', approved on 19 July 1878, was a sturdy, solid-frame gun with an ejector rod on the right side of the barrel, a hinged loading gate on the right side of the frame behind the cylinder, and a double-action trigger system. The Webleys are believed to have been the well known Royal Irish Constabulary Model.

The standard of these guns depressed the War Department greatly: one gun in four was rejected by the inspectorate, and most of the Webleys had to be returned to the factory for adjustment or repair. Consequently, the authorities resolved to make revolvers at Enfield. No time was wasted on formalities such as competitive trials, and on 16 July 1879 the Director of Artillery (responsible for weapons design) instructed the superintendent of the Royal Small Arms Factory at Enfield to proceed. The superintendent had presumably been warned in advance, because a set of drawings was produced and approved within sixteen days.

The 'Pistol, Revolver, Breech-Loading, Enfield, .476-inch (Mark I)', adopted in August 1880, combined an extraction system patented by a Welsh-born Philadelphian mechanic named Owen Jones, and Warnant lockwork. The barrel swung downwards around a pivot on the lower front of the frame, drawing the cylinder forwards

on its arbor but leaving the extraction plate static. Movement drew the cylinder off the spent cases, which fell away from the gun as the cylinder reached the limit of its travel forwards – excepting the case in the lowest chamber, which generally stuck between the extractor plate and the frame and had to be knocked free.

Despite passing its trials successfully, the Mark 1 soon encountered accuracy problems: this was because the rifled-mouth chambers failed to align with the rifling in the barrel, and shaved lead from the bullets each time the gun was fired. The lockwork had been nickel-plated internally to prevent rusting, but flakes from the poor quality plating continually jammed the mechanism. Perhaps the worst defect was that the revolver would fire if the hammer was struck sharply in its rebound position. A safety catch was added, but the Mark 1 was soon superseded by a Mark 2, in 1882, which addressed the various faults with some success.

Unfortunately, despite the best of intentions, the committee-designed Enfield revolver was very cumbersome compared with many contemporary designs, it shot poorly owing to a reliance on standard Martini-Henry rifling, and it still failed to extract properly. By 1886 it was clear that it had to be replaced, and trials to find a bet-

A .476 Enfield Mk I revolver (1880), a quirky design due largely to Owen Jones. Tipping the barrel downward pulled the cylinder forward away from the standing breech. Courtesy of the MoD Pattern Room Collection, Royal Ordnance plc, Nottingham.

ter weapon eventually narrowed to a choice between Webley's Government Revolver (or 'W.G. Model 1886') and a break-action Smith & Wesson. Sensibly, as there was little to choose between the guns, the Small Arms Committee recommended the indigenous Webley, and the 'Pistol, Breech-Loading, Revolver, Webley (Mark I)' was sealed on 8 November 1887. An initial order confirmed by the Director of Army Contracts as early as 18 July 1887 called for the manufacture of 10,000 guns.

The Mark I was a minor adaptation of the W.G. revolver, with a 4in barrel and an overall length of about 9.14in. It weighed about 35oz unloaded. The cylinder assembly was retained by a large transverse screw on the barrel lug, and the grips were vulcanite. No sooner had work commenced, however, than the bore diameter was changed in June 1888 from .441 to .446. Confusingly, the gun actually accepted the government .455 Webley and .476 Enfield cartridges. The 'Stirrup Fastener' had been renamed 'Barrel Catch' by the autumn of 1891, and its associated parts re-designated accordingly. An extractor lever spring and pin were added at the same time. As John Carter patented a safety device in this period, to prevent the gun firing from the rebound

position, and as Carter & Whiting sought protection for a two-point cylinder lock – both present on the Mark I – it is apparent that series production did not commence until 1889.

Enough small modifications had been suggested to the Mark I by 1894 to merit approval of a new 'Mark II', embodying the separate recoil shield of the Mark I*, a new hammer with larger spur, a modified barrel latch, and a more graceful butt. The Mark III, approved in October 1897, was a Mark II with a new barrel unit and cylinder assembly intended to give a better cylinder release and to reduce the friction associated with rotation of the cylinder. Small changes were also made to the recoil shield and the extractor lever, though these components remained interchangeable with earlier Marks. Production of the Mark III continued for some time after the Mark IV had been introduced, and certainly lasted for the duration of the Second South African War.

The Mark IV was the first of the service-pattern Webleys to be produced solely in .455 calibre; earlier Marks had been chambered for .442, .455 and .476 ammunition as required, but the .455 cartridge had been standardized by 1899. The Mark IV revolver is often labelled

A Mk II Enfield revolver. Note the plain grips, which replaced the chequered pattern of the Mk I. Courtesy of Weller & Dufty Ltd, Birmingham.

A .455/476 Webley 'W.G. Army Model' and its brown leather holster, sold by the Army & Navy Co-operative Stores Ltd. The use of Webley's winged-bullet trademark dates it to the turn of the century. Courtesy of Weller & Dufty Ltd, Birmingham.

A .442 Webley Mk I revolver of 1887. Note the bird's head butt and the short barrel. Courtesy of Ian Hogg.

the 'Boer War Model' because its introduction coincided with the outbreak of hostilities, and it armed many of the volunteer units. Excepting the standardization of calibre, few changes had been made compared with the Mark III. However, a better grade of steel had been specified for the frame and barrel, some components were case-hardened to resist wear, and the hammer spur and cylinder locking slots were broadened. The goal was simply to improve reliability without affecting the operation of what had become a tried and well tested weapon.

The Mark V revolver, introduced in 1913, was essentially a Mark IV with a slightly larger cylinder and with corresponding adjustments to the frame; this gave the additional strength necessary to chamber cartridges loaded with smokeless propellant.

Automatic pistols

The Small Arms Committee had tested many automatics prior to 1914, but none had met criteria that included excessive demands on bullet weight and muzzle velocity. The simplest or most effectual guns – such as the FN Brownings – were too low-powered, while the only guns that approached the power requirements (for instance, the clumsy Gabbett Fairfax 'Mars' series of 1901 to 1903) were generally impossibly complicated and awkward to handle.

After the final rejection of the Mars, interest centred on the Colt and Webley pistols. The first .38 Colt had been submitted in December 1902, performing so admirably that the Chief Inspector of Small Arms had noted it 'the best pistol yet submitted'. Trials of a .45 version in January 1906 were similarly impressive.

An improved .45 pistol appeared in July 1910, but the hammer persistently jarred out of contact with the sear and fell on an empty chamber during a 'drop safety' or rough usage test undertaken by HMS *Excellent* in August; damage caused to the lockwork then caused the Colt

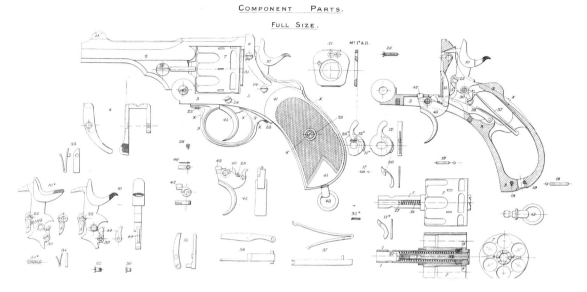

PISTOL. WEBLEY. MARK I. I*& II. C. B.L. REVOLVER.

COMPONENT PARTS.

FULL SIZE.

Drawings of the Mk I, I* and II Webley revolvers, from Instructions to Armourers, *1912.*

The large and excessively cumbersome Gabbett Fairfax 'Mars' pistol was tested extensively by the British Army in the early 1900s but never adopted.

A long-barrelled .455-calibre Webley-Fosbery 'Automatic Revolver'. The barrel and the upper part of the frame slid backward on firing, rotating the cylinder by means of the groove cut in its periphery. Courtesy of Ian Hogg.

The .455 Mk I Webley & Scott automatic pistol of 1913 was an ungainly design, but successful enough to be adopted officially by the British Army.

to fire the next magazineful automatically. As the competing Webley had performed impeccably, the Royal Navy summarily rejected the Colt.

The first .45 Webley pistol, designed by William Whiting, had been submitted to the Chief Inspector of Small Arms in October 1904. Trials had been disappointing, however, and a .38 blowback submitted in April 1909 was equally unacceptable. Then an improved .45-calibre gun

appeared in the summer of 1909, locked by displacing the barrel block diagonally down and back, and opinions changed after the gun had passed a stringent trial. And although the Chief Inspector of Small Arms had rejected the Webley in March 1910 as 'unsuitable for service', the navy demurred, and the 'Pistol, Self Loading, Webley, .455 Mark I (N)' was approved in January 1912.

The army authorities then had a change of heart and decided to issue 100 Webley pistols for trials with the Royal Horse Artillery. Discussion concerning suitable weapons for the gun-horse teams then raged within the regiment, and it is assumed that this provided an ideal reason for a full-scale pistol trial. These pistols had an adjustable backsight patented by W.J. Whiting in 1913, and were numbered in a block taken from the navy series. Fifty had their backstraps cut for shoulder stocks, the others were plain.

The trials were abandoned, incomplete, when World War One began. The .455 Webley pistol was subsequently found to be unreliable, jamming as easily from the effects of mud and dust as from excessive fouling produced by its cordite-loaded ammunition.

Charles Blaskett holds a .310-calibre Martini-action cadet rifle. The photograph was taken prior to the First World War in the studio of Frank A. McNeill, in Adelaide, South Australia, but does not bear a date.

THE BRITISH EMPIRE

Australia

Australian forces were armed with standard British SMLE Mks III and III* rifles made in a government manufactory established in 1912 in Lithgow, New South Wales. The guns duplicated their British prototypes, excepting that most were stocked not in walnut but in a selection of woods indigenous to Australia. As these were almost

Typifying the fighting spirit of the British Empire prior to 1914, these men of the Armed Native Constabulary of Suva, Fiji, carry Martini-Henry rifles.

always softer than walnut, minor changes were made to the bedding and some other components.

Martini-action cadet rifles were also commonly encountered, chambered for the .297/.230 or .310 rimmed cartridges. Writing in *The Gun and Its Development* in 1910, William Greener suggested that .310 'Sharpshooter Cadet Rifles' and .297/.230 'Miniature Patterns' were bought for adults and juniors respectively. Large numbers were acquired by the governments of Victoria and Western Australia from 1900 onwards. The first batches were apparently ordered from Auguste Francotte & Cie in Liège, as the British manufacturers were struggling to satisfy demands of the Second South African War.

Purchases continued after *c.* 1907 on behalf of the Commonwealth of Australia, though these guns were made either by the Birmingham Small Arms Co. Ltd of Small Heath or W.W. Greener Ltd of Birmingham.

Belgian-made guns had military-style stocks with a single barrel band near the muzzle, a cocking indicator on the right side of the receiver, and ramp-and-leaf backsights similar to the Martini-Enfields; British-made examples were similar, but their backsights had SMLE-type protecting wings. Typically, the .310 cadet Martini was 44.75in long, weighed a little under 9lb, and had a 29in barrel rifled with four grooves. A small socket bayonet could be locked around the front-sight block.

A typical Canadian Mk II Ross rifle, with a Harris-type controlled platform magazine. These guns were not particularly successful, largely owing to poor manufacturing standards that caused perpetual modification. Courtesy of Ian Hogg.

Canada

After using the standard British-pattern Snider, Martini-Henry and Lee-Metford rifles, the Canadians elected to follow an independent line by adopting the Ross rifle in 1903. The Ross was perhaps the most vilified of all twentieth-century military rifles, even though it was often a first-class sporter and had an enviable reputation as a competition rifle; as a military weapon it perhaps owed its brief glory to the inability of the British to supply Canadian troops with Lee-Enfields during the Second South African War.

The design was due to Sir Charles Ross, whose first British patent dated from 1893. The straight-pull bolt action was an adaptation of the 1890-pattern Austrian Mannlicher. The earliest or 1897-patent 'Magazine Sporting Rifle' was not particularly successful, though it was made in small numbers in both Britain and the USA. The operating handle lay at the extreme rear of the receiver, and a combination of cam-lugs and helical cam-tracks between the sleeve and the bolt caused the locking lugs to revolve into engagement with the receiver when the bolt handle was pulled straight back. Rotation of the bolt-sleeve was prevented by ribs sliding in guideways in the receiver. A single-column magazine could accept a clip of four .303 cartridges.

A military version of the improved or 1900-pattern Ross sporting rifle was submitted for trials with the Canadian militia in 1901, but was easily defeated in an endurance test negotiated by a competing Lee-Enfield. The Canadians were all but obliged to adopt the Ross, however, because the British were unable to supply Lee-Enfields,

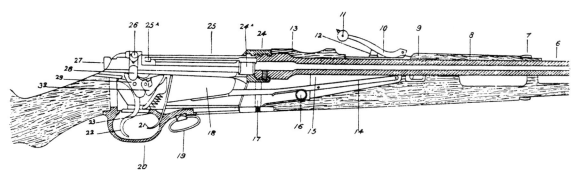

A longitudinal section of the Ross rifle. Note the inordinate length of the magazine-platform arm (14). From the Text Book of Small Arms, *1909 edition.*

Afghan fighting men pose with a selection of British weaponry, principally Lee-Enfield rifles. As at least some of the guns are SMLEs, it seems likely that the picture dates from the early 1920s. However, the tribesmen's equipment is typical of the 1900–14 era.

and so the pattern for the 'Rifle, Ross, .303-inch, Mark 1' was sealed in April 1902. A contract calling for the manufacture of 12,000 rifles was signed in March 1903, and the foun-dations of the Ross Rifle Company factory were laid in Quebec.

The first of these rifles was delivered to the Canadian army in 1905, but series production was only possible if parts were used that were made by sub-contractors across the border in the USA.

The 1905-type action relied on helical ribs on the bolt engaging grooves inside the bolt sleeve. When the sleeve was pulled back, the ribs rotated the locking lugs of the bolt body out of the receiver wall. However, though the Ross worked reasonably well when clean, lubricated, and firing good quality ammunition, war in the trenches only served to emphasize how easily even the supposedly improved 1910-type mechanism could be jammed by mud or heat generated during rapid fire.

Thus although the action was unusually strong and could be operated very rapidly in conditions that were helpful, serious problems soon became apparent. As early as 1906 part of a bolt had been blown back into the face of a member of the Royal North-West Mounted Police, and a series of accidents prompted more than one investi-gation. Those involving 1905-type actions usually arose

when the locking lugs failed to engage, or the trigger released the striker before the breech was properly locked. The bolt of the 1910-pattern guns, however, could be rotated under the extractor after the bolt sleeve had been removed from the bolt-way. Though the bolt sleeve would re-enter the receiver, the bolt could not then lock on the closing stroke. When the gun fired, the bolt slammed back – and if the bolt stop failed under such a violent impact, the entire bolt would fly back out of the gun directly at the firer's face. Some of the worst accidents befell left-handed firers, but even right-handers rarely escaped unscathed.

The British ordered substantial quantities of Mark III Ross rifles in 1914, owing to a shortage of SMLEs, but they were never popular and were rapidly withdrawn from front-line service; 45,000 of them went to the Royal Navy from April 1917 onwards, replacing the unpopular Japanese 6.5mm Arisaka rifles.

Changes were made in 1916 to improve extraction, and the addition of a rivet or screw in the bolt sleeve (begun unofficially by armourers in France) prevented bolts being wrongly assembled. However, the improvements came too late to prevent the unpopular Ross being replaced by the short Lee-Enfield in the autumn of 1915. Enshrouded in controversy, the Ross Rifle Company ceased trading in March 1917, and its assets were seized by the Canadian government; however, it petitioned successfully for compensation, receiving $2 million shortly after the war had ended.

India

The Indian Army – a separate entity from the British Army in India – was initially armed from Britain. Early in the twentieth century, however, powder mills in the town of Ishapore were converted to an arms factory, and the first of a series of 'India Pattern' (IP) or 'Special to India' (SI) weapons was approved. These customarily followed British prototypes, but modifications were made to suit local conditions: for example, butt plates were altered to allow pull-throughs and cleaning material to be carried in rifles that were not similarly equipped for Home Service.

Indian-made rifles were distinguished by butt-socket marks such as ISHAPORE and 'I.P.'; they also bore a crowned 'E.R.I.' cypher (1905–10) or 'G.R.I.' (1910–18). Property marks included an 'I' beneath a broad arrow, and stock roundels displayed names such as 'Ferozepore' or 'Allahabad'.

The 'Carbine, India Pattern', approved on 8 January 1904, was issued to the Sappers & Miners with the P/1888 sword bayonet. A standard, rifle-type nosecap was fitted with a Martini-pattern swivel, a second swivel being added on the under edge of the butt. Survivors were re-chambered in 1924 for .303 Mk VII cartridges, and the backsight graduations were altered. The maximum sighting distance was 1,000yd (914m).

A 'Rifle, India Pattern, Single-shot' was approved by the Secretary of State for India in December 1909, and 2,000 full-length guns destined for Frontier Levies had been made at Enfield when World War One began. The magazine well was filled with a sturdy wood block, and a special trigger guard/magazine plate was used.

FRANCE

Rifles

The Gras Rifle

Just as the Franco-Prussian War of 1870–1 had persuaded the Germans that the days of the Dreyse Zündnadelgewehre (needle rifles) were over, so the introduction of the 1871-pattern Mauser rifle made the French realize that the 1866-type Chassepot needle-guns were also obsolescent. Though the Chassepot was much more efficient ballistically than the Dreyse, its annular india-rubber obturating washer rapidly lost elasticity and could distintegrate during prolonged fire.

Trials undertaken in 1872 with a Dutch Beaumont rifle demonstrated the value of metallic-case ammunition, and the submission in May 1873 of an appropriately converted Chassepot by Captain Basile Gras was a turning point. The Gras bolt was comparatively simple, with a separate head carrying the extractor and a satisfactory lock being provided simply by the abutment of the bolt-handle rib against the receiver

French North African colonial tribesmen pose with an 11mm Gras artillery musketoon.

The 11mm Gras rifle was an adaptation of the obsolescent Chassepot needle gun, the earliest examples being conversions. This is a gendarmerie rifle, with an additional barrel band and a flattened bolt handle turned down against the stock-side. Courtesy of the MoD Pattern Room Collection, Royal Ordnance plc, Nottingham.

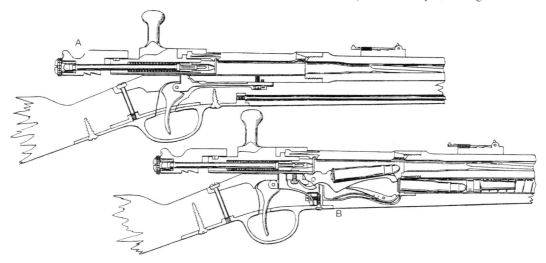

A comparison between the action of the single-shot Gras rifle (A) and the tube-magazine Kropatschek (B). Note the similarity of the bolts. Drawings by André Jandot from James E. Hicks' French Military Firearms 1717–1938.

bridge. Because there was no ejector, spent cases were simply tipped from the boltway by the head of a screw doubling as the bolt stop.

In a final trial with Gras and Beaumont rifles undertaken in April 1874, the Dutch design was abandoned, and the *Fusil d'Infanterie Mle 1874* was immediately ordered into series production. It was essentially similar to the Chassepot – indeed, many 'new' guns were simply converted from their needle-fire predecessors (and known as 'Mle 1866/74'). Conversions can usually be identified by manufacturers' marks dating prior to 1874.

New guns were made in several differing forms. The basic infantry rifle had two barrel-retaining bands and a bar-and-tenon on the right side of the muzzle for the Mle 1874 épée bayonet; the cavalry rifle was essentially similar, but had an additional band, the bolt handle turned down against the stock side, and it lacked a bayonet fitting. The gendarmerie carbine was practically identical to the cavalry rifle, but accepted a special socket bayonet. The artillery short rifle, or *Mousqueton d'Artillerie*, had a short barrel and a single band, and the right side of the muzzle was adapted to accept a sword bayonet.

Magazine Rifles

Tests undertaken by the French Navy in mid-summer 1877 resolved in favour of the Kropatschek. After approval of a cartridge-stop or cut-off mechanism, the trials rifle was adopted on 28 June 1878 to replace ageing M1866 (Chassepot) needle-guns that survived in navy service. Made in Austria in 1878–9 by Osterreichische Waffenfabriks-Gesellschaft of Steyr, the *Fusil de la Marine Mle 1878* was little more than a single shot M1874 Gras action amalgamated with a tube magazine in the fore-end, inspired by the Swiss Vetterli. About

– were adapted Gras actions fitted into new one-piece stocks deep enough to contain the magazine tube, and were easily distinguished by a prominent grasping groove in the fore-end. They had a single barrel band and a nosecap, with a bayonet bar on the right side of the muzzle. The cut-off lever rotated in a depression in the stock behind the bolt handle.

Newly made M1884 rifles had a cleaning rod let into the left side of the stock, the nosecap was clinched inwards, and the magazine tube protruded beneath the muzzle. The metal parts of army rifles were browned, whereas those of 1878-pattern naval

The 11mm-calibre 1878-pattern Kropatschek navy rifle, with a tube magazine beneath the barrel. Note that these guns had one-piece stocks. Courtesy of Hans-Bert Lockhoven.

25,000 guns were made. They were locked by the bolt-guide rib abutting the receiver ahead of the bridge as the bolt handle was turned downwards; they were 1,244mm long, weighed about 4.5kg empty, and had a 743mm barrel with four-groove rifling. The magazine held seven rounds, and the ramp-and-leaf backsights were graduated to 1,800m. Performance included a muzzle velocity of about 455m/sec with 11 × 59mm ball cartridges. There were two barrel bands, a bayonet lug on the right side of the nosecap, and swivels under the rear band and butt.

The success of the navy rifle inspired the army to develop a similar gun. Developed in 1883 by two staff members of the Châtellerault arms factory, arms inspector Close and Commandant Lespinasse, the *Fusil d'Infanterie Mle 1884* was little more than a French-made M1878. The earliest guns – 'Mle 74/84' or 'Mle 74/80 M.84'

rifles had been polished to resist corrosion.

Chambering the standard 11 × 59mm Gras cartridge, the M1884 shared the single-lug locking system of its predecessors. The guns were 1,244mm long, weighed 4.26kg empty, and had 743mm barrels rifled with four grooves. The tube magazine within the fore-end held eight rounds, and the backsight was graduated to 1,900m. The M1884 was rapidly superseded by the M1885, which had a massive receiver separating butt and fore-end, and a cut-off protruding from the bottom of a prominent housing milled in the right side of the receiver ahead of the trigger.

Though more than 50,000 Kropatschek rifles were used in France, their service life was greatly curtailed by the development of the 8mm smokeless propellant cartridge, credited to government chemist Paul Vieille. This generated chamber pressures that were too high for the simple Gras-type bolt of the Kropatschek to withstand in safe-

The experimental 1885-pattern French army rifle was a development of the navy's Kropatschek, with a distinctive slab-sided receiver separating the butt from the fore-end. Courtesy of Hans-Bert Lockhoven.

The 8mm Lebel rifle of 1886 was no great improvement on the 1885-pattern guns mechanically, but introduced a revolutionary small-calibre cartridge loaded with smokeless propellant. This picture shows the tipping cartridge-elevator in the bottom of the receiver. Courtesy of Ian Hogg.

The M1886/93 Lebel rifle. Drawing by John Walter.

ty. An improved bolt system, with two asymmetrical lugs on a detachable bolt head, was perfected in 1885–6 by the *Commission d'Étude des Armes à Répétition* to become the M1886 ('Lebel') rifle.

The *Fusil d'Infanterie Mle 1886* was known colloquially as the 'Lebel', after the commandant of the École Normale de Tir, who had personally directed trials undertaken in the Camp de Châlons. Its worst feature was the tube magazine, retained at the insistence of a government keen that any new rifle should hold at least as many cartridges as the German M71/84 Mauser. The Lebel bolt was basically that of the M1874 (Gras), but lugs on the separate bolt head locked horizontally into the

receiver behind the chamber. The two-piece stock of the perfected Kropatschek was retained, but the nosecap was adapted to accept an épée bayonet with a slender cruciform blade and a locking collar beneath the muzzle ring.

The Berthier Rifle

The origins of this weapon lay in a desire to equip French cavalrymen with a suitable magazine carbine. Adolphe Berthier adapted the Mle 86 (Lebel) action to accept an Austrian Mannlicher-style magazine in 1887, but approval to build a prototype infantry rifle was withheld until May 1888 while experiments with Lebel-type carbines were being undertaken. When these failed, attention turned to the Berthier, and encouraging trials were held in Fort Mont-Valerien. Carbines were approved in 1890 for the cavalry, cuirassiers and gendarmerie, the cuirassier pattern having an extraordinarily curved combless butt suited to firers wearing a breastplate; a short rifle or Mousqueton followed in 1892 for artillerymen. The guns shared similar actions, but were stocked differently. Bayonets were not issued with cavalry carbines, which were stocked virtually to the muzzle, but the gendarmerie pattern accepted an épée bayonet and the short rifle could be fitted with a sturdy sword bayonet.

The guns were very successful – they were much easier to load than the Lebel – and were popular with soldiers. Rifles were approved for sharpshooters in Indo-China and Senegal, the *Fusil des Tirailleurs Indo-Chinois* (M1902) and the *Fusil des Tirailleurs Senégalais* (1907) respectively, even though the tube-magazine M1886/93 Lebel remained the principal weapon of the line infantry.

The bolt of the Berthier resembled the Lebel pattern, though the lugs locked vertically and modifications were made to feed from a clip-loaded box magazine. The magazine was one of the poorer features of the design, its capacity restricted partly by the shape of the clumsy 8mm service cartridge, and partly by a desire to envelop the magazine in the stock.

Rigorous service during World War One soon revealed the weakness of the slender stocks, and also that, possibly owing to the lightweight construction, accuracy was not particularly good. The sturdier M1886/93 rifles were retained customarily for grenade-launching and sniping, even in units where the Berthier had been issued.

Other Rifles

The turning-bolt design credited to Commandant Louis Daudetau was patented in Britain in December 1890. The rifles were chambered for a variety of cartridges, but no great success was encountered in France even though a 6.5 × 53.5mm version was supplied in quantity to the French navy at the turn of the century. Others went to Portugal in 1899–1900, where they were apparently used for field trials prior to the emergence of the Mannlicher-Schönauer and then the Vergueiro-Mauser. Daudetau rifles and carbines were sold to El Salvador and Paraguay in the late 1890s, while Uruguay selected the 6.5 × 53.5 No. 12 Daudetau cartridge for weapons converted from 1871-type Mausers in Saint-Denis. Production ended in the early 1900s after about 5,000 had been made, but Daudetau-action sporting rifles were still being made in the 1920s.

The *École Normal de Tir* ('ENT') at Châlons was, in effect, the school of infantry and was deeply involved in the development of small arms. By the 1890s, enough designers and engineers had joined the staff for work on weapons to begin. Two types of ENT turning-bolt 6mm rifles were tested in 1896, with two-piece stocks but an otherwise Berthieresque profile; a 7mm gun was tried in 1898, with a pump-type actuator under the action beneath the chamber; and a 6mm straight pull gun of 1901 relied on a bar-lock moved laterally by a pivoting lever running back along the right side of the pistol grip.

The French Daudetau navy rifle of 1895, inspired by the introduction of the Lee straight-pull design in the USA, fired a 6.5mm cartridge. It was not particularly successful and failed to displace the Mle 86/93 Lebel. Courtesy of Hans-Bert Lockhoven.

The 1917-pattern semi-automatic rifle, often known as the 'RSC' after its promoters, was successful enough to see service in the First World War. It was, however, large and clumsy. Courtesy of Ian Hogg.

ENT also developed semi-automatic rifles prior to 1914, including several gas-operated Rossignol designs with retractable locking lugs and a selection of short-recoil designs credited to Belgrand, Chezaud or Vallarnaud. None of these guns was especially successful, nor did long-recoil prototypes developed by the *Commission Technique de Versailles* (CTV) and the *Établissement Technique de l'Artillerie de Puteaux* (APX) fare much better. Like most comparable semi-automatic rifles developed elsewhere, French designs were usually too complicated and too prone to excessive breakages to succeed.

Next came the 8mm Fusil C8, derived *c.* 1908 from experiments begun by Chauchat and Sutter two years earlier. Made in small quantities for field trials, the long-recoil C8 was locked by rotating an interrupted screw on the bolt head into seats in the receiver. The magazine accepted a three-round Berthier clip.

The semi-automatic *Section Technique de l'Artillerie* rifle, STA No. 4 (later reclassified 'Fusil A1'), was a gas-operated Pralon-Meunier design dating in its original guise from 1897. It was also locked with interrupted-thread lugs. A series of experimental rifles culminated in STA No. 6 (or 7mm Fusil A6), used in small numbers during World War One.

Machine-guns

The French were the first army in Europe to adopt a machine-gun, accepting the De Reffye (improved Montigny) *Mitrailleuse* in 1869. This was really a 'battery gun', a collection of rifle barrels in a cylindrical casing; it was loaded by inserting cartridges into a perforated plate, offering this plate up to the breech so that a cartridge entered each chamber, placing a breech block with multiple firing pins behind the plate, and then pulling a lever to operate the firing pins in succession.

The *Mitrailleuse* was expected to perform great feats of destruction in the Franco-Prussian War; however, at that stage of development, machine-guns had not entered into tactical thinking and the French deployed them as artillery. Unfortunately they lacked the range of field guns, and, emplaced well forward of normal artillery positions, they attracted counter-fire from Prussian artillery that destroyed most of them before they could take effect. In the few instances where commanders deployed them intelligently, the machine-guns did indeed effect great destruction – but not enough to salvage their reputation.

The failure of the *Mitrailleuse* in the war of 1870–71 was still rankling when the first truly automatic guns appeared in the 1880s, and as Maxim was not French, there was little hope of his gun being adopted by the French Army; as late as 1895, Ateliers de Puteaux was still unsuccessfully promoting a modernized Gatling gun. Fortunately for the French Army, the French-made Hotchkiss appeared in 1897. The Hotchkiss company had been offered a gas-operated design by an Austrian, Adolf von Odkolek zu Augezd, and had acquired the rights to what was soon developed into a quirky but efficient machine-gun.

After a successful test in 1897, the French army requested minor improvements and then adopted the weapon as the *Mitrailleuse Hotchkiss*

Hotchkiss made mechanically-operated machine-guns and essentially similar machine-cannon. Extremely popular in naval service, this 37mm version is shown on a typical landing carriage. Courtesy of Ian Hogg.

A typical 1914-pattern 8mm Hotchkiss machine-gun, favoured by the French army during the First World War. Courtesy of Ian Hogg.

Modele 1900. Guns of this type had their baptism of fire in Japanese hands during the Russo-Japanese War (1904–5), where reports filed by neutral observers did much to promote Hotchkiss sales. But the French Army, as parsimonious as most armies of the day, believed that money could be saved by developing guns of its own. Experiments with the Puteaux, or APX (1905), and the Saint-Étienne (1907) ended in disaster, however, and in 1914, desperately short of serviceable weapons, the authorities found no alternative but to revert to the Hotchkiss.

Handguns

The French army, with extensive experience of the Lefaucheux pinfires, remained wedded to the revolver for many years. The first effectual 'modern' design was the M1873, now often known by the names of the designers Chamelot & Delvigne. A six-cartridge chamber could be loaded through a swinging gate on the rear right side of the frame, and unloaded with the help of a reciprocating rod on the right side of the barrel. The rimmed 11 × 17mm 1873-pattern cartridge was a centrefire pattern giving a muzzle velocity of about 130m/sec.

Nearly 340,000 1873-pattern revolvers were made in the Saint-Étienne factory between 1873 and 1885. There was also a navy pattern which, unlike the standard army guns, had the cylinder modified to chamber either the M1870 or M1873 11mm cartridges. The M1874 was similar, but destined for officers and senior NCOs; the surface of its cylinder was fluted instead of plain. Production in the period 1875 to 1885 amounted to about 35,000 for the army, plus about 1,300 dual-cartridge guns (for naval officers) made in 1878, 1880 and 1882 only.

The first Chamelot-Delvigne revolvers were sturdy and reliable, but widely regarded as too heavy and slow to load compared with the auto-extracting Smith & Wessons that gained common currency, particularly in Russia, during the 1870s and 1880s. A series of French trials committees experimented with lighter guns throughout the 1880s, issuing the semi-experimental 1887-pattern gun in some numbers, before settling on the Modèle d'Ordonnance *1892*, widely but misleadingly known as the 'Lebel'. This was an 8mm-calibre six-shot pattern with a cylinder, mounted on a yoke, which swung out of the right side of the frame. This feature was specifically designed to allow cavalrymen to hold the gun and the reins in their left hand while reloading with the right; however, it made the task awkward for foot soldiers.

Made by the Manufacture d'Armes de Saint-Étienne (military issue) and the Manufacture Française d'Armes et Cycles de Saint-Étienne (commercial patterns), the M1892 remained the principal service weapon in 1914 even though extensive experimentation with semi-automatic pistols had been undertaken. However, the French found themselves so short of weapons that huge quantities of simple 7.65mm blowback Ruby-type pistols were ordered in Spain early in 1915.

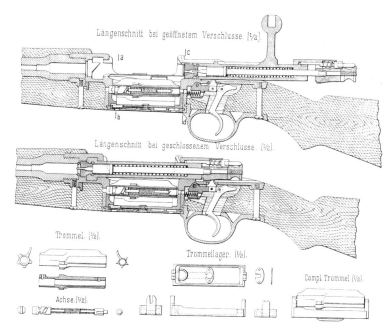

Longitudinal sections of the 1903-pattern 6.5mm Mannlicher-Schönauer rifle, extensively used by the Greek army during the First World War. Note the spring-driven spool magazine. From Konrad von Kromar, Repetier- und Handfeuerwaffen der Systeme Ferdinand Ritter von Mannlicher (Vienna, 1900).

A typical 1871-pattern 10.35mm Vetterli rifle. Note the tangent-pattern back sight. Courtesy of the MoD Pattern Room Collection, Royal Ordnance plc, Nottingham.

The 10.35mm M1871/87 Vetterli-Vitali rifle was a conversion of earlier single-shot guns. Note the box magazine protruding beneath the stock ahead of the trigger guard; the odd shape was due to the cartridge-tray follower rod, which moved vertically. Courtesy of the MoD Pattern Room Collection, Royal Ordnance plc, Nottingham.

GREECE

Adopted in 1876 to replace the unsuccessful indigenous Mylonas, the 11 × 59mm single-shot Gras rifle was made in Steyr by Osterreichische Waffenfabriks-Gesellschaft; 57,000 rifles and 6,000 carbines had been delivered by the end of 1877. Many found their way in the early twentieth century to lesser Balkan states – Montenegro, for example – after being displaced by magazine rifles. Others were taken out of store to serve second-line troops during the Balkan wars.

The Gras was superseded by 1888- and 1895-pattern Mannlichers supplied in small numbers by Osterreichische Waffenfabriks-Gesellschaft, and then in 1903 by the 6.5 × 54mm Mannlicher-Schönauer rifle. It was hoped, with some justification, that the five-round spool magazine would feed more precisely than box patterns. The rifle soon acquired a reputation for smooth operation and reliability, and remained in service until the 1940s.

ITALY

Rifles

The unification of Italy created standardization problems in ordnance circles. Rigorous trials undertaken in 1868–9 convinced the Italians of the merits of the Swiss Vetterli breech, but not of the tube magazine. Italy had a larger army than Switzerland, and the cost of re-arming with magazine rifles was prohibitive. The first Italian weapons, therefore, were single-loaders.

Metallic-cartridge rifles
Although the single-shot 10.35mm M1870 Vetterli – made in rifle, short rifle and carbine forms – was successful enough in service, the advent elsewhere of magazine rifles forced the Italian authorities to begin trials. The army was not especially keen to issue guns of this type on a large scale; the navy was more accommodating, however, and the M1882 navy rifle, the *Fucile di Marina Mo. 1882* or 'Vetterli-Bertoldo', was made in small numbers by the Reale Fabbrica d'Armi Terni.

The M1882 shared the action of the 1870-pattern army rifle, but had an eight-round tube magazine beneath the barrel. A typical example was 1,210mm long, weighed 4.05kg empty, and had a 730mm barrel rifled in the usual four-groove style. The backsight was a quadrant pattern graduated to 1,400m, and the muzzle had a lug for a sword bayonet.

Dislike of tube magazines impelled the army to upgrade single-shot M1870 rifles into M1870/87 repeaters by adding a four-round box magazine beneath the action. The conversion was known colloquially as the 'Vetterli-Vitali', acknowledging the designer of the magazine. Guns of this type remained in service for many years, particularly with native levies in Somaliland and Eritrea. After the defeat of these Italian colonial forces in

1941, many thousands of Vetterli-Vitali rifles were shipped back to Britain to equip the Home Guard and the Army Cadet Force.

Small-bore magazine rifles
The Italians soon realized that even their new Vetterli-Vitali rifles were obsolescent. The advent of the 8mm M1886 Lebel in France and, particularly, the adoption of the 8mm M1888 Mannlicher by arch-rival Austria-Hungary, forced them into commission of an infantry weapon. Work began in the School of Musketry, Parma, at the end of 1888 under the presidency of General Gustavo Parravicino. In December 1889, the committee reported on trials with more than fifty rifles;

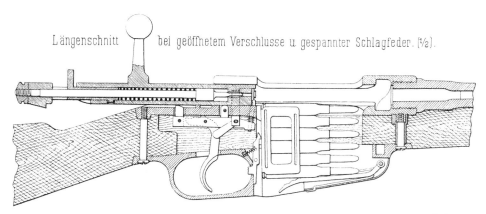

Längenschnitt bei geöffnetem Verschlusse u. gespannter Schlagfeder. (½).

Längenschnitt bei geschlossenem Verschlusse u. gespannter Schlagfeder. (½).

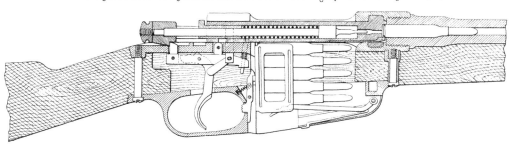

Longitudinal sections of the 6.5mm Mannlicher-Carcano rifle, which remained the service rifle of the Italian army until the end of the Second World War. Note the clip-loaded box magazine and the simplicity of the bolt; unlike many Mannlicher-style clips, the Italian pattern can be loaded either way up. From Konrad von Kromar, Repetier- und Handfeuerwaffen der Systeme Ferdinand Ritter von Mannlicher (Vienna, 1900).

This gas-operated prototype 6.5mm Cei-Rigotti rifle, dating from the early 1900s, was tested in Britain. Note the exposure of the operating rod on the right side of the breech. Courtesy of the MoD Pattern Room Collection, Royal Ordnance plc, Nottingham.

however, none had proved to be ideal. A decision followed in March 1890 to adopt a 6.5mm cartridge, and ten differing breech systems were tested for suitability; a report preferring the Mannlicher magazine system to Lee, Mauser and other rivals was submitted in April 1891.

A modified Mannlicher developed in Reale Fabbrica d'Armi de Torino by a team led by Salvatore Carcano, the Fucile di Fanteria Modello 1891, was adopted on 29 March 1892. Carcano, the principal inspector of the Turin arms factory, contributed a bolt adapted from Mauser's 1889 Belgian design with an additional bolt-sleeve safety mechanism. In fact the only truly Mannlicher feature to be retained by the designing committee was the magazine, though the clip was reversible and contained one cartridge more than normal.

The M1891 rifle had a full-length stock, a projecting magazine case, a split-bridge receiver, and a tangent backsight. A wooden hand-guard cov-

ered the barrel from the front of the backsight to the barrel band. Rifles were accompanied by cavalry and gendarmerie carbines, and by the oddly named 'Carbine for Special Troops' (*Carabina per Truppi Speciali*) or 'Carabina TS' – in fact this was no more than a short rifle for engineers and artillery, with a lateral lug beneath the nosecap for a quirky sword bayonet.

The Cei-Rigotti Rifle

In 1895, Captain Amerigo Cei-Rigotti of the Bersagliere invented a gas-operated selective-fire carbine that attracted widespread interest in European military circles. Gas was led into a cylinder, about half-way along the barrel, to operate a short-stroke piston from which a tappet curved up to strike an elongated operating rod connected to the bolt. A lug on the head of the operating rod acted in a cam-track in the bolt, dis-

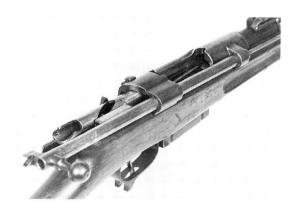

Another view of the Cei-Rigotti rifle, with the breech open. Courtesy of the MoD Pattern Room Collection, Royal Ordnance plc, Nottingham.

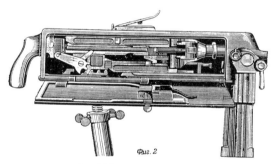

Рис. 139. Пулемет Перино обр. 1909 г.

A Drawing of the action of the Perino machine-gun. From V.G. Federov, Evolyutsiya Strelkovogo Oruzhiya (1938).

engaging the locking lugs from recesses in the barrel as the rod ran back. The operating system was essentially similar to that of the US M1 carbine of 1941. A simple change-lever gave single shots or automatic fire, and the detachable box magazines held up to fifty rounds.

The Cei-Rigotti was demonstrated in the British Royal Small Arms Factory, Enfield, in March 1901. Several series of cartridges were fired at a 24ft (7m)-wide target at a distance of 200yd (180m), and the gun, set to fire automatically, then fired ten rounds in less than two seconds. However, owing to excessive jamming, the Cei-Rigotti was rejected. Development work is believed to have continued for some years, but by 1914 the rifle and associated machine-guns had disappeared into history.

Machine-guns

Like most European armies, the Italians experimented with mechanically operated guns in the 1870s and 1880s, and between 1885 and 1887 purchased small quantities of three-barrel Nordenfelt and two-barrel Gardner guns chambering the standard 10.35mm Vetterli cartridge. Known as the 'N' and 'G' patterns respectively, they were confined largely to fortifications and warships.

A few 10.35mm Maxim guns 'M', purchased from 1887 onwards, were subjected to extensive trials, but large-scale purchases seem to have been deferred indefinitely in the hope of discovering an Italian design. One eventually appeared: the Perino. Patented in 1900 by Guiseppe Perino, this interesting weapon operated by a combination of recoil and gas action. The breech was locked by a bell-crank lever mechanism, giving a very positive action, and the feed originally relied on a metal chain carried on a drum on the side of the gun; each link of the chain carried a cartridge. The feed box of later Perino guns contained five twelve-round trays, and was perpetuated by many other Italian designs.

The Italian government was keen to promote indigenous inventions – quite rightly, as the Perino was serviceable enough for its day – but it wasted too much time in endless trials against the Maxim, the Vickers the Colt and their rivals. When a decision was finally reached, World War One was looming and the Italians had to take what they could get. When fighting began in earnest, the Perino was abandoned in favour of the Revelli-designed FIAT machine-gun (see Part Three), whilst Hotchkiss, Maxim and Colt guns were acquired in near-desperation in France and the USA.

2 Eastern Europe and Japan

JAPAN

Rifles

Contact with Chinese troops who carried Mauser, Snider and Chassepot rifles highlighted the poverty of the Japanese arms industry, and this led to the creation of a technical commission in 1875. Major Tsuneyoshi Murata was despatched to France, Germany, Switzerland, the Netherlands and Italy in 1876 and 1877, and by combining features suggested by the principal European rifles, he successfully created the first Japanese-made breech-loader.

At least 100,000 Meiji 13th Year Type Murata rifles, also known as 'M1880', were made in the period 1880–86 by the Koishikawa ordnance factory on the outskirts of Tokyo. They chambered an 11 × 60mm rimmed cartridge, giving a muzzle velocity of about 1,485ft/sec, and were locked by the bolt-guide rib abutting the receiver ahead of the bridge. The guns were 51.55in overall, weighed 9.1lb, had 33in barrels with five-groove rifling turning to the left, and could accept a sword bayonet. The Meiji 16th Year Type cavalry

carbine (1883) had a 20in barrel and a stock extending to the muzzle. It weighed merely 7.15lb.

The single-shot Murata was superseded by the Meiji 22nd Year Type infantry rifle (1889) and the Meiji 27th Year Type cavalry carbine (1894), which had eight- and six-round tube magazines beneath the barrel respectively. The rifle was 47.5in long, weighed 8.7lb empty, and had a 29.5in barrel rifled with four grooves turning to the right; the carbine was just 37.5in long and weighed 6.85lb. They chambered an 8mm rimmed cartridge which gave a muzzle velocity, in the rifle at least, of 1,850ft/sec.

A typical Meiji 22nd Year ('Murata') rifle, introduced in 1889. The tube magazine beneath the barrel and elements of the bolt suggest French influence. Courtesy of Ian Hogg.

The open breech of the Meiji 30th Year rifle of 1897, better known as the 'Arisaka'. This view shows how the bolt handle turns down into a seat in the receiver-bridge, but not the distinctive hook which protrudes from the left side of the cocking piece. Pressing the small catch inside the trigger guard releases the magazine floorplate.

The Arisaka

Japanese soldiers embroiled in the Sino-Japanese War (1894) encountered the German Gewehr 88 in combat for the first time, and soon discovered that their tube-magazine Murata rifles were far less efficient than guns with clip-loaded box magazines. A committee chaired by Colonel Nariake Arisaka, appointed to develop a new rifle, soon concluded that the Mauser action was preferable, and a few thousand Meiji 29th Year Type trials rifles (1896) were made in the Koishikawa factory. The guns chambered a 6.5 × 50 semi-rimmed cartridge, giving a muzzle velocity of about 2,500ft/sec. They were 50.05in long, weighed about 9lb, and had 31in barrels with six-groove Metford polygonal rifling. The charger-loaded box magazine, contained within the stock, held five rounds, but the most distinctive feature was the safety hook protruding from the cocking piece. Trials rifles also lacked a hand-guard.

Field trials suggested minor improvements, and the *Meiji 30th Year Type* rifle (1897) was approved in 1899. Except for a single barrel band instead of two, and a deeper pistol-grip, the gun was difficult to distinguish from its predecessor.

The 1897-pattern rifle and an associated carbine served during the Russo-Japanese War (1904–5), supplemented by the unsuccessful Meiji 35th Year Type rifle of 1902, but these were then superseded by the *Meiji 38th Year Type* rifle of 1905. Issued from 1907 onwards, the rifle was well made and of excellent material, and the perfected Arisaka action proved to be exceptionally strong and durable. The Mauser twin-lug lock and a Mauser-type trigger were joined by a reciprocating bolt cover and a characteristically Japanese stock. Owing to a shortage of Western-style stock blanks, most butts had a separate wedge-shaped toe pinned and glued in place.

The rifle was soon joined by a Meiji 38th Year Type carbine, and ultimately, in 1911, by a Meiji 44th Year Type cavalry carbine distinguished by a folding bayonet attached to a bulky nosecap. The guns served throughout World War One, though Japanese land forces were scarcely involved once the German protectorate of Kiautschou had fallen. Many Arisaka weapons were sold in the period 1914–17 to alleviate shortages in Russia and Britain; their stories are told in Part Three.

Automatic Weapons

The Russo-Japanese war of 1904–05 was the first conflict in which machine-guns were employed by both sides in significant numbers, and the Japanese Army used the French Hotchkiss to great effect. Kijiro Nambu then used the 1914 pattern Hotchkiss to design a gun suitable for Japanese manufacture, and the resulting 'Taisho 3rd Year' was a close copy of the original, chambered for the 6.5mm Arisaka rifle cartridge. The only obvious external differences between this and the French gun lie in the barrel finning and the fittings on the tripod. It was adopted in 1914,

The 8mm-calibre Japanese Meiji 26th Year type revolver (1893) was a break-open pattern, inspired by the Smith & Wesson practice of the 1870s. Note the absence of a hammer spur, suiting the gun only to double-action fire. Courtesy of Ian Hogg.

The 'Type Nambu' pistol was made in two basic patterns; this is the 7mm version, officially known as 'Type B' but now more commonly labelled the 'officer's model'. Courtesy of Ian Hogg.

and some of the original weapons continued in service throughout World War Two. The Taisho 3rd Year Type inherited the merits of reliability and strength from its French ancestor, but it also inherited the need for lubricated ammunition, always a possible source of trouble in dusty conditions. Like the models which followed it, the Taisho 3rd Year Type had sockets in the tripod feet through which the crew passed poles so they could carry the gun and tripod in one lift – a feature unique to Japanese machine-guns.

Handguns

The principal Japanese service weapon was the Meiji 26th Year Type revolver of 1893, a 9mm six-shot weapon developed by a military commission. The basic action had been adapted from the break-open Smith & Wessons supplied in large numbers to Japan in the 1870s. One identifying feature was the absence of a spur on the hammer, intended to protect cavalrymen from accidents.

Though the revolver remained the principal weapon encountered in Japanese hands prior to 1914, substantial quantities of Nambu-type (*Nambu shiki*) semi-automatic pistols had been made. Under development since the early 1900s, the standard 8mm 'Type A' had been acquired by the Japanese army and the navy; several hundred had even been exported to Siam before World War One began. The minuscule 7mm 'Type B' pistol had become popular with officers, even though it was a poor man-stopper.

Nambu pistols were all recoil-operated, compressing a single coil spring in a chamber on the left side of the receiver, and had a detachable box magazine in the butt. Though externally similar to the Parabellum (Luger) pistol, close inspection reveals that the spring-chamber formed an integral part of the frame.

RUSSIA

Rifles

In the early 1860s the Russians were seeking an effective method of converting their huge

Calibre

The calibre of most pre-1917 Russian firearms was expressed in 'Lines', an indigenous measurement equal to 1/10in: hence the 'Three-Line Rifle' had a calibre of 0.3in. Sights were customarily graduated in arshin (paces), each equalling 28in.

inventory of cap-lock muzzle-loaders, and experimented with a selection of breech-loaders; they finally opted for a design submitted by the Bohemian gunmaker Sylvestr Krnka.

At least 350,000 M1869 Krnka infantry rifles were made in the imperial manufactories in Izhevsk, Sestroretsk and Tula between 1870 and 1875, initially simply by converting old 1856-pattern rifle-muskets. Chambering a 15.24 × 21mm rimmed cartridge, giving a muzzle velocity of about 1,075ft/sec with a 570-grain bullet, they were locked by swinging the breech-block laterally, and fired by a sturdy inertia-type striker struck by a new hammer mounted on existing back-action lock plates.

A typical Krnka rifle was 52.75in long, weighed 9.9lb empty, and had a 35.6in barrel rifled with four grooves. A socket bayonet could be locked around the front-sight base when required. The Dragoon Rifle shared the action of the infantry rifle, but was merely 48.15in long and weighed 7.6lb.

The Krnka, nothing more than an expedient, was supplemented by the 1868-pattern Berdan rifle, about 30,000 single-shot infantry rifles being made in 1869–70 in Hartford, Connecticut, by Colt's Patent Fire Arms Mfg Co. Chambered for a 10.6 × 57.5mm rimmed cartridge giving a muzzle velocity of about 1,450ft/sec, they relied on a pivoting breech-block locked behind the chamber when the linear striker ran forwards after the firer had pressed the trigger. The guns were 53in overall, weighed 9.37lb, and had 32.5in barrels rifled with six grooves. Their leaf-type backsights were graduated to 1,400 paces, and a socket bayonet could be locked around the front-sight base.

The original Berdan was not particularly successful in service, and was soon superseded.

At the time of its adoption in 1871, the 4.2-Line (10.6mm) Berdan II bolt-action rifle was among the most powerful being issued in Europe, the flatness of its trajectory worrying the British and French in particular. Production was slow, however, and the Russians did not manage to re-equip even front-line infantrymen until the mid-1870s. Some guns were fitted with a Krnka quick-loader in 1877, consisting of a ten-round canvas cartridge box strapped to a plate on the left side of the fore-end ahead of the chamber. Experiments with quick-loaders and magazine attachments for the Berdan rifle continued for many years. On 1 July 1914, the Berdan inventory still stood at 362,400 7.62mm and 10.67mm rifles, plus a small number of 7.62mm carbines.

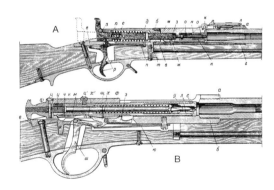

Longitudinal sections of the Berdan I (A) and Berdan II (B) rifles. The Berdan I, made in the USA by Colt, had a bolt-locked block that lifted upward at the rear; and the Berdan II had a conventional bolt mechanism. From V.G. Federov, Evolyutsiya Strelkovogo Oruzhiya *(Moscow, 1938).*

Magazine rifles

Trials undertaken at the Oranienbaum proving ground in 1888 with a selection of rifles resolved in favour of the single-shot Lutkovskiy and Mosin submissions – and this was surprising, given the presence of a magazine-feed Mauser. Fortunately for the Russians, a five-shot version of the Mosin rifle appeared in 1890,

A typical 1891-pattern 7.62mm Mosin-Nagant rifle, with the original flat-leaf back sight. Courtesy of Ian Hogg.

to be tested against a .35-calibre Nagant. Throughout the summer and autumn of 1890, 300 Mosin rifles, 100 Nagants and 300 Berdans lined-down to 7.62mm were submitted to exhaustive testing. Eventually the trials commission elected to combine the Mosin bolt mechanism, which owed much to the French Lebel, with the efficient magazine system and feed-interruptor mechanism of the Nagant. The resulting 'Obr. 1891g' or 'Three-Line Rifle' was adopted in April 1891, only later becoming known as the 'Mosin-Nagant'.

Duly satisfied, the Main Artillery Commission recommended that the principal ordnance factories should immediately begin tooling for mass-production. The comparative backwardness of the arms industry persuaded the Russians to equip the Tula factory with machines purchased from Greenwood & Batley of Leeds, then copy the plant layout to enable Izhevsk and Sestroretsk to begin production. Consequently, more than 80 million roubles were budgeted to allow 3.29 million guns to be made, whilst an additional 74 million roubles were to be spent on new

cartridge-making facilities and a semi-smokeless propellant manufactory.

The production schedules were hopelessly optimistic: many of the vital machine-tools took longer to arrive in Russia than had been anticipated, and teething troubles persisted. Though production began in Tula in 1892, only 1,439 rifles had been made by the end of the year – and as certain key components had not been finalized, even these were classed as trainers.

Desperate to re-arm their line infantrymen, the Russians ordered 503,000 rifles from the French government early in 1892 (Russia and France had particularly close ties in this period). The guns were to be made in the factory in Châtellerault for 59 francs apiece, and were all to be delivered by the last day of 1895 to prevent penalty clauses being invoked; 503,539 completed rifles arrived on time.

Tula was ready to begin series production in the spring of 1893, and 191,984 1891-type rifles were assembled by the end of the year. With tooling in Izhevsk and Sestroretsk under way, progress seemed assured. During the first phase

A longitudinal section of the Russian Mosin-Nagant rifle. One of the best features of the design was a cartridge-depressor in the magazine, which prevented the clumsy rimmed cartridges misfeeding.

of rearmament (1892–96), 1,470,470 combat rifles and 32,443 trainers were made in the Russian arms factories; nearly two million more were delivered during the second phase, which lasted until 1903.

Mosin-Nagant rifles performed acceptably during the Russo-Japanese War (1904–5), but were found to be poorly sighted; in addition, firing with the socket bayonet attached to the muzzle ruined accuracy. However, the most pressing problems had arisen with the Russian artillery, and investment was directed away from small arms. This had no real effect at first, owing to the reduction of men under arms after 1905 and the return of many guns to store.

used. Much of the skilled workforce had been laid off, or diverted to tasks that were believed to be of greater importance.

Automatic Rifles

In 1905, Yevgeniy Roshchepei, a 'regimental blacksmith', designed a blowback rifle based on Mosin-Nagant components. However, though the gun was tested at the Oranienbaum proving ground, it found no lasting success; the absence of a breech-lock, allied with the considerable power of the 7.62 × 54mm Russian rifle cartridge, did not endear it to the military mind. It is proba-

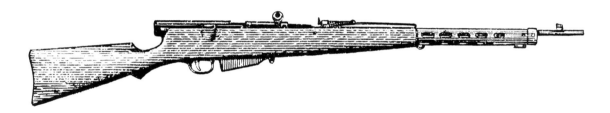

The 1912-pattern Federov automatic rifle was the prototype of the 'Avtomat'. Drawing from V.G. Federov, Evolyutsiya Strelkovogo Oruzhiya (1938).

In 1910, however, a commission headed by Polivanov recommended that a war reserve should be created to satisfy demands for weapons in the event of general mobilization. The War Ministry subsequently established that 4,272,744 rifles would be needed, 3,924,323 7.62mm Mosin-Nagants and 348,421 of the surviving 10.6mm-calibre Berdans. The standing army of the day mustered 1.23 million men, and there were expected to be about 2.54 million conscripts on mobilization. However, Russia mobilized nearly 5.5 million men in 1914, the war reserve disappeared overnight, and weapons of all types were soon in short supply.

Very little had been done since publication of the report of the Polivanov commission to ensure that losses of rifles were made good, and by 1913, only one-eighth of production capacity was being

ble that the Roshchepei gun was difficult to cock, owing to the strength of its recoil springs, and prone to extraction failures.

Vladimir Federov proposed a recoil-operated modification of the Mosin-Nagant as early as 1905, contemporaneously with trials of the Roshchepei rifle, but it may never have been built. A modified design appeared in 1907, relying on pivoting flaps engaging lugs on the bolt to lock the action at the moment of firing. Even the earliest guns of this type were promising enough to allow Federov and Degtyarev, then his principal assistant, to continue work in the Oranienbaum workshops. Though the recoil spring proved too weak to return the bolt when the muzzle was elevated, and extraction was capricious, these seemed minor problems; the prototype had otherwise worked surprisingly well.

The two designers then moved from the Oranienbaum proving ground to the Sestroretsk arms factory, where better facilities were available. New prototypes were prepared in 1908–9, locked by two blocks pivoted on the barrel extension. When the action recoiled, a cam on the standing frame pulled the rear of the locking blocks downwards to release the bolt. Trials showed the Federov rifle to be superior to Tokarev, Browning and Sjøgren rivals, and it was approved for field trials in 1912.

The 1912-pattern Federov was long, very clumsy, and had a butt with a distinctively shaped pistol-grip. The box magazine protruded beneath the stock ahead of the trigger; a selector lay on the top edge of the stock above the trigger; and a wooden hand-guard ran from the backsight to the sheet-metal fore-end. However, trials revealed persistent extraction problems, owing to the awkward shape of the standard 7.62mm rifle cartridge, and only about 150 modified guns were delivered, in small batches, in 1912 and 1913.

The 1913-type rifles chambered the 6.5 × 50 Japanese semi-rimmed carriage, giving a muzzle velocity of about 2,395ft/sec. They were locked by pivoting the blocks on the barrel extension into the bolt, and could fire fully automatically when the selector was set appropriately. They were 49.4in long, weighed 10.15lb, and had 31.5in barrels rifled with six polygonal grooves. A five-round integral box magazine and a 2,000-pace tangent-leaf sight were standardized.

By 1914, it was becoming clear that the 1913-type Federov – even though it was prone to jamming – was the best of the guns under review. Unfortunately, work ceased at the beginning of World War One, in order to free Federov and Degtyarev to supervise mass-production of Mosin-Nagant infantry rifles. However, the merits of automatic rifles were sufficiently clear to persuade the authorities to relent, and in 1915 Federov resumed work. The eventual outcome was the Avtomat, described in detail in Part Three.

Machine-guns

The Russians had been enthusiastic champions of the Gatling gun, known in Russia as the 'Gorloff' after the president of the trials commission, and had experimented with the Nordenfelt for naval use. The first Maxims had been purchased in the early 1890s, chambered for the 7.62 × 54mm rifle cartridge, and small quantities had been pressed into service during the Russo-Japanese War. Hotchkiss machine-guns used by the Japanese attracted great public approval, though this was due more to the skill with which they were handled than their intrinsic merits.

The first regulation-pattern Maxim to be issued in large numbers was the 7.62mm *Pulemet obr. 1905g*, which was distinguished more by its wheeled mount than any unusual features on the gun. It was superseded by the 1910-pattern Maxim, which had a sheet-steel barrel casing instead of phosphor-bronze, and improvements in the feed system. The later Maxims could be found on a lightweight tripod or a wheeled Sokolov mount, originally with two additional folding legs beneath the axle. They served with distinction throughout World War One, reinforced by large numbers of 'Potato Digger' M1895 Colts made under licence by Marlin.

The 7.62mm 1896-type Mauser pistol was popular in Russia, large numbers being purchased for service in the Russo-Japanese War of 1904–5. This particular gun, sold in the USA prior to the First World War, bears the mark of Von Lengerke & Detmold of New York on the left side of the receiver.

The 7.62mm Nagant revolver of 1895 was remarkable for its gas-seal system, achieved by camming the cylinder forward at the moment of firing so that the mouth of the elongated cartridge case could expand to seal the gap between the cylinder and the barrel. This Tula-made example dates from 1941, but many of the earliest guns were made by Em. & L. Nagant Frères in Liège. Courtesy of the MoD Pattern Room Collection, Royal Ordnance plc, Nottingham.

Handguns

The Russians had purchased Smith &Wesson 'Russian Model' revolvers enthusiastically in the 1870s, first from the USA and then, when production capacity could no longer be spared, from Ludwig Loewe of Berlin. Production eventually commenced in Tula.

Guns of this type were made in several patterns, beginning with a long-barrelled 'infantry' type and eventually proceeding to shorter-barrel 'cavalry' guns with prawled backstraps and spurred trigger-guards. Many of these obsolescent handguns survived to serve during World War One as trainers, or on unimportant duties miles from the Eastern Front.

For an army regarded elsewhere in Europe as backward and inefficient, the Russians were surprisingly ready to embrace the semi-automatic pistol. Trials with the Parabellum (Luger) and the FN-Browning had been undertaken with vigour in the early years of the twentieth century, but the most popular proved to be the 7.63mm Mauser C/96. Thousands of these were acquired by army officers, particularly during the Russo-Japanese War of 1904–5, and many others had been acquired in the same era by revolutionaries eager to overthrow the Tsar. Sales figures published by Waffenfabrik Mauser AG in 1910 indicated that

422 pistols had been sold to Russia in 1904, and an additional 1,240 in 1905. Only Germany, the home market, performed better: the totals were 484 for 1904, and 2,741 for 1905. The entire Asian market – which was to become a most enthusiastic consumer of Mauser pistols and lookalikes – took merely 649 in 1904–5.

In 1914, however, the service handgun remained the 1895-pattern Nagant revolver. This seven-shot weapon chambered a special 7.62mm with the case-neck extended to envelop the bullet. This was needed to effect a seal between the case mouth and the bore. To do this, the trigger mechanism cammed the entire cylinder forward at the moment of ignition. The design, one of many similar ideas proposed at the time, had been patented in 1895 by the Nagant brothers of Liège. Many of the first revolvers were made in Belgium, but a duplicate production line installed in the Tula small-arms factory began to make them in 1899 and continued work – amazingly! – until 1943.

It is arguable whether the additional complexity was worth the meagre gain in velocity from sealing the cylinder/bore joint, but the Nagant not only proved to be solid and reliable, in more recent years it has also provided the basis for excellent target revolvers.

3 The United States of America

RIFLES

The American Civil War (1861–5) provided an ideal testing-ground for a variety of breech-loading rifles, and by 1864 the Federal army had decided that a suitable means should be found of converting existing rifle-muskets. The Chief of Ordnance, General Dyer, asked Erskine Allin – then Master Armorer at the National Armory, Springfield – to prepare a suitable design.

Trials completed by April 1865 recommended adoption of the Spencer repeater and the single-shot Peabody, but the end of the Civil War was accompanied by a wholesale reduction in the military budget that made the conversion of muzzle-loaders the only viable option. The prototype Allin rifle performed well enough in the summer of 1865 to be ordered in quantity for field trials, and Springfield Armory had soon converted about five thousand .58 rimfire rifles from 1863-pattern cap-lock rifle-muskets. The new breech-block could be swung up to reveal the chamber, but the alteration proved to be much too complicated. In addition, the ratchet-type extractor was weak and the cartridge was inadequate.

The 1865-pattern Allin rifle was superseded by a simplified gun with its barrel lined down from .58- to .50-calibre. Trials still favoured the Berdan as the best conversion system, with the Peabody being the best 'new rifle', but the Allin design was controversially selected for production. Substantial quantities of .50-70 M1866 rifles were made in Springfield Armory, followed by the improved M1868 (1868–9) and M1870 (1870–2).

In the autumn of 1872 a Board of Officers began trials with rifles chambering a new .45-70-405 centrefire cartridge. By January 1873, more than a hundred submissions had been reduced to twenty-one, and after further testing the US government-sponsored Springfield was adopted for service in May. The purchase of a few Ward-Burton magazine rifles was recommended for the cavalry, but subsequently rejected by the Chief of Ordnance.

Many changes were made to the basic 'Trapdoor Springfield' during a production life lasting twenty years, though none affected the basic operating system. A half-stocked carbine appeared in 1873, followed by a de luxe 'Officer's Rifle' in 1875, specialist target rifles (1881–2), and eventually a smooth-

The .58-calibre Starr carbine was typical of the breechloaders used during the American Civil War (1861–5). Though conceived as a cap-lock, a metallic cartridge-firing conversion appeared in 1864. Courtesy of Wallis & Wallis, Lewes, East Sussex.

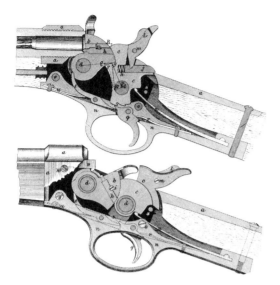

Two cutaway views of the Remington Rolling Block, showing how the tail of the hammer supported the breechblock at the moment of firing.

bore shotgun known as the 'Forager'. The service rifle was radically revised in 1879, without changing its designation, and again in 1884. Short-rifle derivatives were tried extensively in the early 1880s, often fitted with rod bayonets, until the last of the single-shot Allin-breech guns was approved in August 1889 – three years after the French Army had accepted a magazine rifle chambering small-calibre ammunition loaded with smokeless propellant.

Allin-pattern guns remained regulation US Army firearms until the introduction of the Krag-Jørgensen in the early 1890s. They were then gradually withdrawn, serving the National Guard until

c. 1905. Those that remained on the official inventory during and after World War One were stored for the use of state militiamen until the early 1920s.

The First Magazine Rifles

A patent protecting a bolt-action rifle and its detachable box magazine was granted in the USA in November 1879 to James P. Lee. The Lee Arms Company was formed in Bridgeport, Connecticut, and about fifty prototypes – varying considerably in detail – were made in the toolroom of the Sharps Rifle Company. The perfected version had a handle locking down ahead of the receiver bridge. The greatest problems, however, had concerned the design of the magazine spring and the way in which the cartridges were presented to the chamber. The earliest attempts to develop one-piece zigzag springs failed, and the solution was not found until Hugo Borchardt riveted a series of flat spring-steel plates together. The plain-sided Borchardt magazine was patented in March 1882.

The US Navy ordered three hundred Lee rifles, but the collapse of Sharps occurred before anything other than the most basic machining could be done on the receivers, and the contract was passed to E. Remington & Sons.

A typical first-pattern US Navy rifle was 48.5in long, had a 29.5in barrel rifled with three grooves, and weighed about 8lb 8oz empty. The detachable box magazine held five .45-70 rounds, and the ramp-and-leaf backsights were graduated to 1,200yd. Performance included a muzzle velocity of 1,320ft/sec with ball cartridges, and the M1873

This .433 (11mm) Remington Rolling Block rifle, an 1871-pattern Spanish example, is typical of the guns of this type – used in modernized smallbore form by the French and even the British during the First World War.

A typical .45-calibre M1884 'Trapdoor Springfield' rifle, with its M1873 socket bayonet, scabbard and belt-frog. These guns were loaded by lifting the tail of the breech-block, but had a reputation for jamming. Courtesy of Wallis & Wallis, Lewes, Sussex.

A .45-calibre 1882-pattern Remington-Lee rifle; the earlier 1879 type lacked the additional locking lug. Courtesy of Hans-Bert Lockhoven.

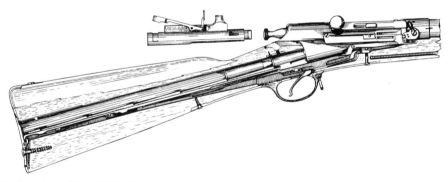

A longitudinal section of the .45 Chaffee-Reece rifle, an unsuccessful competitor of the Remington-Lee in the rifle trials of the early 1880s. Drawing by André Jandot, from J.E. Hicks' U.S. Military Firearms 1776–1945.

socket bayonet could be locked around the front sight when required. The breech was locked simply by allowing the bolt-guide rib to abut the receiver ahead of the bridge, and by a lug entering the receiver wall as the bolt handle was turned down.

A half-cock notch sufficed as an unreliable safety feature, but the Lee rifles were successful enough to convince the US Navy of their merits, and seven hundred additional guns were purchased. These accepted the standard Remington socket bayonet instead of the 1873-pattern Springfield design, and the magazines were made in accordance with a patent granted to Roswell Cook in September 1884. A sliding spring-detent (on the left side) held the cartridges when the magazine was detached from the gun, but was automatically released when the magazine was pushed into the feedwell.

Most of the earlier 1879-type Navy rifles, which had been issued with the plain-sided

The Krag-Jørgensen rifle was adopted in Denmark and Norway in addition to the USA. This is a 6.5mm 1894-pattern Norwegian rifle, with a loading gate that hinges downwards. Courtesy of Ian Hogg.

The action of a modified US Army 1898-pattern .30 Krag-Jørgensen rifle with the experimental Parkhurst & Warren charger-loading system. Courtesy of Ian Hogg.

Borchardt magazines, were altered to receive the Cook pattern in Navy workshops. Modified guns could accept Borchardt or Cook magazines interchangeably, though second-pattern rifles were restricted to the Cook type.

Among the rifles tested by the US Army in the summer of 1882 was Lee-patent 'Gun No. 36', incorporating an improved bolt with the handle locking down behind the receiver bridge. On 4 September 1882, the board reported that Lee No. 36 was preferred to Chaffee-Reece No. 33 and Hotchkiss No. 34, owing to the detachable box magazine and an additional locking lug. A contract for 750 guns was finally agreed with E. Remington & Sons on 31 May 1884, allowing field trials to be undertaken in competition with the Springfield-made Chaffee-Reece and Hotchkiss guns supplied by Winchester.

The 1882-pattern Lee rifles had one-piece stocks, two bands, standard army-type sights, and improved Diss-patent magazines with two prominent cartridge-guide grooves in the sheet-metal

bodies. Unfortunately, in the autumn of 1885, the Chief of Ordnance informed the Secretary of War that whilst the Lee had performed better than its rivals, most respondents preferred the single-shot .45-70 Springfield!

Eventually, worried by advances in Europe, the US Army announced a competition to find a suitable small-bore magazine rifle. Trials with more than fifty guns were concluded in August 1892, when the Krag-Jørgensen was chosen in preference to the Lee and the Mauser simply because fresh cartridges could be inserted in the

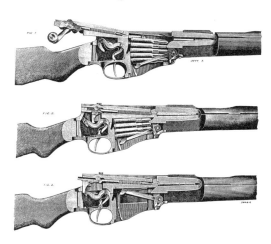

The 6mm M1895 Lee Navy Rifle relied on a straight-pull bolt. However the opening stroke was awkward and the guns were never popular. They had soon been replaced by Krag-Jørgensens. These three engravings, from Engineering, *show the action open (top) and closed in the fired (centre) and cocked (bottom) positions.*

A photograph of the Lee Navy Rifle action, open. Courtesy of Ian Hogg.

A typical 1899-pattern Remington-Lee rifle, chambered for small-calibre smokeless ammunition. The action is shown cocked. Note also the tangent-type back sight. The cleaning rod is missing from its customary position beneath the barrel.

magazine when the bolt was shut on a loaded chamber.

About 24,560 M1892 Krag-Jørgensen rifles, or 'US Magazine Rifles, Caliber .30, Model of 1892', were made by the National Armory in Springfield, Massachusetts, between 1894 and 1897. They chambered a rimmed .30-40 cartridge generating a muzzle velocity of about 2,000ft/sec, relying on a single lug on the bolt head engaging a recess in the receiver to lock the breech. The guns were about 49in long, weighed 9.38lb empty, and had 30in barrels with four-groove concentric rifling turning to the right. A five-round pan magazine – virtually a box magazine laid on its side – ran transversely across the underside of the action, beneath the bolt, and fed the cartridges up to a feedway on the left side of the bolt.

It was loaded by opening a hinged door that formed the base of the magazine and carried the spring and follower, thus allowing loose rounds to be dropped into the feedway. When the door was closed, the spring pressed the cartridges across the aperture in the receiver until they could be caught

by the left side of the bolt head during the loading stroke. The magazine door could be opened at any time to add cartridges, which gave the Krag an advantage over clip- or charger-loading rivals.

So many adaptations and improvements were made to the original pattern that it was eventually reclassified 'M1896'; this was followed by the last and most common of the rifles, the M1898, originally destined for an unsuccessful high-power cartridge, which differed in the design and machining of the receiver. More than 324,000 M1898 Krags had been made in Springfield Armory when work ceased in 1904.

There were also a number of half-stocked Krag-Jorgensen carbines. The first were made for trials in 1893, simply by shortening M1892 rifles by about 8in. A cleaning rod was carried in the butt, a saddle ring appeared on the left side of the wrist, and the nosecap lacked a bayonet lug. The M1896 pattern was followed by a series of improved guns, most of the changes involving sights and the design of the fore-end. The M1899 was the most common, about 36,000 being made

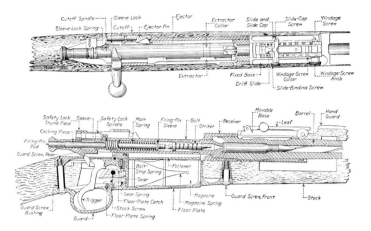

Longitudinal sections of the M1903 'Springfield' rifle, a modified Mauser with a five-round magazine carried almost entirely within the stock.

in Springfield prior to 1904; guns of this type had a longer fore-end than their predecessors, and, after 1902, the tip of the hand-guard was raised to prevent the saddle scabbard damaging the back-sight. In addition, about ten thousand full-length rifles were converted prior to 1914 to carbine-length for issue in the Philippines. Unlike US Army carbines, the guns destined for the Philippines accepted the standard sword bayonet.

The Springfield

The experiences of the Spanish-American War showed that Spanish Mausers were superior to the Krag-Jorgensen. On 2 October 1900, there-fore, a Board of Officers convened at Springfield Armory to test an experimental weapon, and at least a hundred 'Model of 1900' rifles were made in the National Armory in 1901.

Chambered for an experimental .30 calibre rimless cartridge, giving a muzzle velocity of 2,300ft/sec with a 220-grain bullet, they relied on two lugs on the bolt head locking in recesses in the receiver behind the chamber as the bolt han-dle was turned down; a 'safety lug' turned down ahead of the receiver bridge. The guns were 49.25in long, weighed 9.47lb with their integral rod bayonets, and had 30in barrels rifled with

four grooves. The box magazine could be loaded from a five-round charger.

Approval was given in 1902 for the manufac-ture of five thousand improved M1901 rifles in Springfield, by adapting existing machinery, but only a hundred M1901 rifles had been made when it was realized that full-scale production would disrupt work on the Krag-Jorgensen. However, the Krag's inability to handle high-pressure ammunition remained a worry in US Army ordnance circles; experiments therefore continued with a short rifle, inspired by the intro-duction in Britain of the SMLE, and the upshot was that the 'US Magazine Rifle, Caliber .30, Model of 1903' was duly approved. Better known as the 'Springfield' after the principal manufac-turer, the modified 1906-pattern M1903 was the main weapon of the US Army when World War One began in Europe, and also of the American Expeditionary Force in April 1917. It is described in greater detail in Part Two.

HANDGUNS

The US armed forces had been equipped with revolvers since the middle of the nineteenth cen-tury, first with cap-lock Colts and then a variety

A longitudinal section and exterior view of the 1892-pattern Colt revolver, the first swing-cylinder pattern to be adopted by the US Army. Extensive teething troubles were cured by reversing the rotation of the cylinder to prevent it attempting to turn itself out of the frame.

of Colt and Smith & Wesson cartridge-firers. When the Spanish-American War began in the summer of 1898, substantial quantities of shortened ex-cavalry .45 M1873 ('Peacemaker') Colts remained in service, particularly with the artillery; however, the regulation pattern was a modernized form of the .38 M1892.

In its original form, this swing-cylinder Colt design had been accepted by the US Navy in 1889; teething troubles had been overcome by altering the rotation of the cylinder from anti-clockwise to clockwise (viewed from the rear), and by adding a safety mechanism to prevent the gun firing before the cylinder was properly locked into the frame, resulting in a sturdy and reliable weapon. However, the .38 bullet proved to be a bad man-stopper, and experience against fanatical tribesmen in the Philippines convinced the authorities that something more potent was needed. A short-term solution was provided by a modernized form of the 1878-pattern double-action .45 Colt, issued as the 'M1902', but interest in the first generation of semi-automatic pistols had been

aroused by an encouraging test of the Borchardt pistol-carbine in 1897 and the emergence of the first designs credited to John M. Browning.

Several prototypes had been produced in the mid-1890s, one embodying the original 'Browning Dropping Link'. This used barrel recoil to disengage lugs on the barrel from recesses in the underside of the slide, dropping the barrel on a pivoting linkage. Early guns used two 'parallel motion' links, one at the muzzle and one at the breech. These were not especially successful, but were reliable enough to beat the Parabellum and the Savage in the US trials of 1906–7. Browning persisted, and in 1909 introduced a modification in which only a rear link was used. This strong and efficient design was subsequently adopted on 29 March 1911 as the 'US Pistol, Caliber .45, Model of 1911'.

Wear in the barrel bushing and the tolerances necessary to swing the barrel in its housing made the early Colt-Brownings less accurate than some of their rivals, but the Browning breech system had the merits of simplicity, reliability and unusual strength; one gun fired six thousand consecutive rounds without misfires or parts breakages. The US M1911 service pistol was very popular and was destined to be produced in large numbers: 75,000 guns made by Colt's Patent Fire Arms Mfg Co. and Springfield Armory were in store or on issue when the US Army entered World War One late in 1917, but there

This 1905-pattern .45 Colt-Browning pistol led to the M1911, one of the sturdiest and most reliable semi-automatic pistols ever to have been adopted for military service.

The M1911 US Army Colt-Browning had attracted interest elsewhere when the First World War began. These are Norwegian 11.35mm M/1912 (Colt-made) and M/1914 (Kongsberg) guns. Courtesy of Masami Tokoi, Düsseldorf.

were 643,755 by the Armistice in November 1918. It is a tribute to the strength and durability of the Browning design that the US Army should have retained it through both world wars.

THE EARLY MACHINE GUNS

The first mechanically operated gun to find lasting success was patented in November 1862 by Dr Richard Jordan Gatling. Originally made in Cincinnati, Ohio, the first .58-calibre pattern fired standard combustible cartridges inserted in integrally capped carriers. Though a multiple barrel cluster had been developed for the DeBrame Revolver Cannon of 1861, the Gatling was the earliest gun of its class to prove useful. Even though only the uppermost barrel fired, it achieved an impressive fire-rate by firing six times for each turn of the crank handle.

The chequered early history has been told by Wahl & Toppel in *The Gatling Gun*, and only the rudiments need be repeated here. Though used successfully by state militiamen during the American Civil War, the gun was not tested by the US Army until January 1865 – whereupon, much impressed, the authorities ordered the development of a 1in version. On 24 August 1866, the gun

was formally approved for service with the US Army: fifty .50-calibre and a similar number of 1in guns were acquired. Made by Colt's Patent Fire Arms Manufacturing Company, these 'Model 1865' Gatlings had a cam-sleeve inside the breech casing to retract the breech bolts. Consequently, the latter revolved with the barrels.

They fired .50-70-450 centrefire cartridges from tin box magazines that fitted over the feed hopper. Traverse was controlled by a lateral screw under the breech; elevation was altered with a screw-wheel beneath the breech. The breech-bolts of the improved M1871 could be removed through the cascabel plate for inspection or repair. An improved curved box magazine was used, though most guns would also accept a drum magazine patented in April 1872 by L.M. Broadwell. The Broadwell drum consisted of a cluster of twenty vertical magazines formed into a single unit, each containing twenty cartridges; as each portion was emptied, another was rotated into position manually. The M1871 Gatling also had an oscillator, which traversed the gun automatically through an arc of about 6 degrees either side of the centreline as the crank handle was turned.

The US Navy tested .50-calibre Gatlings at Fort Madison in the autumn of 1873, when 100,000 cartridges were fired through one gun in three days. Contemporaneous US Army trials at Fort Monroe, with 1in and .42-calibre guns, also finished favourably; consequently, the .45-70 M1874 was adopted on 1 July 1874.

Smaller and lighter than its predecessors, the M1874 had a hopper and breech housing of bronze rather than wrought iron. The special breech-bolts had been patented in April 1872, and the improved oscillator could be set either to traverse a target automatically or to act as a windage adjustment. A headspace adjustor was added to the central spindle at the front of the gun, which was potentially dangerous: so many accidents occurred that a crank lock had to be fitted, and the firers were forbidden to adjust the headspace nuts unless the crank lock was engaged. The improved feed hopper lay to the left

Gatling Guns with Accles drum magazines customarily also had their barrel-clusters encased in a bronze sleeve. From Engineering, *25 April 1884.*

of the gun's centreline, and the sights were shifted to the right side of the frame.

Two M1874 patterns were made: 'musket length', generally with ten 32in barrels, 49in overall and weighing about 525lb with the standard wheeled carriage; and the so-called 'Camel Gun', generally mounted on a 40lb tripod, which had 18in barrels, was 35.5in long and weighed about 135lb without its mount.

A variety of essentially similar guns followed, though there were many differing model-dates. The first of the so-called 'Bulldog' Gatlings, introduced in 1877, had short bronze-encased barrels and a direct drive system in which the crank handle was attached directly to the rear of the central axis rod protruding through the cascabel plate. This raised the rate of fire to previously unattainable rates. One ten-barrel gun tested by the US Navy in August 1876 fired a thousand rounds in 1min 19sec, attaining 996 hits on a 200yd (180m) target.

The M1879 had a special quick-adjustable yoke-pattern elevator, locked by a friction brake instead of a screwed-thread; this allowed an elevation of 30 degrees, a depression of 15 and a traverse of about 40 degrees either side of the centreline. The gun had ten 32in barrels, measured 49in overall, and weighed about 200lb; although it was generally mounted on the standard wheeled carriage, a few were equipped with light tripods.

The M1881 introduced a feed system patented in September 1881 by Gatling employee Lucien F. Bruce, comprising a bronze frame with two 'T'-slotted tracks to accept the rims of the .45-70 cartridges. These tracks could be loaded continuously during firing, one automatically falling into place (under gravity) when the other track had been expended. The gravity feed was effective enough under normal conditions, but it did not work efficiently at excessive angles of depression or elevation. The Accles Positive Feed, patented in Britain in 1881, was another answer, in which a large, vertical ring magazine, holding 104 .45-70 rounds, relied on a propellor plate – driven by the gun feed – to move cartridges down through the body under the guidance of helical grooves on the end plates. Unfortunately the magazine was cumbersome and easily damaged, and the US Army abandoned it in 1898, preferring an improved Bruce Feed.

After a selection of guns had been acquired in the 1880s, the M1893 Gatling appeared. It was the first to chamber the new .30 government cartridge (.30-40 Krag) and had a 'Gatling Positive Feed', a strip-feed system patented by Clement Broderick and John Vankeirsbilck in September 1893. Service experience soon showed that the thin metal cartridge strips were too weak, and by 1898 they had been replaced by the Bruce Feed.

In 1894, a Navy trial of Gatling, Gardner, Maxim, Robertson, Skoda and Accles guns resolved in favour of the automatic Maxim, though one member of the trial board filed a minority opinion in favour of the Gatling. But though the writing was clearly on the wall for manually operated machine-guns, the US Army still bought them: indeed, in the Spanish-

American War of 1898, Captain John 'Machine-Gun' Parker had five .30-calibre Gatlings at the Battle of San Juan Hill, and as a result the Gatling is honoured as the first machine-gun to be used by the United States against a foreign power.

The last US Army Gatling gun was the M1903, which was simply the .30-40 M1900 altered to handle the .30-03 cartridge. Most guns were conversions, but forty additional new ones were purchased to replace guns worn out in the Spanish-American War and the Philippine Insurrection. Most were subsequently converted for the .30-06 cartridge. Customarily assigned to static roles in fortifications for the last few years of their lives, they were declared obsolescent in 1912; however, they were only discarded after the end of World War One.

The first automatic machine-guns to be adopted by the United States were a batch of a hundred 37mm Maxim 'Pom-Pom' cannons purchased by the US Navy in 1895; these were mounted in fighting tops and similar elevated locations on warships, partly as a defence against torpedo boats, but also to sweep the decks of hostile ships. They remained in service until the last of the American pre-dreadnought warships were scrapped in the 1920s.

The US Army was able to test Maxim guns in the early 1890s, but the inventory of serviceable Gatling guns was large enough to prevent large-scale purchases, and the first automatic to be adopted was the 1895-pattern Colt designed by John M. Browning. Whereas Maxim had embraced recoil operation, Browning, well aware of muzzle blast, used the gas pressing behind the bullet as his source of power. An arm was pivoted downwards beneath the barrel by propellant gas escaping through a hole in the underside of the barrel after the bullet had passed.

The arm swung down in an arc to drive an operating rod extending back into the receiver to turn and then open the bolt. A spring then returned the bolt, loading a round from a cloth belt as it did so, and the swinging arm returned to its closed position ready for the next shot. The arc-like arm movement prevented the Colt being used close to the ground; if set too low, it threw up earth and clouds of dust, a habit that earned it the sobriquet 'potato digger'.

For all its idiosyncrasies, the Colt was reliable and effective; it was deployed in the Spanish-American War in .236 and .30-40, and even though by 1914 it had been superseded in US Army service by the Maxim, it was taken to France in that year by the Canadian Army. Large quantities were even made by Marlin for the Russians in 1915–17.

The first US Army .30-03 M1904 Maxim machine-guns – the Maxim having been the victor of a series of protracted trials – were supplied by Vickers, Son & Maxim in Britain. However, a manufacturing licence was obtained and the balance of the order for 282 guns emanated from Springfield Armory.

The Maxim was reliable and could sustain fire seemingly for ever, but it was taken into action on mule-back and demanded a squad of five men.

The US Army adopted the Maxim Gun in 1904, but initial purchases were few and far between. This drawing shows a typical pre-1900 gun on a wheeled carriage.

The US Army wanted something that one man could carry and two men could use, and finally selected the Hotchkiss light machine-gun developed in France in 1907–8; it was known to the Americans as the 'Bénet-Mercié Machine-Rifle M1909'. Machine-rifles of this type saw action in 1916 during the border wars with Mexico; however, they received such adverse publicity after one particular night attack that they became known as the 'Daylight Guns' because it was rumoured, quite wrongly, that the strip-feed system could not be mastered in the dark.

PART TWO: THE GUNS

4 Belgium

Belgian service weapons can often be identified by the royal cyphers. These generally take the form of a crowned cursive or Roman letter, for example 'A' for Albert. The guns also bear an encircled 'GB' (*Gouvernement Belge*) and inspectors' marks in the form of capital letters surmounted by crowns or stars.

HANDGUNS

9mm Model 1878/86 Revolver

The original revolver made in Liège by Emile & Leon Nagant was adopted by the Belgian army on 10 June 1878, initially to arm artillery officers and the customs service. It had a single-action trigger mechanism, a fluted cylinder and an octagonal barrel fitted into a prominent bolster on the frame. Next came the lightened double-action M1883, for cavalry officers, with a plain-surface cylinder and a short 'flattened octagon' barrel.

Pistolet-Revolver Nagant, Modele 1878/86

Synonym:	'M1886 Belgian Nagant revolver'
Length:	270mm (10.63in)
Weight:	940g (2.06lb), empty
Barrel length:	140mm (5.51in)
Chambering:	9 × 23mm, rimmed ('Belgian Nagant')
Rifling type:	four-groove, concentric, RH
Magazine type:	rotating cylinder
Magazine capacity:	six rounds
Loading system:	single cartridges
Front sight:	open blade
Backsight:	fixed notch
Muzzle velocity:	198m/sec (650ft/sec)

Both guns chambered a 9mm centrefire cartridge.

The M1878/86 was essentially similar to its predecessors, but had simpler lockwork, a rebounding hammer and an octagonal barrel that attached directly to the short-faced frame. Like the other

A typical 1900-pattern 7.65mm FN-Browning semi-automatic pistol. Courtesy of FN Herstal SA.

Pistolet Browning, Modele 1900	
Synonym:	'M1900 FN-Browning'
Adoption date:	3 July 1900
Length:	164mm (6.46in)
Weight:	0.630kg (1lb 6oz), empty
Barrel length:	102mm (4.02in)
Chambering:	7.65 × 17mm, semi-rimmed
Rifling type:	six groove, concentric, RH
Magazine type:	detachable box in butt
Magazine capacity:	seven rounds
Front sight:	open blade
Backsight:	fixed notch
Muzzle velocity:	290m/sec (950ft/sec)

The 9mm M1903 FN-Browning pistol replaced the 1900 pattern in Belgian service, and had also been adopted in Sweden prior to the First World War. Courtesy of FN Herstal SA.

Pistolet Browning Modele 1903	
Synonym:	'M1903 FN-Browning'
Length:	207mm (8.15in)
Weight:	935g (2lb 1oz), empty
Barrel length:	118mm (4.65in)
Chambering:	9 × 20mm Browning Long, semi-rimmed
Rifling type:	four groove, concentric, RH
Magazine type:	detachable box in butt
Magazine capacity:	seven rounds
Front sight:	open blade
Backsight:	fixed notch
Muzzle velocity:	329m/sec (1,050ft/sec)

Nagants, it was loaded with one cartridge at a time through a gate on the right side. A rod, stowed beneath the barrel, could be swung out on a yoke to push empty cases from the chambers, one at a time, through the loading gate behind the cylinder.

7.65mm Model 1900 Pistol

Made in accordance with patents granted to John Browning in 1897, prototypes of this gun were made by Fabrique Nationale d'Armes de Guerre (FN) of Herstal-lèz-Liège. About four thousand 'M1899' guns were made before the manufacturing pattern was finally settled. The original guns are larger than the M1900, have plain frames and unusually small grips, and lack the lanyard loop customarily found on the butt of the later weapons.

The perfected FN-Browning was tested successfully by the Belgian army, defeating the Borchardt-Luger and a Mannlicher in the final elimination trials largely owing to its simplicity. It was adopted to arm officers and some sword-carrying NCOs, and an order for about twenty thousand was given to Fabrique Nationale. Issues were extended in October 1901 to the gendarmerie and some mounted artillerymen, and then, in May 1905, to NCOs of the cavalry. In

Three drawings, including a longitudinal section, of the 9mm M1903 FN-Browning. From Revue de l'Armée Belge, 1903.

FABRIQUE NATIONALE HERSTAL LIEGE on the left side of the slide, above a cartouche containing a pistol and the FN monogram; the monogram and BREVETE S.G.D.G. (*Sans Garantie du Gouvernement*, 'without government guarantee') appeared in a panel raised from the left side of the frame. A small radial-lever safety catch lay on the left rear of the frame, accompanied by FEU ('fire') and SÛR ('safe').

The machining of the raised panel on the frame changed noticeably after substantial quantities of guns had been made, reaching the back of the trigger-guard instead of midway. The grips were enlarged, six retraction grooves became five, and a lanyard loop was added to the butt. The slide mark became FABRIQUE NATIONALE D'ARMES DE GUERRE HERSTAL BELGIQUE above the pistol/monogram cartouche, which was repeated on the left side of the frame above BROWNING'S-PATENT and BREVETE S.G.D.G.

9mm Model 1903 Pistol

This was a substantial improvement on the 1900-pattern FN-Browning, embodying a similar blowback mechanism but with the return spring concentric with the barrel and the barrel retained in the frame by a series of lugs – simple and very effective. It chambered the 9mm Browning Long cartridge, which was considered to be the most powerful that could be safely fired from any pistol lacking a positive breech lock. Consequently, though retaining a family resemblance, the M1903 was larger and more elegant than its 1900-pattern predecessor. Owing to its simplicity, it was widely copied in Spain until the Spanish Civil War began in 1936.

The M1903 was adopted by the Swedish army prior to 1914, the first M/07 pistols being purchased from Fabrique Nationale, and later ones emanating from the Huskvarna factory. Guns were also purchased on behalf of Russian

October 1910, all men carrying the earlier Nagant revolvers were ordered to exchange them for Browning pistols; when World War One began, even the officers of the Garde Civique were carrying pistols.

Production of 1900-type guns was discontinued in 1911. Nearly 725,000 had been made, though most had been sold commercially. The earliest guns were marked municipal police forces prior to World War One. Belgian military purchases were small, confined to replacement of worn or damaged M1900 FN-Brownings. Production of the pistol ceased when the Germans occupied Liège in August 1914, but resumed on a small scale in 1920 and continued until 1927; work continued in Sweden, however, until the early 1940s.

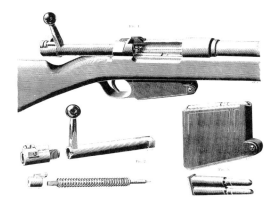

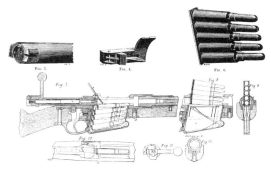

Drawings of the M1889 Mauser rifle. From Engineering, *3 April 1891.*

RIFLES

7.65mm Fusil d'Infanterie Modèle 1889

After extensive testing in the late 1880s the authorities decided to adopt this much-improved Mauser rifle. Tooling had begun by the end of

January 1891, and, on 31 December, Fabrique Nationale delivered the first four rifles to the Ministry of War. The 'Fusil à Répétition, système Mauser, Modèle de 1889' was formally adopted on 6 February 1892. It was the first true small-calibre Mauser. The one-piece bolt was derived from that of the Gew. 88 – with two symmetrical locking lugs – but the handle turned down behind the solid bridge of the receiver, and a cocking-piece housing or bolt-shroud was screwed into the rear of the perfected bolt.

The charger-loaded magazine was an improvement on Mannlicher clip patterns, as the charger was not essential to the action. Consequently the magazine was simpler, less prone to mis-feed, and could be replenished with single rounds. A suitable guide was milled into the leading edge of the receiver bridge, its companion being formed

Fusil d'Infanterie Mle 1889	
Synonym:	'M1889 Belgian Mauser infantry rifle'
Adoption date:	6 February 1892
Length:	1,276mm (50.25in) Length with M1889 sword bayonet attached: 1,518mm (59.75in)
Weight:	4.097kg (9lb 0oz), without sling Weight with M1889 sword bayonet attached: 4.352kg (9lb 9oz)
Barrel length:	779mm (30.67in)
Chambering:	7.65 × 53mm, rimless ('Belgian Mauser')
Rifling type:	four-groove, concentric, RH
Magazine type:	single-row protruding box
Magazine capacity:	five rounds
Loading system:	charger or loose rounds
Front sight:	open blade
Backsight:	leaf-and-slider type
Minimum backsight setting:	100m (109yd)
Maximum backsight setting:	2000m (2,187yd) Muzzle velocity: 620m/sec (2,034 ft/sec)

A typical 7.65mm M1889 Mauser rifle.

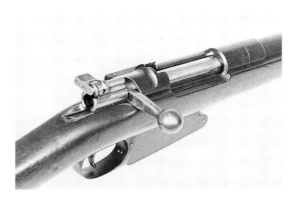

The bolt mechanism of the 1889-pattern Belgian Mausers. Courtesy of Ian Hogg.

by an extension of the spring-loaded bolt stop to hold the charger in place. Spent chargers were thrown clear as the bolt closed.

The rifle had a straight-wristed, one-piece stock; a housing for the follower-arm pivot projected from the lower front edge of the magazine case. A single spring-retained barrel band and a nosecap with a bayonet lug on its underside were used, but the barrel had a full-length annular jacket inspired by the Gew. 88. Sling swivels lay beneath the barrel band and on the under-edge of the butt.

By 30 June 1893, more than forty thousand Mle 89 rifles had been delivered to the army; daily production had stabilized at 250 rifles, 25,000 bullets and 25,000 cartridge cases. The last of the 150,000 rifles was delivered on 31 December 1894.

Another Belgian government contract for 1889-type rifles was given to Fabrique Nationale in June 1903, followed by another in November 1906.

Large numbers of Mle 89 rifles were seized by the Germans when World War One began. Many were issued without alteration, but some were apparently converted to fire the standard German 8 × 57mm cartridge. The remnants of the Belgian army fighting alongside the French placed production contracts with Hopkins & Allen after the fall of Belgium. In addition, a syndicate of exiles acquired facilities to make Mle 89 rifles in England; these are marked simply ETAT BELGE' and 'BIRMINGHAM' above the chamber.

Most guns were made prior to the German invasion of Belgium, by Fabrique Nationale d'Armes de Guerre of Herstal-lèz-Liège and the state small-arms factory, Fabrique d'Armes de l'État of Liège. Some were also apparently the work of Anciens Établissements Pieper of Herstal-lèz-Liège. A few thousand were made by Hopkins & Allen of Norwich, Connecticut, in 1914–16; a very few were also made in Britain during World War One.

7.65mm Fusil de la Garde Civique Modèle 1889

The M1889 Civil Guard rifle, adopted on 11 February 1896 for the Corps Spéciaux de la Garde Civique, was essentially similar to the standard infantry rifle (above), but the bolt handle was turned down and the accompanying bayonet had a blade of 11.8in instead of the standard 9.8in.

7.65mm Carabine de Cavallerie Modèle 1889

Made by Fabrique d'Armes de l'État of Liège, *c.* 1892–1914, the standard Mauser-type cavalry carbine was simply a much shortened form of the infantry rifle. The bolt handle was turned downwards, the backsight was mounted on the chamber reinforce, and the fore-end extended only to the barrel band. This exposed a considerable length of the barrel jacket and cleaning rod. A slotted plate was screwed to the left side of the butt to accept a stud on the carrying harness. Early carbines had a distinctive pivoting cover to protect the stud slot, but this was eventually abandoned.

Carabine pour le Gendarmerie à Pied et de l'Artillerie de Fortresse, Mle 1889	
Synonym:	'Belgian M1889 carbine for dismounted gendarmerie and fortress artillery'
Adoption date:	9 May 1904
Length:	1,045mm (41.14in)
Weight:	3.53kg (7.75lb), without sling
Barrel length:	550mm (21.65in)
Chambering:	7.65 × 53mm, rimless
Rifling type:	four-groove, concentric, RH
Magazine type:	single-row protruding box
Magazine capacity:	five rounds
Loading system:	charger or loose rounds
Front sight:	open blade
Backsight:	leaf-and-slider type
Minimum backsight setting:	100m (109yd)
Maximum backsight setting:	1,200m (1,310yd)
Muzzle velocity:	585m/sec (1,919ft/sec)

A Belgian Mauser-pattern gendarmerie and fortress-artillery carbine, M1889. Most guns of this type had their bolt handles turned down against the stock. Courtesy of Hans-Bert Lockhoven.

Carabine de Cavallerie Mle 1889	
Synonym:	'Belgian M1889 Mauser cavalry carbine'
Adoption date:	1892
Length:	885mm (34.85in)
Weight	3.062kg (6lb 12oz), without sling
Barrel length:	400mm (15.75in)
Chambering:	7.65 × 53mm, rimless
Rifling type:	four-groove, concentric, RH
Magazine type:	single-row protruding box
Magazine capacity:	five rounds
Loading system:	charger or loose rounds
Front sight:	open blade
Backsight:	leaf-and-slider type
Minimum backsight setting:	100m (109yd)
Maximum backsight setting:	1900m (2078yd)
Muzzle velocity:	559m/sec (1,835ft/sec)

7.65mm Carabine des Enfants de Troupe, Modèle 1889

The cadet rifle, made in small numbers by the Fabrique d'Armes de l'État prior to 1914, was similar to the carbine issued to dismounted gendarmerie and fortress artillery, but had a straight bolt handle and the barrel band lay midway between the backsight base and the nosecap. Few were made.

7.65mm Carabine pour le Gendarmerie à Pied et de l'Artillerie de Fortresse, Modèle 1889

The work of Fabrique d'Armes de l'État, *c.* 1899–1914, this short-barrelled Mauser shared the action, stock and barrel band/nosecap of the infantry rifle. The barrel band lay closer to the nosecap than the backsight base, distinguishing it from the otherwise similar cadet carbine. The bolt handle was generally turned downwards. Described as *avec yatagan*, the gun took a long-bladed bayonet. In 1916, however, surviving bayonets in the hands of the gendarmerie were replaced by the M1916 épée type.

7.65mm Carabine pour Gendarmerie à Cheval Modèle 1889

A minor variant of the cavalry carbine, made by Fabrique d'Armes de l'État prior to World War One, this had a conventional-length stock. However, the barrel band all but abutted the nosecap, and a sling swivel on the band was used in conjunction with a bracket screwed to the right side of the butt. A long-blade ('yatagan') version of the M1889 knife bayonet was issued until World War One, when it was replaced by the M1916 épée with a shortened M1882 (Comblain) blade.

Carabine pour le Gendarmerie à Pied et de l'Artillerie de Fortresse, Mle 1889	
Synonym:	'Belgian M1889 carbine for dismounted gendarmerie and fortress artillery'
Adoption date:	9 May 1904
Length:	1,045mm (41.14in)
Weight:	3.53kg (7.75lb), without sling
Barrel length:	550mm (21.65in)
Chambering:	7.65 × 53mm, rimless
Rifling type:	four-groove, concentric, RH
Magazine type:	single-row protruding box
Magazine capacity:	five rounds
Loading system:	charger or loose rounds
Front sight:	open blade
Backsight:	leaf-and-slider type
Minimum backsight setting:	100m (109yd)
Maximum backsight setting:	1,200m (1,310yd)
Muzzle velocity:	585m/sec (1,919ft/sec)

7.65mm Carbine pour les Cyclistes de la Garde Civique Modèle 1898

Made in small numbers by Fabrique d'Armes de l'État until *c.* 1912, this was based on the 1898-pattern Mauser action and, therefore, differed appreciably from the other Belgian service rifles. Though the data were generally similar to the Gendarmerie & Fortress Artillery carbine, the barrel jacket was discarded, the sights were graduated from 300m to 1,200m, and a special bayonet was used; apparently the gun had a modified safety mechanism that could not be applied when it was cocked. A sling bar lay on the left side of the band, and a swivel was attached to the left side of the butt.

Carabine pour Gendarmerie à Cheval Mle 1889	
Synonym:	'Belgian M1889 carbine for mounted police'
Adoption date:	1904
Length:	885mm (34.84in)
Weight:	3.05kg (6.75lb), without sling
Barrel length:	400mm (15.75in)
Chambering:	7.65 × 53mm, rimless
Rifling type:	four-groove, concentric, RH
Magazine type:	single-row protruding box
Magazine capacity:	five rounds
Loading system:	charger or loose rounds
Front sight:	open blade
Backsight:	leaf-and-slider type
Minimum backsight setting:	100m (109yd)
Maximum backsight setting:	1,900m (2,078yd)
Muzzle velocity:	560m/sec (1,837ft/sec)

MACHINE-GUNS

7.65mm Mitrailleuse Maxim, Modèle 1900

Manufactured by Deutsche Waffen- und Munitionsfabrik of Berlin, this was the standard Maxim pattern of the day (more details will be found in the British section), with a smooth phosphor-bronze water jacket, with the internal toggle mechanism breaking downwards, and the fusée spring casing on the left side of the receiver turned upwards.

7.65mm Mitrailleuse Maxim Modèle 1909

Sometimes listed mistakenly as the 'M1910', this was the standard DWM-made pattern of the day. The Belgian gun was little more than an export model of the German army Maschinengewehr 08 (MG. 08); indeed, when the Germans captured them in 1914, only the barrel and breech-block needed to be changed to enable ex-Belgian guns to fire the 8 × 57mm cartridge. The M1909 Maxim was appreciably lighter than its 1900-pattern predecessor, owing to improvements made in many individual components, and the water jacket was plain steel instead of phosphor bronze.

7.65mm Fusil Mitrailleur Modèle 1909

A few Benet-Mercié type Hotchkiss light machine-guns, chambered for the standard Belgian 7.65 × 53mm rimless cartridge, were purchased *c.* 1910 to arm the cyclists attached to the Chasseur squadrons. They were identical with their French prototypes excepting for calibre; details will be in the French section. They were apparently replaced by Lewis Guns (below) prior to World War One.

7.65mm Fusil Mitrailleur Lewis Modèle 1913

When Colonel Lewis failed to persuade the US Army that merit lay in his machine-gun, like John Browning before him, he beat a path to Europe. A promising demonstration persuaded the Belgians, struggling with Benét-Mercié Hotchkisses and semi-experimental Berthiers, to adopt the Lewis Gun – largely because it could be used by one man.

Société Anonyme Belge Armes Automatique Lewis was formed on 13 November 1912 at the

---

Mitrailleuse Maxim Mle 1900

Synonym:	'M1900 Belgian Maxim'
Length:	1,180mm (46.46in)
Weight of gun:	18.0kg (39.69lb), empty
Weight of mount:	31.9kg (70.5lb)
Barrel length:	717mm (28.22in)
Chambering:	7.65 × 53mm, rimless
Rifling type:	four-groove, concentric, RH
Feed type:	fabric belt
Belt capacity:	250 rounds
Selector:	none, automatic fire only
Cyclic rate:	450rd/min
Front sight:	open blade
Backsight:	leaf-and-slider type
Minimum backsight setting:	300m (328yd)
Maximum backsight setting:	2,500m (2,735yd)
Muzzle velocity:	650m/sec (2,132ft/sec)

Mitrailleuse Maxim Mle 1909

Synonym:	'M1909 Belgian Maxim'
Length:	1,175mm (46.25in)
Weight of gun:	18.0kg (39.69lb), empty
Weight of mount:	26.50kg (58.31lb)
Barrel length:	720mm (28.35in)
Chambering:	7.65 × 53mm, rimless
Rifling type:	four-groove, concentric, RH
Feed type:	fabric belt
Belt capacity:	250 rounds
Selector:	none, automatic fire only
Cyclic rate:	450rd/min
Front sight:	open blade
Backsight:	leaf-and-slider type
Minimum backsight setting:	300m (328yd)
Maximum backsight setting:	2,500m (2,735yd)
Muzzle velocity:	650m/sec (2,132ft/sec)

A Belgian M1904 Maxim machine-gun crew. The soldier on the right carries an M1909 Mauser rifle and a standard 1889-pattern sword bayonet.

suggestion of an entrepreneur, Joseph Waterkeyn, who fronted a consortium keen to finance Lewis's work in return for rights to 'Europe and the entire Eastern Hemisphere'. In May 1913, Lewis returned to the Birmingham Small Arms Co. Ltd to purchase gun barrels. Development of the prototype Lewis Guns had been undertaken in the BSA toolroom when the inventor had first visited Europe; impressed by the potential that lay in the machine-gun, BSA now acquired 'Britain and the Empire' rights from the Belgian syndicate – a fortuitous involvement which, when World War One began, ensured that production could be maintained even though Belgium had been overrun.

Belgian Lewis Guns lacked the standard large-diameter barrel jacket containing the forced-air cooling system, but did have a forty-seven-round pan magazine above the breech.

Fusil Mitrailleur Lewis Mle 1913	
Synonym:	'Belgian Lewis Gun'
Length:	1,285mm (50.63in)
Weight of gun:	11.79kg (26.0lb) empty
Barrel length:	667mm (26.25in)
Chambering:	7.65 × 53mm, rimless
Rifling type:	four-groove, concentric, RH
Feed type:	horizontal pan magazine
Belt capacity:	forty-seven rounds
Selector:	none, automatic fire only
Cyclic rate:	550rd/min
Front sight:	open blade
Backsight:	leaf-and-slider type
Minimum backsight setting:	200m (219yd)
Maximum backsight setting:	2,000m (2,187yd)
Muzzle velocity:	620m/sec (2,034ft/sec)

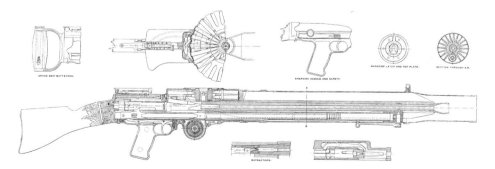

A longitudinal section of a Lewis Gun, from Engineering, *8 November 1912.*

5   Great Britain

British rifles often display 'W▲D', signifying the War Department. This superseded the Board of Ordnance ('B▲O') in the mid-nineteenth century. 'V.R.' ('Victoria Regina') may appear on guns made between 1888 and 1901; later alternatives include 'E.R.' ('Edwardius Rex'), 1901–10; and 'G.R.' ('Georgius Rex'), 1910–36.

Guns made by the Royal Small Arms Factory at Enfield Lock were usually marked 'ENFIELD' or 'EFD'. Guns made in BSA's Small Heath factory bore the marks 'B.S.A. & M. CO.' (Birmingham Small Arms & Munitions Company) until 1897, when the company reverted to the original 'B.S.A.' marks. Those made by the London Small Arms Co. Ltd were marked 'L.S.A. CO.' or alternatively, 'L.S.A. CO. LD.' Rarer marks include ' V.S.M.' for Vickers, Sons & Maxim Ltd (on charger-loading Lee conversions only, 1911–12); 'S.S.A.' for the Standard Small Arms Company, Birmingham (1916–18);

and 'N.R.F.' for its short-lived successor, the National Rifle Factory No. 1 (1918–19 only).

Designation marks take the form 'I' or 'II*' for Marks I and II* respectively, the 'star' being the standard method of indicating a minor improvement not warranting a change of Mark number. 'M.E.', M.H.' and 'M.M.' represent Martini-Enfield, Martini-Henry and Martini-Metford respectively. Prefixes 'A.C.' and 'C.C.' denote artillery and cavalry carbines, though the marks can be difficult to decipher: 'II C. I', for example, is a 'Mark II Carbine (type unspecified), First Class'.

When the Lee-Enfield appeared, it was so similar to the Lee-Metford that the prefix 'L.E.' was used to distinguish it. Thereafter, a series of descriptive prefixes had to be used: 'C.L.L.E.' for 'Charger-loading Lee-Enfield'; 'COND.L.E.' for 'Converted Lee-Enfield' (not 'condemned'!); and 'SHT.L.E.' for 'Short Lee Enfield'.

A .455 Webley Mk V revolver.
Courtesy of Ian Hogg.

HANDGUNS

Pistols, Revolver, .455, Webley, Mks IV and V

The Mark IV was issued just in time for the Second South African War. Improvements on the earlier designs were minimal and largely internal. The body, barrel and cylinder were made of a special grade of mild steel, the ratchet on the extractor was case-hardened, and the point of the lifting pawl was water-hardened to increase its life. The spur of the hammer was lightened to reduce lock time, the cylinder locking slots were broadened, and the edges of the body were rounded. A total of 36,756 Mk IV revolvers had been made prior to 1904.

The Mark V, adopted on 9 December 1913 and approved for manufacture in June 1914, was strengthened for cordite ammunition. Consequently, its cylinder had a diameter of 1.745in instead of 1.718in, and the body was relieved appropriately. An additional recognition feature was provided by the rear edge of the cylinder, which was rounded instead of squared.

Many Mark III and Mark IV revolvers were upgraded to Mark V standard when returned for repair, parts of the frame being cut away at the bottom of the cylinder aperture. After May 1915, Land Service guns were given 6in barrels and a new 9.12in cleaning rod (carried separately) was approved. It is believed that about 20,000 of an original order for 23,600 Mk V Webley revolvers had been made when production stopped in 1915.

Pistol, Revolver, Webley, .455 Mark IV	
Synonym:	'Webley revolver Mk IV'
Approval date:	21 July 1899
Length:	9.25in (235mm)
Weight:	2.25lb (1,020g)
Barrel length:	4.0in (102mm)
Chambering:	.455in, rimmed
Rifling type:	seven groove, concentric, RH
Magazine type:	rotating cylinder
Magazine capacity:	six rounds
Loading system:	loose rounds, or Webley Patent (or similar) quick-loader
Frontsight:	open barleycorn
Backsight:	fixed notch
Muzzle velocity:	705ft/sec (215m/sec)

RIFLES

Rifles, Charger-Loading, Magazine, Lee-Enfield

The first British small-arms cartridge to be loaded with smokeless propellant, the .303 Mk I Cordite (approved in November 1890), appeared almost as soon as the perfected Lee-Metford rifle had been issued; however, it proved to wear Metford rifling much too quickly. Trials with a variety of profiles eventually allowed the British authorities to approve new concentric 'Enfield' rifling with five square-shouldered grooves instead of the shallow seven-sided Metford pattern.

Sealed in the autumn of 1895, the 'Rifle, Magazine, Lee-Enfield, .303-inch, Mark I' had new rifling and the front sight moved to the left,

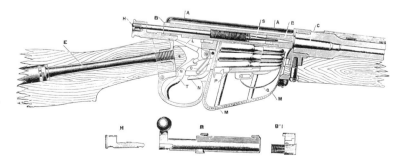

A longitudinal section of the British commercial Lee-Speed action. From W.W. Greener, The Gun and Its Development *(ninth edition, 1910).*

A Long Lee-Enfield Mk I* rifle of 1895. Note the absence of charger-guides on the receiver, which allowed a sheet-steel bolt cover to be fitted. Courtesy of Ian Hogg.

Rifle, Magazine, Lee-Enfield, .303in, Mark I

Synonym:	'Long Lee-Enfield Mk I'
Adoption date:	11 November 1895
Length:	49.5in (1,257mm)
Weight:	9lb 4oz (4.2kg) empty, without sling
Barrel length:	30.5/16in (770mm)
Chambering:	.303 (7.7 × 56mm), rimmed
Rifling type:	five-groove, concentric, LH
Magazine type:	detachable staggered-row protruding box
Magazine capacity:	ten rounds
Loading system:	loose rounds
Front sight:	open barleycorn
Backsight:	stepped-base leaf-and-slider type
Minimum backsight setting:	200yd (183m)
Maximum backsight setting:	2,000yd (1,829m), with long-range sights to 2,800yd (2,560m)
Muzzle velocity:	2,060ft/sec (628m/sec)

The open action of the Mk I* Lee-Enfield rifle, showing the bolt head, the cut-off (with a rolled-tube finger piece) and the bolt-cover. Courtesy of Ian Hogg.

compensating for the tendency of the bullet to drift to the right; otherwise the Lee-Enfield was all but identical mechanically with the Lee-Metford.

The Mark I* Lee-Enfield could be identified by the absence of a clearing rod and the associated channel beneath the fore-end; Mark I rifles modified to Mark I* standards customarily have a fillet of wood in the groove, but about 590,000 new Mark I* rifles were made by the government small-arms factories in Enfield and Sparkbrook, by the Birmingham Small Arms & Metal Co. Ltd, and by the London Small Arms Co. Ltd.

The pull-off was reduced to match that of the SMLE (5–7lb) from February 1906 onwards, but the first batches of many guns converted to accept .22 rimfire aiming tubes ('A.T.') appeared in 1907.

Rifle, Magazine, Charger-Loading, Lee-Enfield, .303in, Mark I.
Approved in 1914, this 'Naval Service' pattern resembled the Charger-Loading Mark I* rifle, and had an identical charger bridge. The original sights were adapted for Mark VII ammunition, suitably altered 1,900yd leaves being marked 'C.L.'.

Rifle, Magazine, Charger-Loading, Lee-Enfield, .303in, Mark I*.
Sealed on 2 October 1914, this naval service gun was simply an original Mark I* Lee-Enfield adapted to Charger-Loading Mark I (N) standards.

Rifle, Magazine, Charger-Loading, Lee-Enfield, .303in, Mark II*.
Approval of the bridge-type charger guides allowed this gun to be sealed on 1 July 1907. By 1913, more than 300,000 original Mark I and I* rifles had been adapted by Enfield, Vickers, BSA and LSA.

A typical .303 Charger-Loading Lee-Enfield (CLLE) rifle. Note the guides, one on the right side of the bolt head and the other on the front left side of the receiver bridge. Courtesy of Ian Hogg.

The Lee-Enfield Mk I carbine of 1896 had a short barrel, a safety catch on the cocking piece, and a six-round magazine to prevent snagging on the saddle scabbard. Courtesy of Wallis & Wallis, Lewes, Sussex.

Carbines, Magazine, Lee-Enfield

A Lee-Metford carbine was sealed in June 1894 to replace the Martini-action carbines issued to

Carbine, Magazine, Lee-Enfield, Cavalry, .303in, Mark I	
Synonym:	'Lee-Enfield cavalry carbine'
Adoption date:	17 August 1896
Length:	39.15/16in (1,014mm)
Weight:	7lb 7oz (3.37kg) empty, without sling
Barrel length:	20.75in (527mm)
Chambering:	.303 (7.7 × 56mm), rimmed
Rifling type:	five-groove, concentric, LH
Magazine type:	detachable staggered-row protruding box
Magazine capacity:	six rounds
Loading system:	loose rounds
Front sight:	open barleycorn
Backsight:	leaf-and-slider
Minimum backsight setting:	200yd (183m)
Maximum backsight setting:	2,000yd (1,829m)
Muzzle velocity:	1,940ft/sec (591m/sec)

cavalry, artillery and engineer units, but only 18,700 were made in the Royal Small Arms Factory, Enfield Lock, before an essentially similar Mark I Lee-Enfield was approved in 1896. A Mark I* carbine, sealed in August 1899, differed from its predecessor only in the omission of the clearing rod.

Though the carbines served with distinction in South Africa, production (totalling just 40,000) ended with the introduction of the sturdier and more efficient SMLE, and they were gradually replaced in the course of the war. Some, however, still equipped Yeomanry cavalrymen in 1914. Oddly, the carbines were never formally declared obsolete: their demise was signalled in the List of Changes A1274 of 19 August 1925, which said simply that 'Carbines will be rendered incapable of firing small arms ammunition and will be used for drill purposes and for issue to the Officer Training Corps'.

Rifle, Short, Magazine, Lee-Enfield, .303in, Mark I

A satisfactory short rifle had been perfected by the end of 1902, changes from the prototypes

'Infantry of the Line for the Front': a postcard (no. 4318) published by Raphael Tuck & Sons of London as part of a series entitled 'The European War, 1914'. The men are clearly carrying full-length Lee-Enfield rifles, though the clarity is not sufficient to determine whether they are charger-loading conversions. Author's collection.

Rifle, Short, Magazine, Lee-Enfield Mark I	
Synonym:	'SMLE Mk I'
Adoption date:	23 December 1902 (but see text)
Length:	44.9/16in (1,132mm)
Length with bayonet attached:	61.11/16in (1,567mm) with P/07 sword type
Weight:	8lb 2oz (3.69kg), empty, without sling Weight with P/1907 bayonet attached: 9lb 3oz (4.167kg)
Barrel length:	25.3/16in (640mm)
Chambering:	.303in (7.7 × 56mm), rimmed
Rifling type:	five-groove, concentric, LH
Magazine type:	staggered-row protruding detachable box
Magazine capacity:	ten rounds
Loading system:	charger or loose rounds
Front sight:	protected blade
Backsight:	tangent leaf/slider type
Minimum backsight setting:	200yd (183m)
Maximum backsight setting:	2,000yd (1,829m), with long-range sights to 2,800yd (2,560m)
Muzzle velocity:	2,060 ft/sec (628m/sec)

including the addition of an 'eared' front sight and modifications to the hand-guard running the length of the barrel. Approved in December 1902, the gun entered production immediately; however, so many minor alterations were required that the pattern was re-sealed on 14 September 1903, and again in September 1906.

Cut-offs were fitted to rifles made for naval service from August 1903 onwards, then extended to land service from October 1906. A shortened lead from the chamber to the bore was also in this period, and an improved 'U'-notch replaced the 'V' on the backsight leaf in 1907.

About 363,000 SMLE Mark I rifles were made by the Royal Small Arms Factories in Enfield Lock and Sparkbrook; by the Birmingham Small Arms Co. Ltd, Small Heath; and by the London Small Arms Co. Ltd in Bow.

Rifle, Short, Magazine, Lee-Enfield, .303in, Mark 1*

Adopted on 27 March 1906, this SMLE had a trap in the butt plate for the oil bottle and pull-through, a swivel on the butt, and a modified magazine. More than sixty thousand guns were made in the Enfield factory, and another three thousand 'India Pattern' examples in Ishapore. Data were similar to the Mark I, though the Mark I* was marginally longer and weighed an additional 5oz (140g).

The Converted Short, Magazine, Lee-Enfield rifles

The guns are listed here by 'Mark' instead of introduction date. 'Cond. Mk II' and 'Cond. Mk II*' rifles were the earliest, but many other conversions were sanctioned during World War One (see Section Three). Surviving 'Cond. Mk I**', 'Cond. Mk II**' and 'Cond. Mk II***' SMLEs were re-sighted for Mark VII ball ammunition and given bridge-type charger guides in 1912; appropriate changes were made in the stock; and the front-sight protectors were straightened.

*Rifle, Short, Magazine, Lee-Enfield, .303in, Converted Mark I**.* Accepted for naval service in January 1908, this was transformed by ordnance depots in Chatham, Plymouth and Portsmouth. The guns retained the original charger guides on the bridge and bolt head, but had Mark III sights. A large 'N' appeared on the left side of the receiver shoe.

Rifle, Short, Magazine, Lee-Enfield, .303in, Converted Mark II. Sealed in January 1903, although final approval was withheld until November, this was an adaptation of the Mark I

Rifle, Short, Magazine, Lee-Enfield, .303in, Converted Mark II	
Adoption date:	16 January 1903 (see text)
Length:	44.9/16 (1,132mm)
	Length with P/1907 sword bayonet attached: 61.11/16in (1,567mm)
Weight:	8lb 2oz (3.700kg), empty, without sling
	Weight with P/1907 bayonet attached: 9lb 3oz (4.167kg)
Barrel length:	25.3/16in (640mm)
Chambering:	303in (7.7 × 56mm), rimmed
Rifling type:	five-groove, concentric, LH
Magazine type:	detachable staggered-row protruding box
Magazine capacity:	ten rounds
Loading system:	charger or loose rounds
Front sight:	protected blade
Backsight:	tangent leaf/slider type
Minimum backsight setting:	200yd (183m)
Maximum backsight setting:	2000yd (1,829m), with long-range sights to 2,800yd (2,560m)

or Mark I* long Lee-Enfields, and a few old Mark II or II* Lee-Metfords. A new short barrel were fitted; charger guides were added to the receiver and bolt head; new sights appeared; and the stock was greatly modified. Improvements subsequently made in the Converted Mark II* eventually forced changes in the design of the

A 'Sealed Pattern' SMLE Converted Mk II rifle, 1903. Courtesy of Ian Hogg.

A typical .303 SMLE Mk III rifle. Courtesy of Ian Hogg.

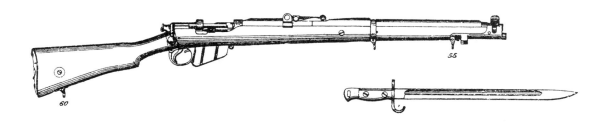

A longitudinal section (right) *and an exterior view* (above) *of the SMLE Mk III rifle. From the* Text Book of Small Arms, *1909.*

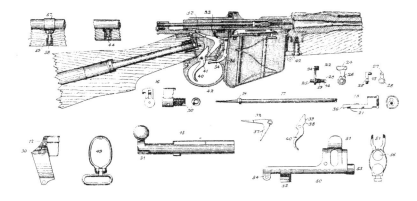

Converted Mark II, which was re-sealed in September 1906.

Rifle, Short, Magazine, Lee-Enfield, .303in, Converted Mark II*. Approved on 15 March 1906, this was adapted from old Lee-Metfords (Marks II, II*) or Lee-Enfields (Marks I, I*) but was otherwise comparable with the standard SMLE Mark I*. Its weight averaged 8lb 7oz, or 9lb 7oz with the P/1907 bayonet attached.

Rifle, Short, Magazine, Lee-Enfield, .303in, Converted Mark II**. Modified by the navy ordnance depots in Chatham, Plymouth and Portsmouth, these were accepted into naval service from July 1908 onwards. They were similar to the Converted Mark I**, with two-piece charger guides.

Rifle, Short, Magazine, Lee-Enfield, .303in, Converted Mark II***. These short rifles appeared in 1909; they differed from the Converted Mark II** in only minor detail.

Rifle, Short, Magazine, Lee-Enfield, .303in, Converted Mark IV. Sealed on 17 June 1907, the 'SMLE Cond. Mark IV' was little more than the Converted Mark II improved to SMLE Mark III

Rifle, Short, Magazine, Lee-Enfield, Mark III

Synonyms:	'Mk III SMLE' , 'Rifle No. 1 Mk 3' (after 1926 only)
Approval date:	26 January 1907
Length:	44.5in (1,130mm); Length with bayonet attached:61.7in (1,567mm), with P/07 sword type
Weight:	8lb 10oz (3.93kg) empty, without sling. Weight with P/1907 bayonet attached: 9lb 11oz (4.39kg)
Barrel length:	25.3/16in (640mm)
Chambering:	.303in (7.7 × 56mm), rimmed
Rifling type:	five-groove, concentric, LH
Magazine type:	staggered-row protruding detachable box
Magazine capacity:	ten rounds
Loading system:	charger or loose rounds
Front sight:	protected blade
Backsight:	tangent leaf/slider type
Minimum backsight setting:	200yd (183m)

Rifle, Short, Magazine, Lee-Enfield, Mark III *continued:*

Maximum backsight setting:	2,000yd (1,829m), with long range sights to 2,800yd (2,560m)
Muzzle velocity:	2,230ft/sec (680m/sec)

standards. It weighed 8lb 14oz without the bayonet.

Rifle, Short, Magazine, Lee-Enfield, 303in, Mark III

Field service soon showed that the bolt-head charge guide quickly worked loose, and monoblock guides on the receiver bridge were developed experimentally in 1906. Eventually, Enfield-pattern charger guides and an improved Watkin & Speed sights were adopted, the nosecap

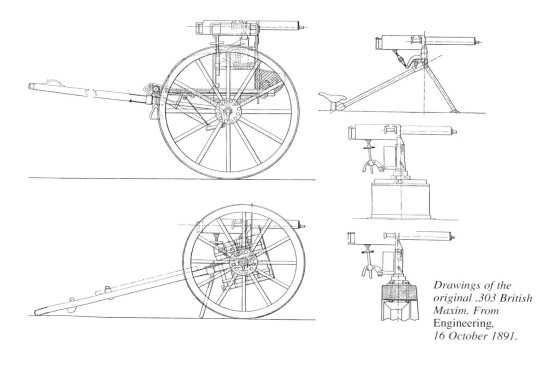

Drawings of the original .303 British Maxim. From Engineering, *16 October 1891.*

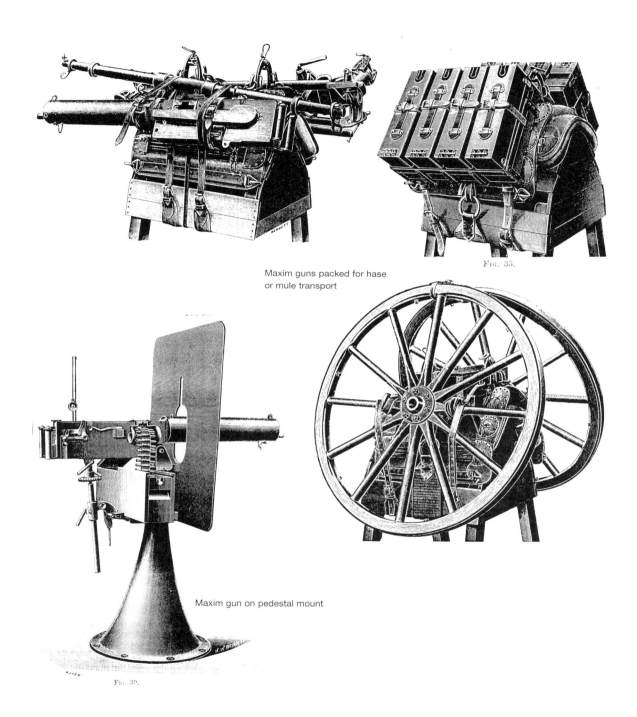

Maxim guns packed for hase
or mule transport

FIG. 35.

Maxim gun on pedestal mount

FIG. 39.

Drawings of Maxim machine-guns and their mountings, from Engineering, *18 March 1898.*

was refined, and more efficient backsight protectors appeared. This advanced the rifle designation to 'Mark III'.

The sights underwent a wholesale revision after 1910, owing to the adoption of a high-velocity cartridge in this year, and changes had soon been made in the magazine and receiver body to ensure that the new, pointed Mark VII bullet fed properly. Changes to the long-range dial sight (on the left side of the fore-end) were initially made by altering the existing graduations, but newly made, post-1911 rifles had new dial plates.

Earlier Rifles

Large quantities of obsolescent Martini-pattern rifles in the hands of the Royal Navy, the Territorial Army, recruiting depots and ancillary units were withdrawn into store as the SMLE rifles became available in quantity. They were joined by essentially similar .303 carbines withdrawn from the artillery, cavalry and engineers – only to be re-issued when World War One began.

MACHINE-GUNS

Gun, Machine, Maxim, .303, Mark I

The introductory notice of this weapon described it as 'similar to the .45in model'; indeed, the only significant changes lay in the calibre and the feed mechanism. The receiver was made of steel, the water jacket and cartridge-feed guides were phosphor-bronze, and the gun was in every respect a typical recoil-operated Maxim. According to the *Vocabulary of Ordnance Stores*, 1912, each new gun cost £64 15s 0d and £64 17s 6.

A frame or 'extension' to the rear of the barrel contained a toggle joint, attached to the breech-block (at the front) and the axis-shaft of the crank handle (at the rear). When the gun fired, the barrel and the barrel extension recoiled about an

Gun, Machine, Maxim, .303in, Mark I	
Synonym:	'British Army .303 Maxim Gun'
Adoption date:	19 June 1889
Length:	42.375in (1,076mm)
Weight of gun:	60lb (27.21kg), empty
Weight of mount:	not known
Barrel length:	28.00in (1,102mm)
Chambering:	.303in (7.7 × 56mm), rimmed
Rifling type:	five-groove, concentric, RH
Feed type:	fabric belt
Belt capacity:	250 rounds
Cyclic rate of fire:	400rd/min
Selector:	none, automatic fire only
Front sight:	open barleycorn
Backsight:	leaf-and-slider type
Velocity:	1,800ft/sec (549m/sec)

A .450 Mk I Maxim Gun on its 'overbank' carriage ('Carriage, Parapet, Machine-Gun, Maxim, .45 Martini-Henry Chamber, Mark I'), approved in January 1889. The gun could be locked at any height along the rack attached to the support-pole, benefiting from protection provided by a trench, an earth bank or a parapet. Courtesy of Ian Hogg.

A water-cooled .303 Mk I Vickers Gun on its tripod mount, accompanied by a condenser tank and an ammunition-belt box.

Gun, Machine, Vickers, .303in, Mark I

Synonym:	'British Army Vickers Gun'
Adoption date:	26 November 1912
Length:	45.5in (1,155mm)
Weight:	40lb (18.1kg), with water jacket filled
Weight of mount:	50lb (22.68kg)
Barrel length:	28.5in (723mm)
Chambering:	303in (7.7 × 56mm), rimmed
Rifling type:	four-groove, concentric, RH
Feed type:	webbing or fabric belt
Feed capacity:	250 rounds
Cyclic rate of fire:	450rd/min
Frontsight:	open blade
Backsight:	leaf-and-slider type
Muzzle velocity:	2,450ft/sec (745m/sec)

---

inch before coming to a halt, allowing the bullet to leave the barrel. The movement of the barrel inside the water jacket was permitted by 'stuffing boxes' packed with asbestos cord, retained by a coil spring around the barrel.

The crank handle turned as it struck a projection, breaking the toggle open and allowing it to fold downwards. A spring then returned the barrel and barrel extension to their forward position, but the breech-block continued to move backwards until the toggle had completely folded and the hammer had been cocked.

Meanwhile, a claw on the breech-block had drawn a cartridge backwards from the belt, over the barrel, during the opening movement; an arm then forced the cartridge down onto the face of the bolt, displacing a spent case downwards. Pressure from the 'fusée spring' then propelled the breech-block forwards, rotating the crank-shaft and lifting the toggle. The forward movement of the breech-block also rammed the new round into the chamber and drove a spent case into the discharge tube beneath the barrel. The

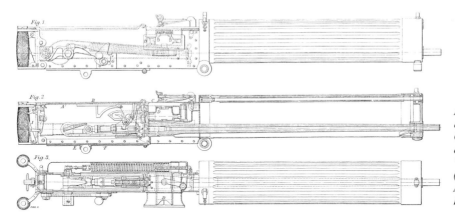

A longitudinal section of the Mk I Vickers Gun. From British official drawing 'S.A.I.D. 2062' ('Superintendent, Armament Inspection Department').

toggle locked as the breech closed, allowing another shot to be fired if the trigger was still being pressed.

The belt was fed by pawls, driven by the backward movement of the barrel extension, that gripped and pulled individual cartridges sideways until each could be aligned in turn with the bolt claw.

Gun, Machine-Vickers, .303in, Mark I

Developed in the mid-1900s, the Vickers was simply a Maxim gun with an inverted locking mechanism – the toggle breaks upward – and lighter components. The Mark I was the only 'Land Service' pattern ever approved, a testimony to its efficiency. It was not declared obsolete until April 1968, having seen service in armoured vehicles and in aircraft. Seven special 'Marks' and a selection of 'starred' sub-variants were introduced, all of them after 1918.

Like many comparable designs of its era, the Vickers machine-gun was comparatively cumbersome: a gun with a full water jacket and a 'Mounting, Machine-Gun, Tripod, Mark IV', sealed on 23 January 1906 to replace Maxim carriages, weighed more than 90lb (40.8kg).

The cyclic rate was nominally 450rd/min, though individual guns sometimes fired considerably faster. The water jacket held seven pints, evaporating at a rate of a pint per thousand rounds once fire had been sustained at a rate of 200–250rpm for three minutes and the water had begun to boil. Steam was led off through a hose into a can, where it condensed to water that could be poured back into the jacket.

The barrel could be changed by elevating the gun, pulling the barrel backwards, and inserting a large cork in the aperture in the front of the barrel jacket. The gun could then be depressed and the barrel withdrawn. The new barrel was simply pushed forwards, relying on asbestos string wrapped in grooves to act as a seal and eventually knocking the cork out. Depressing the gun allowed residual water to drain from the bore, and another ten thousand rounds could be fired.

The Vickers Gun was extremely reliable and, like comparable water-cooled weapons, capable of prodigious feats of endurance. However, unless suitable precautions were taken, clouds of steam hung over the gun in cold weather and the muzzle flash was easily detectable during sustained fire at night. Suppressor tubes were issued in 1915–16, but tended to retain so many propellant fumes that periodic ignition produced an awesome flash that could be seen for miles! Colloquially known as 'stovepipes', the tubes were soon officially abandoned; besides, many gunners had already thrown them away.

6 The British Empire

ROSS RIFLES, 1905 TYPE

The first 'Rifles, Ross, .303in, Mark I' were delivered to the Canadian Department of Militia and Defence in August 1905. They had pistol-grip stocks, and nosecaps with bayonet lugs and piling swivels; one sling swivel lay on the barrel band, with the other beneath the butt. The elongated 2,500yd leaf of the original Mark I backsight, which predictably proved to be too fragile, was rapidly replaced by a sturdier 2,200yd Mark II pattern.

One of the most distinctive features of the Ross was its magazine, which embodied 'Harris's Controlled Platform'. A depressor on the right side of the fore-end behind the backsight allowed cartridges to be dropped into the magazine, instead of forcing them individually against the follower spring. The cut-off lever protruded from the right side of the stock above the trigger-guard.

Note: in 1912, the Canadians re-designated the 30.5in-barrelled Mark II** as the 'Rifle, Ross, Mark II', the 28in-barrelled Marks II*** and II***** as 'Rifles, Short, Ross, Mark II', and all other short-barrel guns as 'Rifles, Short, Ross, Mark I' to disguise the changes that were being constantly made.

Rifle, Magazine, Ross, .303, Mark II. Delivered from February 1907 onwards, this retained the Harris magazine, but had a longer hand-guard than the Mark I, and the barrel band was moved towards the nosecap. The sides of the receiver were raised, the bolt sleeve was

Rifle, Ross, .303in, Mark I	
Synonym:	'Ross Military Model 1905'
Adoption date:	not known
Length:	52.0in (1,321mm)
	Length with bayonet attached:
	58.8in (1,494mm)
Weight:	8lb 1oz (3.657kg) empty,
	without sling
Weight with bayonet attached:	9lb 1oz (4.12kg)
Barrel length:	28.0in (711mm)
Chambering:	.303in (7.7 × 56mm), rimmed
Rifling type:	four-groove, concentric, RH
Bore diameter:	0.300in (7.62mm)
Depth of grooves:	0.0055in (0.140mm)
Width of grooves:	not known
Pitch of rifling:	one turn in 10.00in (254mm), RH
Magazine type:	staggered-row internal box
Magazine capacity:	five rounds
Loading system:	loose rounds
Front sight:	open barleycorn?
Backsight:	tangent type
Minimum backsight setting:	100yd (91m)
Maximum backsight setting:	2,200yd (2,012m)
Muzzle velocity:	2,060ft/sec (628m/sec)

improved, the cut-off lever lay within the trigger-guard, and the rear swivel was moved to a new position. An improved Mark III backsight was introduced in 1907, with a distinctive flat-top elevator bar.

Rifle, Magazine, Ross, .303, Mark II. A modified Mark I, this had changes to the magazine lever and a new German-style tangent-pattern backsight with a rotating-collar micrometer system that permitted the sight to be elevated in 10yd increments.

Rifle, Magazine, Ross, .303, Mark II**. After a tremendous number of minor changes had been made, this gun appeared with a 30.5in barrel, an improved 'flag' safety catch instead of a press-catch, a longer nosecap, and a broader barrel band. The cut-off mechanism was discarded. Most Mark II** rifles were fitted with leaf-type backsights made by the Sutherland Sight Company ('Canada Tool & Specialty Company' from the end of 1910 onwards), positioned midway between the receiver ring and the barrel band.

Rifle, Magazine, Ross, .303, Mark II***. Introduced in 1910, this had a 28in barrel and its Sutherland sight placed much more closely to the receiver ring. The cut-off reappeared, and the safety system reverted to a press-catch.

Rifle, Magazine, Ross, .303, Mark II*****. Accepted in the autumn of 1910, this could be identified by a simpler housing immediately behind the Sutherland sight.

ROSS RIFLES, 1910 TYPE

The Mark III Ross, the principal weapon of the Canadian Expeditionary Force in 1914, had a new 1910-patent 'triple-thread, interrupted screw, double-bearing cam bolt head' that locked vertically instead of horizontally (to improve the feed stroke), and a charger-loaded box magazine instead of the original Harris type. The functions of the magazine cut-off and the bolt stop were

---

Rifle, Magazine, Ross, .303, Mark III

Synonyms:	'Ross Military Model 1910' or (misleadingly) 'Model 1912'
Adoption date:	July 1911
Length:	50.50in (1,282mm)
Weight:	9.88lb (4.48kg), without sling
Barrel length:	30.50in (775mm)
Chambering:	.303in (7.7 × 56mm), rimmed
Rifling type:	four-groove, concentric, LH
Magazine type:	staggered-row protruding box
Magazine capacity:	five rounds
Loading system:	charger or loose rounds
Front sight:	adjustable blade
Backsight:	tangent aperture type
Velocity:	2,600ft/sec (790m/sec)

---

combined in a small lever on the left side of the receiver bridge.

The unwieldy Ross was instantly recognizable by the protruding magazine housing and the shallow pistol-grip, and originally it had a folding aperture backsight on the receiver bridge. The modified Mark IIIB ('British Pattern' or '3B'), was approved in October 1915, with a simplified backsight and an SMLE-type cut off.

The problems that afflicted the Ross are well known, particularly the danger of a wrongly assembled bolt. Combat on the Western Front soon revealed that the guns extracted very poorly — this is now known to have been due to differences in chamber dimensioning — and they were replaced in 1916 by SMLEs. However, Ross rifles fitted with American 1908 or 1913-model Warner & Swasey telescope sights (offset to the left to clear the charger guides) made fine sniping rifles.

7 France

HANDGUNS

11mm Revolvers Modèle 1873 and Modèle 1874

The genesis of these revolvers has been given in Part One, and substantial numbers survived to serve during World War One. Issued to NCOs and men, the Mle 1873 was a solid frame weapon of the type usually known as 'Chamelot-Delvigne' owing to the design of the double-action lockwork. Loaded through a swinging gate on the right side of the frame – behind the cylinder – it also had a permanently mounted ejector rod on the right side of the barrel, aligned with the gate. The barrel was part-round, part-hexagonal, and the cylinder had a smooth surface. The 1874-pattern, issued principally to officers and the senior NCOs who carried swords

or sabres, was chemically browned (instead of bright-polished) and had a fluted cylinder. The officers' revolver was about 170g lighter than the troopers' issue.

The 11mm-calibre Chamelot-Delvigne revolver was a sturdy design that remained in limited service with the French armed forces (notably in the colonies) in 1914. This is the 1874-pattern officer's model, with a fluted cylinder; the M1873 for rank-and-file had a plain cylinder. Courtesy of Ian Hogg.

Revolver Mle 1873	
Synonym:	'M1873 French Chamelot-Delvigne revolver'
Length:	242mm (9.53in)
Weight:	1.22kg (2.69lb), empty
Barrel length:	115mm (4.53in)
Chambering:	11 × 17.5mm, rimmed ('French Ordnance')
Rifling type:	four-groove, concentric, RH
Magazine type:	rotating cylinder
Magazine capacity:	six rounds
Front sight:	open blade
Backsight:	fixed open notch
Muzzle velocity:	190m/sec (623ft/sec) with M1873/90 ammunition

Revolver Mle 1892	
Synonym:	'Modele d'Ordonnance' or 'Lebel'
Length:	240mm (9.45in)
Weight:	840g (1.85lb), empty
Barrel length:	117mm (4.61in)
Chambering:	8 × 27mm, rimmed ('Lebel revolver')
Rifling type:	six-groove, concentric, RH
Magazine type:	rotating cylinder
Magazine capacity:	six rounds
Front sight:	open blade
Backsight:	fixed open notch
Muzzle velocity:	218m/sec (715ft/sec)

The 8mm 1892-pattern 'Modèle d'Ordonnance' revolver, also often mistakenly known as the 'Lebel', was a conventional solid-frame design with a cylinder that swung to the right on its yoke. Courtesy of Ian Hogg.

8mm Revolver Modèle 1892

Popularly called the 'Lebel', apparently simply by virtue of being the same calibre as the M1886 infantry rifle, the replacement for the M1873 and M1874 was a solid frame, double action revolver with a side-opening cylinder inspired by the contemporaneous 1889-pattern US Navy Colt. Oddly, the M1892 cylinder opened to the right, making reloading a tortuous business for right-handed firers – however, as noted in Part One, this was due to the requirements of the cavalry. Excepting this particular quirk, the M1892 was a sound and effective design. The entire left side of the frame could be hinged open to reveal the lockwork, a useful feature if the gun needed to be cleaned or repaired. The 8mm cartridge was weak, judged by combat standards, but the guns served the French well; the last was not discarded by the customs services until the 1960s. Most of the service-issue revolvers had been made by the state manufactory in Saint-Étienne,

but many others were made for the commercial market by Manufacture Française d'Armes et Cycles ('Manufrance').

RIFLES

French rifles bear very distinctive marks. Inscriptions such as 'MANUFACTURE D'ARMES' often appear on the receiver above the name of the arsenal, e.g. a cursive 'St Etienne' ahead of a designation such as 'MLE. 1874' or 'MLE. 1886–93'. An 'MA' mark appears on the right side of the barrel alongside the breech, together with the initial of the factory and the date ('S 1886' for 'Saint-Étienne, 1886'). The left side of the barrel displays a serial number such as 'G49693' underneath and to the rear of the backsight base; the number is repeated in whole or in part on most of the pieces, together with inspectors' marks that take the form of small raised letters in squares, circles or diamonds.

8mm Fusil des Tirailleurs Indo-Chinois, Modèle 1902

This rifle was introduced to arm colonial troops in Annam, Cambodia and Tonkin in French Indo-China. Lighter, handier and more efficient than the M1886 Lebel, it was the first Berthier rifle to be issued in quantity in the French armed forces. The action was essentially that of the M1890 cavalry carbine, with the bolt handle bent downwards, but the production life of the rifle was shortened by the introduction of the Mle 07/15 (Part Three). Original guns were sighted for the Balle 1886 M, to use up existing supplies of ammunition, but the sights were altered after 1909 for the Balle 1886 D. The original sight was retained, but the new leaf was graduated to 2,400m (2,625yd) and customarily marked 'N'. Some sights were newly made, but most seem to have been alterations.

Fusil des Tirailleurs Indo-Chinois Mle 1902

Synonym:	'M1902 Berthier Indo-China sharpshooter's rifle'
Length:	1,125mm (44.35in)
Length with bayonet attached:	1,645mm (64.75in)
Weight:	3.62kg (7lb 15oz), without sling
Weight with bayonet attached:	4.0kg (8lb 13oz), without sling
Barrel length:	632mm (24.9in)
Chambering:	8 × 51mm, rimmed
Rifling type:	four-groove, concentric, LH
Magazine type:	internal box
Magazine capacity:	three rounds
Loading system:	clip
Front sight:	open barleycorn
Backsight:	leaf-and-slider type
Minimum backsight setting:	250m (273yd)
Maximum backsight setting:	2,000m (2,187yd)
Muzzle velocity:	632m/sec (2,073ft/sec)

8mm Fusil des Tirailleurs Sénégalais, Modèle 1907

The Mle 02 rifle was ideally suited to the small stature of the French colonial units raised in the Far East, and its success persuaded the authorities

Fusil des Tirailleurs Sénégalais Mle 1907

Synonym:	'M1907 French Berthier Senegalese sharpshooters' rifle'
Length:	1,305mm (51.38in)
Length with bayonet attached:	1,825mm (71.85in)
Weight:	3.83kg (8lb 7oz), without sling
Weight with bayonet attached:	4.22kg (9lb 5oz), without sling
Barrel length:	803mm (31.6in)
Chambering:	8 × 51mm, rimmed
Rifling type:	four-groove, concentric, LH
Magazine type:	internal box
Magazine capacity:	three rounds
Loading system:	clip
Front sight:	open barleycorn
Backsight:	leaf-and-slider type
Minimum backsight setting:	250m (273yd)
Maximum backsight setting:	2,000m (2,187yd)
Muzzle velocity:	632m/sec (2,073ft/sec)

to adopt a modified full size gun for the Senegalese sharpshooters in 1907. Made by the state manufactory in Saint-Étienne, the Mle 07 lacked a cleaning rod, as the relevant equipment was carried separately. Sights were initially graduated for the Balle 1886 M, and the bolt handle was bent downwards; from 1910 onwards, the backsights of surviving guns were altered to 2,400m (2,625yd) for the Balle 1886 D.

The Mle 1886/93 rifle, better known as the 'Lebel', was obsolescent by 1914. Its principal weakness was the tube magazine beneath the barrel, which could only be safely loaded with flat-nose bullets. Courtesy of Ian Hogg.

8mm Fusil d'Infanterie, Modèle 1886/93

The original Lebel rifle, the M1886, was adopted on 22 April 1887. The butt and the fore-end were separated by a massive machined-steel receiver, the butt being bolted to the tangs. Swivels lay beneath the butt and the barrel band. Retained by a spring let into the right side of the fore-end, the nosecap had a boss beneath the muzzle to enter the bayonet pommel; two tenons under the barrel entered the back of the bayonet hilt to increase rigidity.

A radial cut-off lever was set in the right side of the receiver above the front of the trigger-guard, and the original backsight base was simply tin-soldered onto the barrel. However, no sooner had the new rifles entered service than backsight bases began to work loose; a sturdier design, with claws extending down around the barrel, was approved in 1892.

The perfected M1886/93 ('Mle 1886 M.93') rifle had a lighter striker-retainer in the cocking piece, and a stacking rod was added on the right side of the nosecap. A special non-rotating obturator or *tampon masque* was added to the bolt head behind the locking lugs to deflect escaping propellant gas if the case-head should fail. Backsights were adapted from 1901 onwards for the high-velocity Balle 1898 D, new leaves being graduated to 2,400m, and the superfluous 'safety notch' on the cocking piece was abandoned in 1902.

Though the clip-loaded Berthier rifles were technically superior to the tube-magazine Lebel, the M1886/93 was sturdier. When World War One began, the Lebel was equipping most front-line infantry units, though colonial troops carried their special Berthiers. Only during 1917 did the Lebel

A French infantryman of the 40th infantry regiment, with a Lebel rifle. From a patriotic postcard published in Britain shortly after the First World War began.

begin to give way to the M1907/15 and M1916 (Berthier) rifles, yet the old guns were usually retained for marksmen – fitted with × 3 M1916 telescope sights – and grenade-launching. In addition, many of the guns that survived World War One were shortened in the 1930s and re-issued.

It has been estimated that about 3.5–4 million Lebels were made in the state manufactories in Châtellerault, Saint-Étienne and Tulle. A few thousand were made during World War One in the Saint-Denis factory of the privately owned Manufacture d'Armes de Paris.

Fusil d'Infanterie Mle 1886 M.93

Synonym:	'M1886/93 French Lebel rifle'
Date of adoption:	February 1893?
Length:	1,299mm (51.13in)
Length with Mle 86/93 bayonet attached:	1,825mm (71.85in)
Weight:	4.18kg (9lb 3oz), without sling
Weight with Mle 86/93 bayonet attached:	4.58kg (10lb 1oz), without sling
Barrel length:	800mm (31.5in)
Chambering:	8 × 51mm, rimmed
Rifling type:	four-groove, concentric, LH
Magazine type:	under-barrel tube
Magazine capacity:	eight rounds
Loading system:	single rounds
Front sight:	open blade
Backsight:	leaf-and-slider type
Minimum backsight setting:	250m (273yd)
Maximum backsight setting:	2,000m (2,187yd)
Muzzle velocity:	632m/sec (2,073ft/sec)

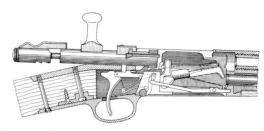

A longitudinal section of the Mle 86/93 Lebel rifle.

Carabine de Cavalerie Mle 1890

Synonym:	'M1890 French Berthier cavalry carbine'
Date of adoption:	March 1890
Length:	945mm (37.2in)
Weight:	2.99kg (6lb 9oz), without sling
Barrel length:	453mm (17.83in)
Chambering:	8 × 51mm, rimmed
Rifling type:	four-groove, concentric, LH
Magazine type:	single-column internal box
Magazine capacity:	three rounds
Loading system:	clip
Front sight:	open blade
Backsight:	leaf-and-slider type
Minimum backsight setting:	250m (273yd)
Maximum backsight setting:	2,000m (2,187yd)
Muzzle velocity:	637m/sec (2,090ft/sec)

8mm Carabine de Cavalerie, Modele 1890

Made by the state manufactory, Saint-Étienne, this was eventually issued to dragoons, hussars and mounted riflemen (chasseurs) and colonial cavalrymen (spahis). The first guns had a conventional stock, a loose sling ring on the left side of the barrel band, and a swivel on the under edge of the butt. They were sighted for the Balle 1886 M. However, from 1901 onwards the sights were revised for the Balle 1886 D, the 2,000m setting being moved from the top edge of the leaf to the body. A sling bar was added to the left side of the butt in 1904, with a fixed ring on the left side of the barrel band.

Carabine de Cuirassiers Mle 1890

Synonym:	'M1890 French Berthier cuirassier carbine'
Date of adoption:	summer 1890?
Length:	945mm (37.2in)
Weight:	2.95kg (6lb 8oz), without sling
Barrel length:	453mm (17.83in)
Chambering:	8 × 51mm, rimmed
Rifling type:	four-groove, concentric, LH
Magazine type:	single-column internal box
Magazine capacity:	three rounds
Loading system:	clip
Front sight:	open blade
Backsight:	leaf-and-slider type
Minimum backsight setting:	250m (273yd)
Maximum backsight setting:	2,000m (2,187yd)
Muzzle velocity:	637m/sec (2,090ft/sec)

A typical M1892 Berthier short rifle, with a three-round magazine. Courtesy of Ian Hogg.

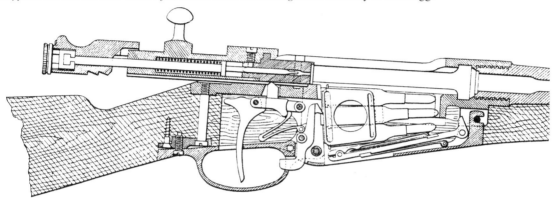

A longitudinal section of the Berthier action, showing the three-round clip. The bolt was essentially similar to that of the Lebel, with a detachable head. From Konrad von Kromar, Repetier- und Handfeuerwaffen der Systeme Ferdinand Ritter von Mannlicher *(Vienna, 1900).*

8mm Carabine de Cuirassiers, Modèle 1890

Sharing the action of the cavalry carbine, this model was introduced to arm the heavy cavalry. It had an extraordinary combless butt suited to firers wearing a steel breast-plate ('cuirass'); the butt plate was leather, instead of iron. The sights were graduated for the Balle 1886 M until 1901, when they were altered for the Balle 1886 D.

8mm Mousqueton d'Artillerie, Modèle 1892

Made exclusively in the government manu-factory in Saint-Étienne, and adopted for artillerymen (and eventually also the customs service), this short rifle was a derivative of the

1890-pattern cavalry carbine. The nosecap and barrel were adapted for a sword bayonet, the cleaning rod was carried in a channel hollowed out of the left side of the fore-end, a sling ring was attached to the left side of the barrel band, and a barred sling recess was cut into the left side of the butt.

Mousqueton d'Artillerie Mle 1892	
Synonym:	'M1892 French Berthier artillery musketoon'
Length:	945mm (37.2in)
Weight:	2.95kg (6lb 8oz), without sling
Barrel length:	453mm (17.83in)
Chambering:	8 × 51mm, rimmed
Rifling type:	four-groove, concentric, LH
Magazine type:	internal box
Magazine capacity:	three rounds
Loading system:	clip
Front sight:	open blade
Backsight:	leaf-and-slider type
Minimum backsight setting:	250m (273yd)
Maximum backsight setting:	2,000m (2,187yd)
Muzzle velocity:	632m/sec (2,073ft/sec)

The action of the 1892-pattern Berthier musketoon, showing the detachable bolt-head and how the flattened undersurface of the grasping knob enabled the bolt handle to be turned down against the stock. Courtesy of Ian Hogg.

MACHINE-GUNS

8mm Mitrailleuse Hotchkiss, Modèle 1900

This was a minor variation of the original or 1897-pattern Hotchkiss, developed from patents granted in the early 1890s to Adolf von Odkolek. A piston moving in a cylinder beneath the barrel, thrust back by residual propellant gas, forced a lug on the bolt body into a locking recess inside

Mitrailleuse Hotchkiss Mle 1900	
Synonym:	'M1900 French Hotchkiss'
Date of adoption:	December 1899 (see text)
Length of gun:	1,305mm (51.38in)
Weight of gun:	26.0kg (57lb 5oz)
Mount weight,	M1900 tripod: 27.0kg (59lb 8oz)
Barrel length:	785mm (30.9in)
Chambering:	8 × 51mm, rimmed
Rifling type:	four-groove, concentric, LH
Feed type:	metal strip
Strip capacity:	twenty-four rounds
Fire selector:	none, automatic only
Cyclic rate:	450rd/min
Front sight:	open blade
Backsight:	leaf-and-slider type
Minimum backsight setting:	200m (219yd)
Maximum backsight setting:	2,000m (2,187yd)
Muzzle velocity:	700m/sec (2,297ft/sec)

the receiver top. The 1897 pattern had overheated too frequently, but by 1900 an answer to the problem had been found, namely in thickening the barrel around the chamber and adding large fins to the rear section of the barrel to increase surface radiation of heat. The feed system relied on a system of sprockets to draw a metal strip into the gun from the right side: as each cartridge was rammed into the chamber, it moved the strip one place to the left. Empty strips were ejected from the left side. Individual cartridges were held in clips on the top surface of each feed-strip.

The Hotchkiss was provisionally adopted in 1899, but tests dragged on for several years. Guns were issued in quantity to the Bataillons des Chasseurs and the Troupes Coloniales in 1905, sighted for the Balle 1886 D and accompanied by a tripod credited to Captain Filloux of the Fonderie de Bourges. However, the progress that was being made with the APX or 'Puteaux' *(q.v.)* derivative brought work on the M1900 Hotchkiss to an early halt.

8mm Mitrailleuse, Modèle 1905

Made by the Ateliers de Puteaux ('APX') – the manufacturer therefore giving the weapon its sobriquet 'Puteaux' – this was an 'in-house' attempt to improve the 1900-pattern Hotchkiss... and, perhaps, avoid paying the full commercial price for each gun.

Among the new features was an unnecessarily complicated rate-of-fire adjuster, also the gas take-off point was moved forwards to the muzzle, and the barrel return spring was mounted

Drawings of the first commercially-successful Hotchkiss machine-gun. From Engineering, *23 April 1897.*

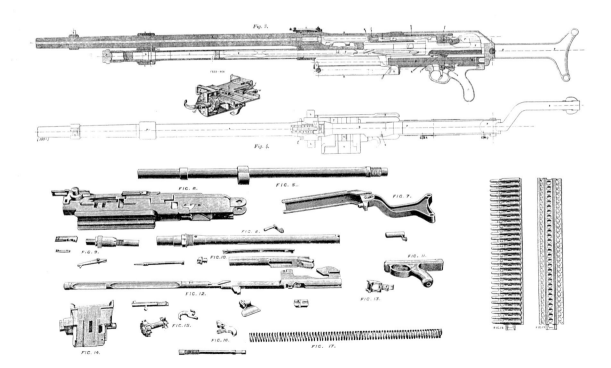

Mitrailleuse Mle 1905	
Synonyms:	'Mitrailleuse dit Puteaux', 'French Puteaux machine-gun'
Adoption date:	1906 (see text)
Length:	1,220mm (48.03in)
Weight:	27.0kg (59lb 8oz)
Mount weight, M1900 tripod:	27.0kg (59lb 8oz)
Barrel length:	840mm (33.07in)
Chambering:	8 × 51mm, rimmed
Rifling type:	six-groove, concentric, LH
Feed type:	metal strip
Belt capacity:	twenty-five rounds
Fire selector:	none, automatic only
Cyclic rate:	variable, 200–600rd/min
Front sight:	open blade
Backsight:	leaf-and-slider type
Minimum backsight setting:	300m (328yd)
Maximum backsight setting:	2,000m (2,187yd)
Muzzle velocity:	700m/sec (2,297ft/sec)

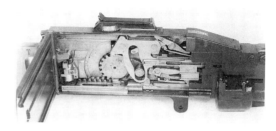

The 1907-model French machine-gun, the Saint-Étienne, was loosely based on the Hotchkisss and shared strip feed. However, the mechanism was altered so that the piston rod was blown forward. This opened the breech by way of the toothed wheel, roller and pivoting cam-plate. This is an Mle 07 T.16, with a drum-type back sight. Courtesy of Ian Hogg.

externally, concentric with the front portion of the barrel. Closely spaced fins surrounded the rear half of the barrel, and the standard mount had no fewer than four folding legs. Changes were even made to the feed, so that the cartridge strips no longer interchanged with the Hotchkiss pattern being issued to the cavalry and the colonial forces even as the APX was being developed.

Adopted 'provisionally' to replace the Hotchkiss, experience rapidly showed the APX to be disastrously inefficient. The rate reducer was particularly prone to breakdown, and the guns were soon relegated to fixed emplacements in fortresses close to the borders with Belgium, Germany and Switzerland, where they could be protected from the dirt of field deployment and cossetted under cover.

8mm Mitrailleuse, Modèle 1907

The failure of the APX (above) left the way clear for the rival Saint-Étienne machine-gun to stake its claim to adoption. Another of the designs based on the Hotchkiss, the Saint-Étienne, incredibly, reversed the backward movement of the gas piston so that it was blown forwards. Rack-and-pinion gear was interposed between the gas piston and the operating rod to ensure that the rod moved back to drive the bolt and feed mechanism. The well tried Hotchkiss flap lock was replaced by a form of over-centre toggle lock; the gas take-off point reverted to the original mid-barrel position; the volume of the gas cylinder could be adjusted to alter the fire rate; and the barrel-return spring lay where it could rapidly overheat, beneath

A Mle 1907 Saint-Étienne machine-gun provides a backdrop for a discussion between a French Poilu and a British Tommy. That they occupy a captured German trench is shown by one Mauser rifle across the Briton's knee and another propped against the parapet.

Mitrailleuse Mle 1907

Synonym:	'Mitrailleuse dit Saint-Étienne', 'French Saint-Étienne machine-gun'
Adoption date:	1907? (See text)
Length:	1,180mm (46.46in)
Weight:	23.8kg (52lb 7oz)
Weight of mount, M1907C tripod:	32.7kg (72lb 1oz)
Barrel length:	800mm (31.50in)
Chambering:	8 × 51mm, rimmed
Rifling type:	four-groove, concentric, LH
Feed type:	metal strip
Belt capacity:	twenty-five rounds
Fire selector:	none, automatic only
Cyclic rate:	variable, 350–600rd/min
Front sight:	open blade
Backsight:	tangent-leaf type
Minimum backsight setting:	200m (219yd)
Maximum backsight setting:	2,000m (2,187yd)
Muzzle velocity:	700m/sec (2,297ft/sec)

the barrel. In fact the strip feed was the only feature that the French government technicians didn't change – which was ironic, since it was the only Hotchkiss feature that was universally disliked.

The first Saint-Étienne machine-guns were introduced to service in 1909, but it was soon evident that they failed to live up to the inflated reputation that had preceded them. The operating mechanism was needlessly complicated and unnecessarily fragile. Changes were made to the sights during World War One, post-1916 drum sights being graduated to 2,400m, but the guns that survived the war were banished to the French colonies.

In addition to the 'Mle 1907 C' tripod, the Saint-Étienne could be mounted on the so-called M1915 'Type Omnibus' tripod associated with the Hotchkiss and a few surviving Puteaux ('APX') machine-guns. This mount weighed about 35kg.

8mm Fusil-Mitrailleuse Hotchkiss, Modèle 1908/13

Chambered for the 8mm Lebel cartridge, this was the French service version of a light machine-gun that was to see service in the USA, Belgium, Britain, Mexico and Sweden prior to 1918. Also known as the 'Benét-Mercié Machine Rifle', it embodied the gas-operated 'fermeture nut' locking system devised by Mercié. This relied on a sleeve with interrupted threads surrounding the chamber mouth, which the action of the gas piston turned to engage corresponding lugs on the bolt head. Unlike the feed strips of the Odkolek-type Hotchkiss guns, the Benét-Mercié patterns carried their cartridges on the underside. Some of the guns used in the air during the early stages of World War One were issued with 'belts' made of four 25-round strips joined together, but predictably these proved to be too cumbersome, and were superseded by 75-round belts made of twenty-five three-round articulated striplets.

Adopted originally as a cavalry weapon, the M1908/13 became the principal weapon of the air service and even of some of the first French tanks; however, it was eventually superseded by the lighter and more battle-worthy Lewis Gun.

Fusil-Mitrailleuse Hotchkiss, Mle 08/13

Synonym:	'M1913 French Hotchkiss light machine-gun'
Adoption date:	June 1913?
Length:	1,190mm (46.85in)
Weight:	12.50kg (27lb 9oz), with bipod
Barrel length:	565mm (22.24in)
Chambering:	8 × 51mm, rimmed
Rifling type:	four-groove, concentric, LH
Feed type:	metal strip
Strip capacity:	twenty-four rounds (see text)
Fire selector:	none?
Front sight:	open blade
Backsight:	tangent-leaf type
Minimum backsight setting:	100m (109yd)
Maximum backsight setting:	2,000m (2,187yd)
Muzzle velocity:	650m/sec (2,133ft/sec)

8 Italy

HANDGUNS

10.35mm Pistola a Rotazione, Modello 1889

The origins of this gun lay in the formation, in 1889, of a military commission under the chairmanship of General Bodeo, charged with replacing the 1872- and 1874-pattern revolvers that served the officers and senior NCOs of the cavalry, the Carabinieri, naval officers, and officers and men of the Train.

A solid frame, double-action design, the M1889 was not especially remarkable – except that it was specifically developed to fire ammunition loaded with smokeless propellant. The Abadie-pattern loading gate was interconnected with the hammer to provide a safety feature, and an ejector rod was carried on a pivoting yoke beneath the barrel. A 'hammer block' was the only mechanical novelty: this prevented the rebounding hammer falling far enough to fire the cartridge unless the trigger was pulled fully back.

Customarily credited to Società Siderugica Glisenti, the original M1889 had an octagonal barrel and a folding trigger; by World War One, however, a variant with a conventional trigger-guard had become universal. It has been suggested that the folding-trigger guns were issued to the rank and file, whereas the trigger-guard guns were destined for officers and senior NCOs. Italian sources, however, do not seem to draw such distinction.

M1889 revolvers were made by Castelli of Brescia, and Metallurgica Bresciana Temprini ('MBT') of Brescia; Società Siderurgica Glisenti of Carcinia; Reale Fabbrica d'Armi Brescia

Pistola a Rotazione, Modello 1889	
Synonym:	'M1889 Italian Bodeo revolver'
Adoption date:	3 June 1891
Length:	235mm (9.25in)
Weight:	950g (2.12lb) empty
Barrel length:	115mm (4.53in)
Chambering:	10.4 × 20mm, rimmed ('Italian Ordnance')
Rifling type:	six-groove, concentric, RH
Magazine type:	rotating cylinder
Magazine capacity:	six rounds
Loading system:	single cartridges
Front sight:	open blade
Backsight:	fixed 'V'-notch
Muzzle velocity:	255m/sec (836ft/sec)

('FAB'); and Vincenzo Bernardelli of Gardone Val Trompia. Others were apparently made in Spain during World War One, by Errasti, Arrostegui and other gunmakers in Eibar. Supplemented by the Glisenti semi-automatic pistol after 1910, the 1889-pattern revolver was made until the early 1930s. Large numbers survived to serve during World War Two.

9mm Pistola Automatica Modello 910

Società Siderugica Glisenti of Carcinia, near Brescia, made M1889 revolvers under contract to the Italian government prior to 1914. Keen to compete with the manufacturers of semi-automatic pistols – the 7.63mm Mauser C/96 had been adopted by the navy in 1899 – Glisenti eventually became associated with an eponymous design. The origins of the Glisenti pistol, howev-

A typical M1889 Bodeo revolver, made by Castelli of Brescia in 1922 but entirely typical of those made during the First World War. Courtesy of Ian Hogg.

er, have still to be properly explained. It is supposed that the design was due to Abiel Revelli, an army officer, but it may have been inspired by the work of the Swiss engineers Häussler & Roch. Rumours of a new Italian service pistol began to circulate as early as 1903, and in 1906, Siderugica Glisenti obtained machine tools from Britain to begin production. However, within a year Glisenti had sold the manufacturing rights to Metallurgica Bresciana gia Tempini ('MBT'), previously the major sub-contractor. Metallurgica Bresciana bought more tools from Germany, and late in 1908 began offering an 'M1906' Brixia pistol. 'Brixia' was the company's tradename.

The 1906-pattern gun was chambered for a unique 7.65 × 22mm bottlenecked cartridge, but this failed to satisfy the Italian army and it was redesigned to accept a 9mm cartridge sharing the dimensions – though not the power – of the German 9mm Parabellum pattern. The new 'M1909' pistol was formally adopted by the Italian army in 1910. Strangely, it became known as the 'Glisenti' even though Metallurgica Bresciana offered an improved Brixia commercially from 1912 onwards.

The breech-lock of these guns consisted of a wedge, pivoting in the frame, which engaged in a recess beneath the bolt. When the gun fired, the barrel, the barrel extension and the bolt ran back about 7mm along the frame top, until the wedge had been turned far enough to disengage the bolt. The barrel unit stopped, held by the depressed locking wedge, and the bolt continued its reciprocation, chambering a new round on the closing stroke. The wedge rose, re-engaged with the bolt, freed the barrel, and the barrel return spring pushed the moving parts back into battery.

By removing a screw in the front of the frame, customarily held by a spring catch, the entire left side of the frame could be removed. Unfortunately this reduced the stiffness of the frame, and removed support from much of the left side of the barrel extension. The side plate would work loose during prolonged firing, and this was a problem – as was the violence of the Glisenti breech, which opened so rapidly (even with the special low power ammunition) that it has been classed more as a 'delayed blowback' than 'fully locked'.

The firing mechanism was also unusual, as the striker was not cocked as the bolt closed. Pressing the trigger pushed the striker back against its spring before releasing it, giving a long and creepy pull. A spring lever was let into the front edge of the grip, but there were no other safety features.

The M1910 remained in production in the government-owned Brescia ordnance factory (Fabbrica d'Armi Brescia, 'FAB') until the early 1920s, although it was supplemented by increasing numbers of Beretta pistols from 1915 onwards.

LONGARMS

6.5mm Fucile di Fanteria, Modello 1891

Better known as the 'Mannlicher-Carcano', this was the result of protracted trials to find a suitable small-calibre infantry rifle, trials that had begun in 1889. The gun had a one-piece straight-wrist stock, and a protruding magazine case that accepted reversible clips.

The bolt and the split-bridge were far simpler than components used on the Mannlichers

A 9mm-calibre M1910 Glisenti pistol, made by Fabbrica d'Armi Brescia in 1910. Courtesy of Weller & Dufty Ltd, Birmingham.

Pistola automatica Mo. 910	
Synonym:	'M1910 Italian Glisenti pistol'
Adoption date:	1910
Length:	218mm (8.58in)
Weight:	860g (30.3oz), empty
Barrel length:	95mm (3.74in)
Chambering:	9 × 19mm Glisenti, rimless
Rifling type:	four-groove, concentric, RH
Magazine type:	detachable single-row box
Magazine capacity:	seven rounds
Loading system:	single cartridges
Front sight:	open barleycorn
Backsight:	fixed open notch
Muzzle velocity:	320m/sec (1,050ft/sec)

derived from the German Gewehr 1888, and the 'safety catch' was nothing but a plate projecting between the rear of the bolt body and the cocking piece. A typically Italian quadrant backsight lay on the barrel ahead of the chamber, there were swivels under the butt and rear band, and a conventional bayonet lug appeared under the nosecap. Maker's marks – for example, a crown above 'R.E. TERNI' – lay on the barrel ahead of the receiver and on the right side of the butt.

The first rifles were issued in the spring of 1894, but the bolt head was almost immediately strengthened pending the introduction of the smokeless M1891/95 cartridge approved in

A typical 6.5mm M1891 Mannlicher-Carcano rifle. Courtesy of Ian Hogg.

Fucile di Fanteria, Mo. 1891

Synonym:	'M1891 Italian Mannlicher-Carcano rifle'
Adoption date:	29 March 1891
Length:	1,289mm (50.75in)
Length with M1891 sword bayonet attached:	1,664mm (65.5in)
Weight:	3.79kg (8lb 6oz), without sling
Weight with M1891 sword bayonet attached:	4.17kg (9lb 3oz)
Barrel length:	781mm (30.75in)
Chambering:	6.5 × 52mm, rimless
Rifling type:	four-groove, concentric, RH
Magazine type:	single-row protruding box
Magazine capacity:	six rounds
Loading system:	reversible clip
Front sight:	open barleycorn
Backsight:	quadrant type
Minimum backsight setting:	500m (547yd)
Maximum backsight setting:	2,000m (2,187yd)
Muzzle velocity:	730m/sec (2,395ft/sec)

The action of a specially cutaway M1891 Mannlicher-Carcano rifle, showing a partially empty clip in the magazine. Courtesy of Ian Hogg.

Production in the Brescia, Terni, Torino and Torre Annunziata ordnance factories is believed to have exceeded 3.5 million guns; when the Armistice was concluded on 11 November 1918, Reale Fabbrica d'Armi Terni alone had made 2,063,750 rifles since 1 January 1915. Work finally ceased in 1937.

6.5mm Moschetto per Cavalleria, Modello 1891

Adopted for cavalry, carabinieri (mounted gendarmerie) and cyclists, this originally had a straight-wrist half-stock, a recoil bolt laterally through the stock beneath the receiver ring, a turned-down bolt handle, and a folding bayonet attached to a special muzzle block. Most moschetti were made in the state-owned Brescia small-arms factory, though at least a few emanated from Terni.

February 1896. The hand-guard was altered in 1905, and improvements to the extractor were sanctioned in 1907.

Monthly production of rifles in the Terni factory had risen to about 2,500 by the spring of 1913, when production of carbines was centred on Brescia and work in the factories in Torino and Torre Annuziata had been run down to virtually nothing. When World War One commenced in the summer of 1914, the Italian army inventory stood at 700,000 Mo. 1891 rifles.

Moschetto per Cavalleria, Mo. 1891	
Synonym:	'M1891 Italian Mannlicher-Carcano cavalry carbine'
Adoption date:	9 June 1893
Length:	953mm (37.52in)
Weight:	3.16kg (6lb 15oz), without sling
Barrel length:	450mm (17.72in)
Chambering:	6.5 × 52mm, rimless
Rifling type:	four-groove, concentric, RH
Magazine type:	single-row protruding box
Magazine capacity:	six rounds
Loading system:	reversible clip
Front sight:	open barleycorn
Backsight:	quadrant type
Minimum backsight setting:	500m (547yd)
Maximum backsight setting:	1,500m (1,640yd)
Muzzle velocity:	635m/sec (2,083ft/sec)

The action of a typical Italian Mannlicher-Carcano short rifle, or moschetto. Note the small tangent-type back sight. Courtesy of Ian Hogg.

The recoil bolt was abandoned in 1900, a hand-guard was added between the backsight and the barrel band/nosecap, and a push-button bayonet attachment mechanism was substituted for a radial lever.

A variant of the cavalry carbine was adopted in the 1890s for the king's bodyguard, the *Squadrone Reali Carabinieri Guardie del Ré*. It could be distinguished by a bolt handle turned downwards against the stock, and a special nose-cap into which the socket bayonet could be reversed. Bolts, nosecaps, magazine bodies and some of the backsight components were gilded, the remaining metal parts being blued.

6.5mm Moschetto per Truppe Speciali, Modello 1891

Adopted for the 'Special Troops' (*Truppe Speciali*), these guns originally had nosecaps similar to the infantry rifles, except that the swivel lay on the rear edge; the other swivel lay beneath the butt. The recoil bolt was abandoned in 1900, when the bolt handle, previously straight, was turned downwards against the stock. A modified nosecap appeared in this period, with a backward extension for the front swivel and a bayonet lug that ran laterally. This accepted a special bayonet with a press-stud protruding from the end of the pommel, and is believed to have been an attempt to prevent an opponent snatching the bayonet from the muzzle.

An 1891-pattern Mannlicher-Carcano cavalry carbine was a half-stocked design with a distinctive folding bayonet. Courtesy of Hans-Bert Lockhoven.

Pre-1908 guns were eventually given new swivels on the left side of the stock, but the work proceeded so slowly that it was not completed until 1913.

MACHINE-GUNS

The Italians were still experimenting with the Perino when World War One began (see Part One), though a few Maxims had been purchased. The 6.5mm FIAT-Revelli, which had pre-war origins, is described in Part Three.

6.5mm Fucile Mitriagliatore Madsen

Two batches of these light machine-guns were purchased from Denmark, in 1908 and 1910. The guns were virtually identical, though Dansk Industri Syndikat AS 'Madsen' regularly made minor cosmetic changes and altered nomenclature to suggest that purchasers were getting the latest technology! Recoil-operated weapons, locked by a dropping breech-block similar to that of the Martini rifle, the Madsen is described in

Moschetto per Truppe Speciali Mo. 1891	
Synonyms:	'Mo. 1891 TS', and 'M1891 Italian Mannlicher-Carrcano short rifle'
Adoption date:	1897
Length:	953mm (37.52in)
Weight:	3.22kg (7lb 1oz), without sling
Barrel length:	450mm (17.72in)
Chambering:	6.5 × 52mm, rimless
Rifling type:	four-groove, concentric, RH
Magazine type:	single-row protruding box
Magazine capacity:	six rounds
Loading system:	reversible clip
Front sight:	open barleycorn
Backsight:	quadrant type
Minimum backsight setting:	500m (547yd)
Maximum backsight setting:	1,500m (1,640yd)
Muzzle velocity:	635m/sec (2,083ft/sec)

greater detail in the Russian section. The Italian examples, however, chambered the standard 6.5 × 52mm M1891/95 service cartridge, developing a muzzle velocity of about 625m/sec (2,050ft/sec), and had a straighter magazine than the sharply curved Russian equivalent.

9 Japan

Prior to 1930, Japanese service weapons were designated according to the reign-period (*nengo*) of each emperor, as from the restoration of 1868; thus, 1890 was the '23rd Year' of the Meiji *nengo*. The system was maintained through the Taisho period (1912–26) and into the Showa era, before being replaced by a calendar based on the mythical foundation of Japan in 660BC. Arsenal identification marks were arbitrary; Tokyo and Kokura used a pile of cannon balls, while Nagoya had two stylized fighting fish. The principal navy mark was a large anchor.

HANDGUNS

9mm Meiji 26th Year Type Revolver

Details of the development of this weapon will be found in Part One. After purchasing guns from abroad, the Japanese developed a gun of their own by mixing components taken from Western designs: thus the lockwork was based on a Galand design, the hinged frame and frame latch were pure Smith & Wesson, a hinged sideplate covering the lockwork was inspired by the proto-types of the French M1892 Modèle d'Ordonnance, and the external shape may be due to Nagant or Rast & Gasser – opinions differ. Owing to the omission of a hammer spur, the revolver can only be fired in self-cocking mode. It chambered a uniquely Japanese rimmed 9mm cartridge.

Meiji 26th Year Type (1893) revolvers were made in the Koishikawa small-arms factory in Tokyo; by the early 1920s the demand had slack-ened, and when much of the production machinery was destroyed by the Tokyo earthquake of 1923, the revolver was abandoned. Surviving examples, however, were still to be found in the hands of second-line troops until 1945.

Meiji 26th Year Type revolver	
Synonym:	'M1893 Japanese revolver'
Adoption date:	1893
Length:	216mm (8.50in)
Weight:	880g (31oz), empty
Barrel length:	120mm (4.71in)
Chambering:	9 × 22mm, rimmed ('Japanese Revolver')
Rifling type:	six-groove, concentric, RH
Magazine type:	rotating cylinder
Magazine capacity:	six rounds
Loading system:	single cartridges
Front sight:	open blade
Backsight:	fixed notch
Muzzle velocity:	195m/sec (640ft/sec)

8mm 'Type Nambu' Pistol

The first semi-automatic handgun to be designed by Captain Kirijo Nambu dated from 1902. It was apparently approved provisionally by the Japanese army in 1904, and entered production in 1906 as the 'Type Nambu'.

Although similar to the Parabellum outwardly, the mechanism of the Nambu resembles that of the Mauser C/96. The barrel and receiver, or 'bar-rel extension', recoil on the frame; a hinged arm attached to the barrel extension is forced up by a ramp in the frame until a lug on its upper surface enters a locking recess in the bolt. The hinged

Type Nambu pistol	
Synonyms:	'Taisho 4th Year Type pistol', and 'Type A Nambu'
Adoption date:	1906?
Length:	228mm (8.98in)
Weight:	880g (31oz), empty
Barrel length:	120mm (4.71in)
Chambering:	8 × 21mm, rimless ('8mm Nambu')
Rifling type:	six-groove, segmental, RH
Magazine type:	detachable box
Magazine capacity:	eight rounds
Loading system:	single cartridges or replacement magazines
Front sight:	open blade
Backsight:	leaf and slider
Minimum backsight setting:	100m (110yd)
Maximum backsight setting:	500m (550yd)
Muzzle velocity:	335m/sec (1,100ft/sec)

arm holds the bolt closed as the action recoils, until it passes off the ramp and drops to free the bolt to run back alone.

A single recoil spring lies in a chamber on the left side of the receiver, alongside the bolt. A grooved cocking grip protruding from the rear of the receiver is attached to the striker running through the centre of the bolt. A pivoting safety lever is set into the front grip strap, and a detachable magazine running up through the butt holds necked 8mm cartridges (also credited to Kijiro Nambu).

The first pistols had an unusually small trigger-guard, wood-bottom magazines, and their butts slotted to receive a shoulder stock. The magazine base was changed to aluminium after about 2,300 guns had been made, the cocking grip was rounded, a swivelling lanyard loop appeared on the lower left side of the butt, and the shoulder-stock slot was abandoned. The trigger-guard was subsequently enlarged, the trigger face was flattened (instead of being bevelled) – and the definitive 'Type Nambu' had been created.

The imperial navy formally adopted the 'Taisho 4th Year Type Pistol' in 1915; however, the Koishikawa facilities could not supply enough guns, and so a contract was given to Tokyo Gasu Denki KK ('Tokyo Gas & Electric Company'). The first 2,000 guns had slotted butts, as the navy considered shoulder stocks to be useful. Work in Koishikawa continued until 1927, and at Tokyo Gasu Denki until 1930. Both manufacturers offered Nambu pistols for commercial sale at the same time as they were fulfilling their military orders.

The 8mm Type Nambu semi-automatic pistol was apparently introduced in 1904, though not officially adopted at this time. This is the perfected 'Type A' version with a large trigger guard, dating, it seems, from c. 1908.

7mm Type Nambu Pistol

Introduced in 1909 to satisfy officers who felt that the standard Type Nambu was too large, this pistol chambered a minuscule 7mm bottle-necked cartridge. Production began in the Koishikawa smallarms factory in about 1910. The earliest guns had wood-bottom magazines, a pinched-in cocking piece and a single-diameter firing pin. After about 450 had been made, the magazine gained an aluminium bottom, the cocking piece was rounded, and a multi-diameter firing pin was introduced.

Production continued until about 1931 in both Koishikawa and Tokyo Gasu Denki factories, but the 'Baby' never achieved widespread popularity, largely because it was almost twice the price of FN-Brownings and comparable imported pistols.

<table>
<tr><td colspan="2">Type B Nambu pistol</td></tr>
<tr><td>Synonyms:</td><td>'Baby Nambu', 'Type B Nambu', 'Officer's Nambu pistol'</td></tr>
<tr><td>Adoption date:</td><td>1910?</td></tr>
<tr><td>Length:</td><td>171mm (6.73in)</td></tr>
<tr><td>Weight:</td><td>590g (21oz), empty</td></tr>
<tr><td>Barrel length:</td><td>83mm (3.27in)</td></tr>
<tr><td>Chambering:</td><td>7 × 20mm, rimless ('7mm Nambu')</td></tr>
<tr><td>Rifling type:</td><td>six-groove, segmental, RH</td></tr>
<tr><td>Magazine type:</td><td>detachable box</td></tr>
<tr><td>Magazine capacity:</td><td>seven rounds</td></tr>
<tr><td>Loading system:</td><td>single cartridges or replacement magazines</td></tr>
<tr><td>Front sight:</td><td>open blade</td></tr>
<tr><td>Backsight:</td><td>fixed U-notch</td></tr>
<tr><td>Muzzle velocity:</td><td>305m/sec (1,000ft/sec)</td></tr>
</table>

RIFLES

6.5mm Meiji 30th Year Type Rifle

Credited to a commission chaired by Colonel Nariake Arisaka, this was an amalgam of features inspired by Western practice. It may be identified by the unusual 'hook safety' lever protruding from the cocking piece. The ejector and extractor were both mounted on the bolt, and the fixed box magazine, contained entirely within the stock, could be loaded through the open action with a Mauser-type charger. More than half a million 1897-pattern rifles had been made in the imperial artillery arsenal, Koishikawa, Tokyo, before about 1907.

<table>
<tr><td colspan="2">Meiji 30th Year Type rifle</td></tr>
<tr><td>Synonym:</td><td>'M1897 Japanese Arisaka rifle'</td></tr>
<tr><td>Adoption date:</td><td>1897</td></tr>
<tr><td>Length:</td><td>50.04in (1,271mm)</td></tr>
<tr><td>Weight:</td><td>9lb 0oz (4.08kg), without sling</td></tr>
<tr><td>Barrel length:</td><td>787mm (30.98in)</td></tr>
<tr><td>Chambering:</td><td>6.5 x 50mm, semi-rim</td></tr>
<tr><td>Rifling type:</td><td>six-groove, segmental, RH</td></tr>
<tr><td>Magazine type:</td><td>staggered-row internal box</td></tr>
<tr><td>Magazine capacity:</td><td>five rounds</td></tr>
<tr><td>Loading system:</td><td>charger or loose cartridges</td></tr>
<tr><td>Cut-off system:</td><td>none</td></tr>
<tr><td>Front sight:</td><td>open barleycorn</td></tr>
<tr><td>Backsight:</td><td>leaf-and-slider type</td></tr>
<tr><td>Minimum backsight setting:</td><td>400m (437yd)</td></tr>
<tr><td>Maximum backsight setting:</td><td>2,000m (2,187yd)</td></tr>
<tr><td>Muzzle velocity:</td><td>775m/sec (2,543ft/sec)</td></tr>
</table>

<table>
<tr><td colspan="2">Meiji 30th Year Type carbine</td></tr>
<tr><td>Synonym:</td><td>'M1897 Japanese Arisaka carbine'</td></tr>
<tr><td>Adoption date:</td><td>1897</td></tr>
<tr><td>Length:</td><td>961mm (37.83in)</td></tr>
<tr><td>Weight:</td><td>3.388kg (7lb 7oz), without sling</td></tr>
<tr><td>Barrel length:</td><td>480mm (18.9in)</td></tr>
<tr><td>Chambering:</td><td>6.5 × 50mm, semi-rim</td></tr>
<tr><td>Rifling type:</td><td>six-groove, segmental, RH</td></tr>
<tr><td>Magazine type:</td><td>staggered-row internal box</td></tr>
<tr><td>Magazine capacity:</td><td>five rounds</td></tr>
<tr><td>Loading system:</td><td>charger or loose cartridges</td></tr>
<tr><td>Front sight:</td><td>open barleycorn</td></tr>
<tr><td>Backsight:</td><td>leaf-and-slider type</td></tr>
<tr><td>Minimum backsight setting:</td><td>400m (437yd)</td></tr>
<tr><td>Maximum backsight setting:</td><td>1,500m (1,640yd)</td></tr>
<tr><td>Muzzle velocity:</td><td>730m/sec (2,395ft/sec)</td></tr>
</table>

A typical Meiji 30th Year Type Arisaka rifle (1897), showing the distinctive finger-spur on the cocking piece which gained this particular rifle the sobriquet 'hook safety'. Courtesy of Hans-Bert Lockhoven.

A Meiji 30th Year Type cavalry carbine. Courtesy of Ian Hogg.

6.5mm Meiji 30th Year Type Carbine

This Arisaka was produced simply by shortening the standard rifle, omitting the hand-guard, and substituting a smaller back sight; mechanically identical with the standard rifle, it accepted the same sword bayonet. At least 40,000 guns of this type were made.

6.5mm Meiji 35th Year Type Rifle

The 30th Year system proved a disappointment in service, and an improved rifle was approved in 1902. The cocking piece was enlarged; a new gas-escape port was added on the bolt; the bolt knob was enlarged; the design of the bolt head and the feed ramp was improved; a sliding spring-loaded breech cover was fitted; the back-sight was changed to a tangent pattern; and the hand-guard was run back as far as the receiver ring.

About 35,000 rifles were made in 1903–6 by the arsenal in Koishikawa. However, though often claimed to have been navy issue, it seems much more likely that the 1902-pattern Arisaka was simply destined to substitute for the 1897 pattern; it is assumed that lessons learned in the Russo-Japanese War showed that more radical changes were required.

Meiji 35th Year Type rifle	
Synonyms:	'M1902 Japanese Arisaka rifle, and 'Japanese Navy Arisaka'
Adoption date:	February 1902
Length:	1,275mm (50.2in)
Weight:	4.07kg (8lb 15oz), without sling
Barrel length:	790mm (31.1in)
Chambering:	6.5 × 50mm, semi-rim
Rifling type:	six-groove, segmental, RH
Magazine type:	staggered-row internal box
Magazine capacity:	five rounds
Loading system:	charger or loose cartridges
Front sight:	open barleycorn
Backsight:	tangent-leaf type
Minimum backsight setting:	400m (437yd)
Maximum backsight setting:	2,000m (2,187yd)
Muzzle velocity:	775m/sec (2,543ft/sec)

The action of the 35th Year Type Arisaka rifle of 1902, with its sheet-steel bolt cover pushed forward over the receiver.

6.5mm Meiji 38th Year Type Rifle

Extensive combat experience in the Russo-Japanese War (1904–5) revealed serious problems with the existing 1897- and 1902-pattern Arisaka service rifles. The bolt-mounted extractor/ejector system was ineffectual, the separate bolt head worked loose, and the mechanism was too easily jammed by dust and mud. By the spring of 1906, therefore, a modified rifle had been developed. Among its features were a simplified bolt, a non-rotating extractor, a reciprocating bolt cover, and a large knurled safety shroud on the cocking piece. Rifles were soon being made in quantity in the imperial artillery arsenal in Koishikawa, Tokyo. Two lugs on the bolt head engaged locking recesses in the receiver as the bolt handle turned down, reinforced by the base of the bolt handle entering its seat in the receiver.

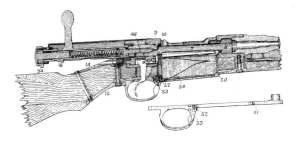

A longitudinal section of the 38th Year Type Arisaka rifle of 1905. From the Text Book of Small Arms, *1909 edition.*

6.5mm Meiji 38th Year Type Carbine

Made by the imperial artillery arsenal in Koishikawa from 1907 onwards, this was issued to cavalrymen until the introduction in 1911 of the Meiji 44th Year Type; production then continued for artillerymen, engineers and Train units. About 215,000 were made in Tokyo prior to the change to prefixed numbers after World War One had ended.

Except for its dimensions, the 1905-pattern carbine was essentially similar to the infantry

Meiji 38th Year Type rifle	
Synonym:	'M1905 Japanese Arisaka rifle'
Adoption date:	May 1907
Length:	1,289mm (50.75in)
Weight:	3.91kg (8lb 10oz), without sling
Barrel length:	795mm (31.3in)
Chambering:	6.5 × 50mm, semi-rim
Rifling type:	six-groove, segmental, RH
Magazine type:	staggered-row internal box
Magazine capacity:	five rounds
Loading system:	charger or loose cartridges
Front sight:	open barleycorn
Backsight:	leaf-and-slider type
Minimum backsight setting:	400m (437yd)
Maximum backsight setting:	2,000m (2,187yd)
Muzzle velocity:	730m/sec (2,396ft/sec)

Meiji 38th Year Type carbine	
Synonym:	'M1905 Japanese Arisaka carbine'
Adoption date:	1907
Length:	963mm (37.91in)
Weight:	3.35kg (7lb 6oz), without sling
Barrel length:	486mm (19.15in)
Chambering:	6.5 × 50mm, semi-rim
Rifling type:	six-groove, segmental, RH
Magazine type:	staggered-row internal box
Magazine capacity:	five rounds
Loading system:	charger or loose cartridges
Front sight:	open barleycorn
Backsight:	leaf-and-slider type
Minimum backsight setting:	400m (437yd)
Maximum backsight setting:	2,000m (2,187yd)
Muzzle velocity:	730m/sec (2,395ft/sec) with M1905 ball ammunition

rifle, with a hand-guard running from the front of the backsight base to the nosecap. It also accepted the standard sword bayonet.

A 38th Year Type cavalry carbine. Courtesy of Ian Hogg.

The action of a 38th Year Type cavalry carbine, showing the diminutive back sight and the sling ring attached to the left side of the barrel band. This gun lacks the cylindrical bolt cover and has a sliver of wood missing from the right side of the stock beneath the chamber.

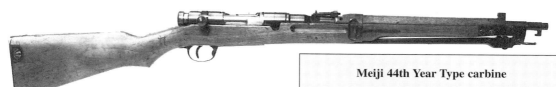

The 44th Year Type Arisaka cavalry carbine, 1911. Note the folding bayonet attached to the nosecap. Courtesy of Ian Hogg.

6.5mm Meiji 44th Year Type Carbine

Made by the Koishikawa manufactory from 1912 onwards, this cavalry carbine superseded the Meiji 38th Year Type (q.v.). It could be distinguished by a folding bayonet attached to an unusually massive nosecap. The earliest bayonet mounting block was very short, with the two lateral retaining bolts close together, but this was changed after World War One had ended. The second-pattern block had fillets that ran backwards along the stock fore-end, and an integral quillon.

Meiji 44th Year Type carbine	
Synonym:	'M1911 Japanese Arisaka cavalry carbine'
Adoption date:	1911
Length:	965mm (38.0in)
Weight:	4.07kg (8lb 15oz), with integral bayonet but without sling
Barrel length:	486mm (19.15in)
Chambering:	6.5 × 50mm, semi-rim
Rifling type:	six-groove, segmental, RH
Magazine type:	staggered-row internal box
Magazine capacity:	five rounds
Loading system:	charger or loose cartridges
Front sight:	open barleycorn
Backsight:	leaf-and-slider type
Minimum backsight setting:	400m (437yd)
Maximum backsight setting:	2,000m (2,187yd)
Muzzle velocity:	730m/sec (2,396ft/sec) with M1905 ball ammunition

The Type 92 (1932) was based on the Taisho 3rd Year Type (1914) machine-gun, little more than a Japanese-made Hotchkiss. Courtesy of Ian Hogg.

MACHINE-GUNS

Japan adopted the Hotchkiss in 1902, using it to good effect in the Russo-Japanese war. A licence was then negotiated to make similar guns in the Koishikawa artillery arsenal, but changes were proposed after only a few hundred French-type 'Meiji 33rd Year Type' ('M1900') weapons had been made.

6.5mm Taisho 3rd Year Type Machine-gun

Adopted in 1914, this should not be confused with the French Modèle 1914 Hotchkiss. The Japanese weapon was based on the licensed copy of the Hotchkiss of 1897 then being made in Koishikawa, altered to suit Japanese manufacturing methods. The gas-operated machine-gun can be identified by double-diameter cooling fins on the barrel (with the larger ones behind the gas port) and by twin spade grips

Taisho 3rd Year Type machine-gun	
Synonym:	'M1914 Japanese Hotchkiss'
Adoption date:	1914
Length:	1,156mm (45.50in)
Weight of gun:	28.12kg (62lb)
Weight of mount:	27.2kg (60lb)
Barrel length:	750mm (29.52in)
Chambering:	6.5 × 50mm, semi-rim
Rifling type:	four-groove, concentric, LH
Feed type:	thirty-round metal strips
Selector:	none, automatic fire only
Front sight:	open blade
Backsight:	leaf-and-slider type
Minimum backsight setting:	300m (328yd)
Maximum backsight setting:	2,000m (2,187yd)
Muzzle velocity:	731m/sec (2,400ft/sec)

instead of the folding pattern that characterized the later Type 92 Hotchkiss derivative; also the tripod had socketed feet. Each socket accepted a carrying pole, allowing the gun to be moved rapidly without detaching the mount – a tactic unique to the Japanese army.

10 Russia

The calibre of most pre-1917 Russian firearms was expressed in 'lines', an indigenous measurement equal to 1/10in (2.5mm); their sights were customarily graduated in arshin (paces), each being equal to about 28in (70cm).

HANDGUNS

.44 Smith & Wesson 'Russian' Model

The Russian army, seeking to equip its cavalry and artillery with a modern revolver, chose a modified Smith & Wesson .44 American Model in 1870. Several important changes were made, culminating in the introduction of a short-barrelled 'Cavalry' pattern with a 'pawl' – a slight spur – on the rear of the grip to prevent it rolling down in the hand under the recoil force; a finger rest was added beneath the trigger-guard at the same time. These modifications were credited to a cavalry officer named Kasavery Ordinetz.

The most important change, though, lay in the cartridge. The diameter of the original .44 S&W bullet was slightly less than that of the bore, allowing it to fit easily into the mouth of the cartridge case, but the Russians insisted on a larger diameter bullet and chambers bored appropriately. This increased the bullet weight, but its tighter fit in the bore contributed to both increased muzzle velocity and vastly improved accuracy.

The contracts placed with Smith & Wesson eventually amounted to 215,704 revolvers, the last being delivered in 1875; however, filling orders of this magnitude so monopolized their Springfield factory that Smith & Wesson lost

A typical 'Russian Model' Smith & Wesson revolver. This is an example of the so-called Cavalry Pattern, with a spurred trigger guard. Courtesy of Ian Hogg.

domestic market dominance to Colt, and it took many years to regain lost ground. Consequently, when the Russians returned in 1881 to order more revolvers, Smith & Wesson preferred to license

Revolver Smit i Vessona	
Synonym:	'S&W No 3 Russian' Model revolver'
Adoption date:	1870
Length:	305mm (12in)
Weight:	1,135g (2.5lb)
Barrel length:	165mm (6.5in)
Chambering:	11.43mm, rimmed ('.44 Russian')
Rifling type:	five-groove, concentric, RH
Magazine type:	rotating cylinder
Magazine capacity:	six rounds
Loading system:	single cartridges
Front sight:	open barleycorn
Backsight:	fixed open notch
Muzzle velocity:	235m/sec (771ft/sec)

manufacture to Ludwig Loewe & Co. of Berlin. Others were made in the Tula ordnance factory, Cyrillic markings on the barrel top serving to distinguish the differing patterns.

7.62mm Nagant revolver, obr. 1895g

Léon Nagant, a Belgian gunsmith, patented a gas-sealing revolver in 1892 – the only one of its type ever to see real success. The Nagant brothers had already contributed to the success of the Mosin-Nagant infantry rifle, and it was doubtless due to this connection that the Russians adopted the patented revolver.

The solid-framed 7.62mm M1895, issued first as a single-action trooper's model and then as a double-action officer's model, had a seven-chamber cylinder. The calibre was chosen deliberately to allow barrel-making machinery to be used for rifles and handguns alike. Realizing that the hitting power of the cartridge was not particularly good, the Russians chose a flat-tip bullet in a quest for improvement.

The cylinder was cammed forward during the cocking movement of the hammer until the coned rear surface of the barrel entered the mouth of the cylinder chamber. An 'abutment' behind the cartridge to be fired then locked the components in place. A distinguishing feature of the Nagant pistol is the abnormally long firing pin necessary to reach across the frame/cylinder gap and pass through the abutment to strike the cartridge primer.

The extended mouth of the special 7.62mm cartridge completely enclosed the bullet. As the cylinder and barrel came together, the shallow-tapered case mouth entered the rear of the barrel; at the moment of firing, the mouth was expanded by gas pressure to bridge any gap that remained between chamber and barrel. This prevented any loss of gas at the cylinder/barrel interface that characterized other revolvers. Argument has always raged about the value of a gas-seal. That gas is sealed in the breech is never doubted, but the marginal improvement in performance is scarcely worth

the additional complication in a military weapon.

The earliest revolvers were supplied from the Nagant factory in Liège, where 7.5mm-calibre versions were offered commercially. The Russians had always intended to make guns of their own, a licence being demanded as a condition of adoption, and the first Tula-made Nagants appeared in 1900. Amazingly, work continued, often on a desultory basis, until 1943; the revolver may have looked ungainly, but it was extremely reliable, and very popular with its users.

The 7.62mm 'gas seal' 1895-pattern Nagant revolver cammed the cylinder forward during the trigger stroke to enable the mouth of the special elongated cartridge to seal the breech at the moment of discharge. This is a Nagant-made example, dating from 1899, but others were made in Tula as late as 1943. Courtesy of Ian Hogg.

Revolver Nagan', obr. 1895g	
Synonym:	'M1895 Russian Gas seal Nagant'
Adoption date:	1895
Length:	235mm (9.25in)
Weight:	810g (28oz), empty
Barrel length:	114mm (4.48in)
Chambering:	7.62 × 28mm, rimmed
Rifling type:	four-groove, concentric, RH
Magazine type:	rotating cylinder
Magazine capacity:	seven rounds
Loading system:	single cartridges
Front sight:	open blade
Backsight:	fixed 'U'-notch
Muzzle velocity:	290m/sec (950ft/sec)

This 7.62mm M1891 Mosin-Nagant rifle has the curved back-sight leaf characteristic of guns altered to fire the light M1908 or 'Type L' bullet. Courtesy of Ian Hogg.

The three major back sights encountered on Mosin-Nagant rifles give a clue to their age. The original 1891-type sight (right) had a flat leaf; the 1908 pattern (centre), for light-bullet ammunition, had a curved leaf; and the 1930 type (left) had a curved 'stepless' tangent-type base. Courtesy of the MoD Pattern Room collection, Royal Ordnance plc, Nottingham.

RIFLES

7.62mm Pekhotniya vintovka obr. 1891g

Recognizable by its length, the design of the magazine and the shape of its butt, this rifle was a combination of a single-shot Mosin and a magazine-feed Nagant submitted to the trials of 1889–90. The split-bridge receiver was octagonal, and a wooden hand-guard covered the barrel from the nosecap to the back barrel band. There were swivels ahead of the magazine and under

Pekhotniya vintovka obr. 1891g	
Synonyms:	Three-Line Rifle', and 'M1891 Russian Mosin-Nagant rifle'
Adoption date:	April 1891
Length:	1,318mm (51.88in)
Length with obr. 1891g bayonet attached:	1,753mm (69in)
Weight:	4.06kg (8lb 15oz), without sling
Weight with obr. 1891g bayonet attached:	4.4kg (9lb 11oz)
Barrel length:	819mm (32.25in)
Chambering:	7.62 × 54mm, rimmed
Rifling type:	four-groove, concentric, RH
Magazine type:	single-row protruding box
Magazine capacity:	five rounds
Loading system:	charger or loose rounds
Front sight:	open barleycorn
Backsight:	leaf-and-slider type
Minimum backsight setting:	400 arshin (284m, 311yd)
Maximum backsight setting:	2,700 arshin (1,920m, 2,099yd)
Muzzle velocity:	605m/sec (1,985ft/sec) with 1891 type ball ammunition

the front band. The oldest guns had a finger rest extending back from the trigger-guard, but this was abandoned in 1894.

Combat experience in the Russo-Japanese War (1904–5) showed that the Mosin-Nagants shot badly at long range, and a new pointed bullet, subsequently designated 'Type L', was introduced in 1908. Backsight leaves that had once been flat, and graduated to 2,700 paces for round-nose bullets, were now graduated to 3,200 paces and curved so that they could fit the original sight bases. A recoil bolt was added through the fore-end above the front of the magazine in this period.

It has been calculated that at least 9.36 million Mosin-Nagant rifles were made prior to 1922, by the ordnance factories in Tula, Sestroretsk and Izhevsk; by Manufacture d'Armes de Châtellerault; by the New England Westinghouse Company; and by the Remington Arms–Union Metallic Cartridge Company.

7.62mm Kazach'ya vintovka obr. 1891g

The Cossack rifle was little more than a shortened infantry rifle with a hand-guard extending as far as the backsight base. The barrel bands were retained by springs; sling slots, protected by blued-steel oval washers, were cut through the butt and the fore-end; and the cleaning rod was changed. Serial numbers had a distinctive 'KA3' prefix. Production of Cossack rifles in the ordnance factories in Tula, Sestroretsk and Izhevsk was greatly reduced after Russian cavalrymen had been unable to dominate well trained Japanese machine-gunners during the Russo-Japanese War. The Russian army inventory still contained 204,390 Cossack rifles on 1 January 1914, but production stopped in 1915.

7.62mm Dragunskaya vintovka obr. 1891g

The dragoon rifle was a near-duplicate of the Cossack rifle, but with a different cleaning rod. It was apparently issued without a bayonet, although the standard socket pattern could be mounted if required. Serial numbers were given no particular

distinction. The introduction of the 1908-pattern ball cartridge led to the substitution of curved-leaf 3,200-pace sights for the original flat 2,700-pace type, work continuing almost until World War One began. The inventory taken on 1 January 1914 included 540,270 dragoon rifles.

Kazach'ya vintovka obr. 1891g	
Synonym:	'M1891 Russian Mosin-Nagant cossack rifle'
Adoption date:	1891?
Length:	1,235mm (48.63in)
Weight:	3.91kg (8lb 10oz), without sling
Barrel length:	759mm (29.88in)
Chambering:	7.62 × 54mm, rimmed
Rifling type:	four-groove, concentric, RH
Magazine type	single-row protruding box
Magazine capacity:	five rounds
Loading system:	charger or loose rounds
Front sight	open barleycorn
Backsight:	leaf-and-slider type
Minimum backsight setting:	400 arshin (284m, 311yd)
Maximum backsight setting:	2,700 arshin (1,920m, 2,099yd)
Muzzle velocity:	605m/sec (1,985ft/sec) with 1891-type ball ammunition

7.62mm Karabina obr. 1907g

Made by the ordnance factories in Tula, Sestroretsk and Izhevsk, the first Mosin-Nagant carbine pattern (also known as '1891/07') was issued to artillerymen and cavalry. It was much shorter than the infantry rifle, and the stock extended so close to the muzzle that the standard socket bayonet could not be mounted.

The diminutive ramp-and-leaf backsight was originally graduated to about 1,600 paces (1,138m, 1,244yd), but the introduction in 1910 of the 1908-pattern 'light bullet' cartridge caused a change in sights. It is suspected that this may

The so-called 'M1910' Mosin-Nagant cavalry carbine. Painting by John Walter.

have been camouflaged by altering the position of the gradations on the existing leaf, and may be the reason why claims have been made that an 'obr. 1910g' carbine also exists. The Mosin-Nagant carbine inventory stood at 118,660 on 1 January 1914.

Karabina obr. 1907g	
Synonyms:	Three-Line Cavalry Carbine' and 'M1907 Russian Mosin-Nagant carbine'
Adoption date:	1907
Length:	1,019mm (40.13in)
Weight:	3.42kg (7lb 8oz), without sling
Barrel length:	509mm (20.04in)
Chambering:	7.62 × 54mm, rimmed
Rifling type:	four-groove, concentric, RH
Magazine type:	single-row protruding box
Magazine capacity:	five rounds
Loading system:	charger or loose rounds
Front sight:	open barleycorn
Backsight:	leaf-and-slider type
Minimum backsight setting:	400 arshin (284m, 311yd)
Maximum backsight setting:	2,000 arshin (1,422m, 1,555yd)
Muzzle velocity:	550m/sec (1,804ft/sec) with 1891-type ball ammunition

7.62mm Pekhotniya vintovka obr. 1870g

With an enormous stock of obsolescent 4.2-line (10.6mm) Berdan rifles, it made sense for the Russians to re-barrel them to fire the 7.62 × 54mm cartridge adopted with the Mosin-Nagant rifle in 1891. These became the 'Three-Line Berdans', conversion being entrusted to contractors in Liège. The rifles received Belgian proof marks, but rarely gave clues to the contractor; Auguste Francotte & Cie, E. & L. Nagant and Anciens Établissements Pieper have all been suggested, as more than 200,000 may have been altered. Alterations initially seem to have been confined to the infantry rifle.

A new barrel was used, greatly strengthened in the chamber area; a new locking-lug recess and raceway were milled in the bottom of the receiver; and a new bolt head with twin locking lugs

7.62mm Pekhotniya vintovka obr. 1870g	
Synonym:	'Dreilineinaya Vintovka Berdana', 'Three-Line Berdan Rifle'
Adoption date:	1895?
Length:	1,322mm (52.05in)
Weight:	4.2kg (9lb 4oz), without sling
Barrel length:	801mm (31.54in)
Chambering:	7.62 × 54mm, rimmed
Rifling type:	four-groove, concentric, RH
Magazine type:	single-row protruding box
Magazine capacity:	five rounds
Loading system:	charger or loose rounds
Front sight:	open barleycorn
Backsight:	leaf-and-slider type
Minimum backsight setting:	400 arshin (284m, 311yd)
Maximum backsight setting:	2,700 arshin (1,920m, 2,099yd)
Muzzle velocity:	605m/sec (1,985ft/sec)

A typical '4.2-Line' (10.6mm) Berdan II rifle. Thousands of these were converted to 7.62mm long before the First World War began.

was fitted to withstand the additional pressure generated by smokeless-propellant ammunition. A standard 2,700-pace 1891-type backsight was fitted.

Though the conversion of Berdan rifles was undertaken in the 1890s, some time elapsed before any carbines were treated similarly – and then only as an expedient while the Mosin-Nagant magazine pattern was being perfected. The work was apparently undertaken in the Tula small-arms factory.

MACHINE-GUNS

7.62mm Pulemet Maxima, obr. 1910g

The first machine-guns to serve the Tsar were supplied from Britain in the 1890s by Vickers Sons & Maxim, but by the end of the Russo-Japanese War in 1905, the indigenous arms industry was capable of producing its own weapons. Assembly began in the Tula small-arms factory in 1905, the first Russian Maxim being the *Pulemet Maxima obr. 1905g* ('PM'); its most distinctive features were a feed-block and water jacket made of bronze.

Next came the 1910 pattern, with a sheet-steel water jacket and alterations in the feed mechanism. The earliest guns had plain jackets, but later examples were fluted to give additional strength; guns made during World War Two were identical, except for a large water-filling port to facilitate rapid refilling or topping up with handfuls of snow.

Most pre-1918 Russian Maxims were accompanied by a mounting credited to a designer named Sokolov, which had a wheeled axle

supporting a large traversing turntable and a 'U'-shaped trail. First-pattern Sokolov mounts had two additional legs, folded away when the gun was being moved, which could be extended forward of the axle to improve stability or to raise the barrel clear of the ground. Other Maxims, however, will be encountered on a tripod mount.

Steel shields could be fitted to the mounts to protect the gunners, but additional weight and marginal protection made them unpopular. A sled was available to help move the gun during the Russian winter, and all the mounts could be fitted with drag ropes.

Pulemet Maxima obr. 1910g	
Synonym:	'M1910 Three-Line Russian Maxim'
Adoption date:	1910
Length:	1,107mm (43.60in)
Weight:	23.8kg (52.5lb)
Weight of mount:	not known
Barrel length:	721mm (28.4in)
Chambering:	7.62 × 54mm, rimmed
Rifling type:	four-groove, concentric, RH
Magazine:	250-round fabric belt
Cyclic rate:	520–580rd/min
Magazine capacity:	five rounds
Loading system:	charger or loose rounds
Front sight:	open barleycorn
Backsight:	leaf-and-slider type
Minimum backsight setting:	400 arshin (284m, 311yd)
Maximum backsight setting:	3,200 arshin (2,720m, 2,488yd)
Muzzle velocity:	863m/sec (2,830ft/sec)

1910-pattern Maxim machine-guns on their wheeled Sokolov mount. The original mount (top) had aditional legs that could be extended to lift the wheels clear of the ground, but a later simplified version (bottom) abandoned them.

7.62mm Pulemet Madsena, obr 1903g

Russia was among the first countries to adopt a light machine-gun for cavalry use, buying Danish Madsens in quantity from the Dansk Rekyriffel Syndikat in 1904 and subsequently making them under licence in a factory in Kovrov.

Originally patented by Julius Rasmussen in 1899, then improved by Jens Schouboe in 1902, the Madsen was really an automatic form of the Peabody-Martini hinged-block action, and had several peculiarities. With no bolt to chamber or extract cartridges, the Madsen was provided with a separate rammer and a powerful extractor. The action worked by recoil, part long and part short, and the movement of the hinged breech-block was controlled by cams and lugs not only on the block but also on a small plate in the side of the

Pulemet Madsena obr. 1903g

Synonym:	'Russian Madsen'
Adoption date:	1904
Length:	1,145mm (45.08in)
Weight:	9.07kg (20lb)
Barrel length:	585mm (23in)
Chambering:	7.62 × 54mm, rimmed
Rifling type:	four-groove, concentric, RH
Magazine type:	overhead curved box
Magazine capacity:	thirty rounds
Loading system:	loose rounds
Front sight:	open blade
Backsight:	leaf-and-slider type
Minimum backsight setting:	400 arshin (284m, 311yd)
Maximum backsight setting:	2,700 arshin (1,920m, 2,100yd)
Muzzle velocity:	825m/sec (2,705ft/sec) with 1891-type ball ammunition

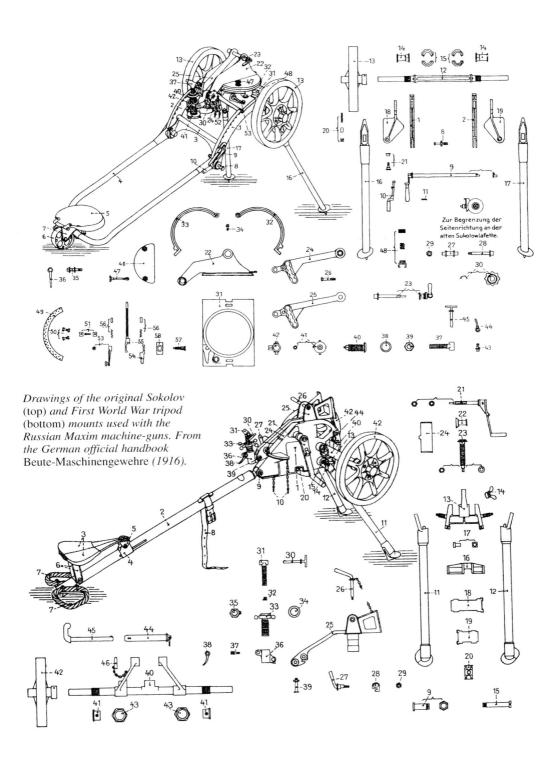

Drawings of the original Sokolov (top) and *First World War tripod (bottom)* mounts used with the Russian Maxim machine-guns. From the German official handbook Beute-Maschinengewehre *(1916).*

Zur Begrenzung der Seitenrichtung an der alten Sukolowlafette.

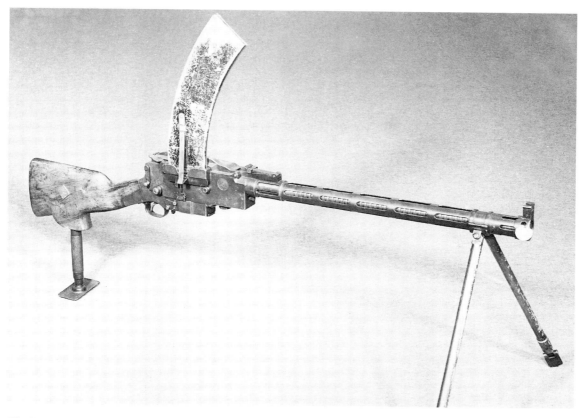

The Russians acquired substantial quantities of 1902-type 7.62mm Madsen machine-guns from Denmark during the Russo-Japanese War, similar to the gun shown here, and made them thereafter in a factory built in Kovrov. Russian-issue 7.62 × 54R Madsens were distinguished by sharply curved magazines. Courtesy of Ian Hogg.

receiver. The top-mounted box magazine inspired many subsequent designs.

The Madsen was not popular with the Russian soldiers, largely because it was difficult to dismantle to clear a jam. The sharply tapering Russian rifle cartridge was not entirely suited to the loading/extraction/ejection cycle, and was prone to rupture. However, the guns were retained by the cavalry for many years; they were also used surprisingly widely on Russian aircraft.

11 The United States of America

HANDGUNS

The United States Army had always been rather more generous with the distribution of pistols than in pre-1914 European armies, where handguns were often more a badge of office than serious weapons. From the Colt M1873 single-action army revolver onwards, a succession of large-calibre patterns had been issued in the US Army; but with the advent of smokeless powder, .38in-calibre was adopted as standard in 1892. The false promise of the high velocity/small calibre combination was exposed during the Philippine Insurrection, forcing a hurried return to .45in.

.45 Colt New Service Revolver, Model 1898

Intended as a military weapon from the outset, the largest of the Colt swing-cylinder guns faced competition from rivals in search of the same market; consequently, some time elapsed before it was purchased in quantity by the US Army. Eventually, however, large numbers were ordered – particularly during World War One – and over 356,000 had been made when work finally ceased in 1944.

Although initially made in .45 Long Colt chambering for US military use, the New Service Revolver was eventually offered commercially in eighteen versions, ranging from .38 to .476 Eley. The general design differed little from the perfected New Army & Navy models of the early 1890s, though minor changes were made to improve robustness and reliability.

.38 Colt Army Special Revolver, Model 1908

Revolvers with cylinders that opened sideways, carried on a yoke or 'crane', had been adopted by the US Navy in 1889 and the US Army in 1892. However, the .38 Colt Army Revolver had serious faults, described in greater detail in Part One, and it wasn't until the Colt Army Special eventually appeared that things improved. The shape of the frame was refined, the front face being sloped back and the lower run deeply curved over the trigger-guard; more of the trigger was exposed; and clockwise rotation tended to push the cylinder into the frame rather than out of it. The hammer was given a loosely pivoted firing pin to minimize breakages, and the barrel length options were restricted to 4.5in and 6in.

This .455 Smith & Wesson 'Triple Lock' revolver, bearing British military marks, was typical of the sturdy and efficient guns being made when the First World War began. Courtesy of Wallis & Wallis, Lewes, East Sussex.

Colt Army Special revolver

Adoption date:	1908
Length:	11.25in (285mm)
Weight:	2lb 4oz (1,020g) empty
Barrel length:	6in (152mm)
Chambering:	.38 Special, rimmed
Rifling type:	six-groove, concentric, LH
Magazine type:	rotating cylinder
Magazine capacity:	six rounds
Front sight:	open blade
Backsight:	groove in frame-top
Muzzle velocity:	865ft/sec (263m/sec)

US Pistol, Caliber .45in, Model of 1911

This was the culmination of trials with semi-automatic pistols made by Colt's Patent Fire Arms Mfg Co. in accordance with patents granted to John Browning in 1897–1909. The M1900, M1902 and M1905 guns had all relied on a cumbersome, parallel-motion locking system using two links; though they had been purchased in small quantities by the US Army and US Navy, often for nothing more than extended trials, none had proved acceptable. Finally, after a tussle with the untried .45 Savage, the perfected 1909-pattern Colt-Browning was victorious.

The secret of its success lay in the substitution of a tipping-barrel locking system controlled by a single link beneath the breech, relying on a bush in the front end of the slide to support the muzzle. As the slide and barrel recoiled, locked together, the link pulled the rear of the barrel downwards to disconnect the locking lugs from their recesses in the inner top surface of the slide. As the barrel began to tilt before the bullet left the muzzle, accuracy was theoretically inferior to the original parallel-ruler system; at the short distances suited to handguns, however, practical experience showed the differences to be insignificant.

The time taken by the US Army to test the Colt-Browning and its rivals was amply repaid by the essential 'rightness' of the M1911, implicit in the fact that no further revisions were found necessary other than the upgrade to M1911A1 standards in the 1920s. The sights were simple and sturdy, manual and grip safeties were provided, and the material was first-class.

A few 1911-pattern pistols were chambered for the .455 Webley & Scott cartridge and supplied to Britain during World War One, some for trans-shipment to Russia and others for the Royal Flying Corps. Most remained in service in 1945.

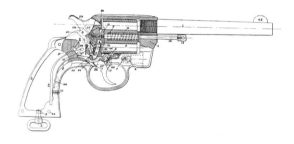

A longitudinal section of the M1894 Colt revolver, from the US Army manual.

US Pistol, Caliber .45, M1911

Synonyms:	'Colt-Browning M1911 pistol' and 'M1911 .45 ACP'
Adoption date:	29 March 1911
Length:	8.5in (216mm)
Weight:	2lb 8oz (1,135g) empty
Barrel length:	5in (127mm)
Chambering:	45 ACP (11.35 × 23mm), rimless
Rifling type:	six-groove, concentric, LH
Magazine type:	detachable box in butt
Magazine capacity:	seven rounds
Front sight:	open blade
Backsight:	fixed square notch
Muzzle velocity:	860ft/sec (262m/sec)

A typical .45 M1911 Colt-Browning pistol.

RIFLES

US Magazine Rifle, Caliber .30, Model of 1903

Series production of .30 M1901 rifles had not begun when the appearance of the British SMLE rifle caused the US Army to think again. Trials undertaken in Springfield Armory showed that the barrel of the 1901-pattern rifle could be reduced to 24in without sacrificing accuracy, and so the barrel, the backsight, the hand-guard, the lower band and the rod bayonet were suitably modified.

The new .30 M1903 rifle was approved in the summer of 1903, and production began immediately. By June 1904, Springfield Armory had made 30,000, and work was beginning in Rock Island Arsenal. However, manufacture was suspended on 11 January 1905: at the beginning of April, the Chief of Staff reported that the short barrel was acceptable, but that a conventional sword bayonet should be substituted for the fragile rod pattern.

Existing rifles were recalled, to be given new stocks and a nosecap with a bayonet lug. An improved 2,400yd backsight was accepted in May 1905, and the hand-guard, front sight and sight cover were all modified in this period.

The 'Cartridge, Ball, Caliber .30, Model of 1906' (otherwise known as .30-06) was approved on 15 October 1906, inspired by the German S-Patrone. Muzzle velocity rose to 2,700ft/sec, allowing the backsight leaves to be altered to 2,850yd. Rechambering existing barrels was comparatively easy, though they were shortened by 0.2in, and a solid tubular backsight mount replaced the original skeletal pattern. A flute was cut in the top surface of the hand-guard in 1910 to improve the sight line; the diameter of the drift adjuster on the backsight was increased; a recoil bolt was added through the stock above the front of the trigger-guard; the butt plate was chequered; and retaining clips were added in the hand-guard.

Sufficient rifles had been made by the beginning of November 1913 to allow work to cease in Rock Island Arsenal until February 1917. When the USA entered World War One, a parkerized finish was adopted to replace traditional browning, and a second recoil bolt – through the stock beneath the chamber – was added in 1918, when the bolt handle was bent slightly backwards. Soon, however, there were reports of serious receiver fractures that culminated in some guns being blown apart; the cause of these fractures was eventually traced to poor heat treatment, and the problem cured by improved manufacturing techniques. The first 'double-treated' Springfield guns appeared some time prior to receiver no. 800,000, made on 20 February 1918; Rock Island Arsenal commenced work with no. 285,507 (11 May 1918).

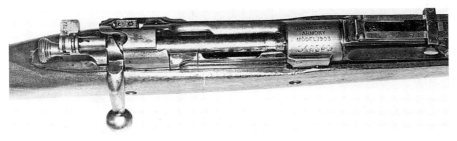

The action of a Springfield-made M1903 rifle, dating from 1908. Note the safety catch attached above the cocking piece. **Courtesy of Ian Hogg.**

A typical .30 M1903 Springfield rifle, chambered for the 1906-pattern cartridge ('.30-06'). This particular gun is cocked.

US Magazine Rifle, .30 M1903	
Synonym:	M1903 US Springfield rifle' and 'M1903 30-06 Springfield'
Adoption date:	19 June 1903
Length:	1,103mm (43.4in)
Weight:	3.85kg (8.5lb)
Barrel length:	615mm (24.21in)
Chambering:	.30 (7.62 × 63mm), rimless ('.30-06')
Rifling type:	four-groove, concentric, RH
Magazine type:	staggered-row internal box
Magazine capacity:	five rounds
Loading system:	charger or loose rounds
Front sight:	open blade
Backsight:	leaf-and-slider type
Minimum backsight setting:	200yd (182m)
Maximum backsight setting:	2,400yd (2,195m)
Muzzle velocity:	701m/sec (2,300ft/sec)

From August 1918 and gun no. 320,000 onwards, Rock Island made receivers of nickel steel in addition to the standard carbon-steel pattern. Nickel-steel receivers bore an 'NS' mark, but this was rarely obvious.

The last rifle to be assembled in Rock Island Armory left the factory in June 1918, though at least another 100,000 receivers were made in 1919–20 and production of barrels continued until about 1922; military production in Springfield Armory had virtually ceased by 1927. Estimates of output vary, but it is believed that about two million M1903 rifles were made.

US Magazine Rifle, Caliber .30, Model of 1898

This was the final major revision of the US Army Krag-Jørgensen, and it differed from its predecessors largely in the refined machining of the bolt mechanism and receiver; the magazine loading gate that was greatly simplified; and the bolt-handle seat that was milled flush with the receiver. The first rifles had the M1898 or Dickson-pattern backsight, with a drift adjustment and a binding screw on the slider. Some were fitted with a headless cocking piece, though this was abandoned in 1900 after complaints that it prevented the striker being re-

US Magazine Rifle, .30, M1898	
Adoption date:	14 March 1898
Length:	1,248mm (49.13in)
Weight:	4.08kg (9lb) empty, without sling
Barrel length:	30in (762mm)
Chambering:	.30 rimmed (7.62 × 59mm, '.30-40 Krag')
Rifling type:	four-groove, concentric, RH
Magazine type:	integral horizontal pan
Magazine capacity:	five rounds
Loading system:	loose rounds
Front sight:	open blade
Backsight:	leaf-and-slider type
Minimum backsight setting:	200yd (182m)
Maximum backsight setting:	2,000yd (2,195m)
Muzzle velocity:	670m/sec (2,200ft/sec)

This .30 M1898 Krag-Jørgensen rifle, an experimental example with the Parkhurst & Warren charger-loading system, is otherwise typical of its type. The unique magazine had a lid that hinged down to provide a loading tray. Courtesy of Ian Hogg.

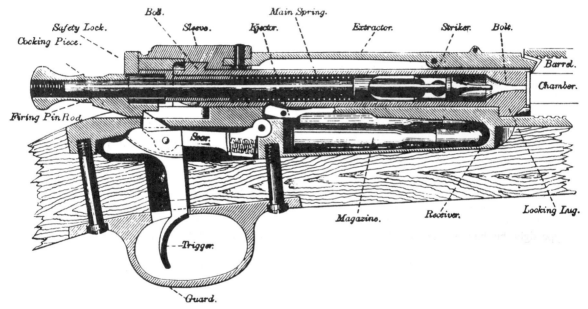

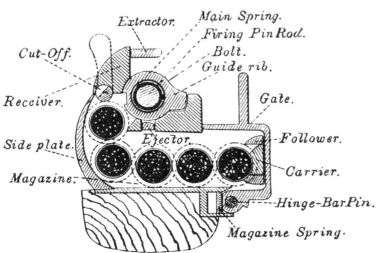

Drawings of the US M1898 Krag-Jørgensen rifle, showing the design of the bolt (above) *and the unique lateral 'pan' or 'tray' magazine* (left). *Most unusually, the Krag could be reloaded even if the bolt was closed.*

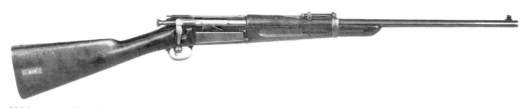

An 1896-pattern Krag-Jørgensen carbine. These guns will be found with a variety of back sights. Courtesy of Ian Hogg.

cocked after a misfire. The magazine cut-off mechanism was reversed from February 1900 onwards (even though it had first been mooted in 1897).

Unfortunately for the US Army, the high-velocity cartridge was too powerful for the Krag action, and a rash of broken locking lugs led to the reintroduction of the standard M1892 cartridge and the development of the M1901 or 'Buffington' sight. This had a stepless base, an elongated leaf graduated to 2,300yd, and an optional peep attached to the slider; bullet-drift adjustments were made simply by loosening a clamp screw and pivoting the entire sight laterally.

The perfected 'Dickson' or 1902-type tangent sight, graduated to 2,000yd, lasted until work on the M1898 rifle ceased in 1904. It resembled the 1898-type sight, but had one sight notch instead of three and a spring plunger in the slider to engage the leaf-edge serrations. Nearly 325,000 M1898 Krag-Jørgensen rifles were made by the National Armory.

MACHINE-GUNS

Three machine-guns made their appearance in the US Army armoury during the first decade of the century: the Colt, the Maxim, and the Benét-Mercié machine-rifle.

Colt Automatic Machine-Gun, Caliber .30, Model of 1895

This gas-operated weapon was made by Colt's Patent Fire Arms Mfg Co. to the designs of John Browning; it had been patented in 1889. Its most remarkable feature was the radial operating lever that pivoted downwards when gas was bled from the muzzle and forced the bolt back to complete the extraction/reloading cycle. This gave a smooth action, though it necessitated a clearance

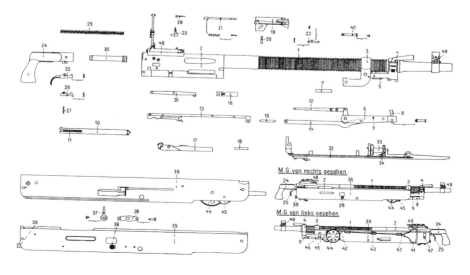

The M1895 Colt machine-gun was still being used in Europe when the First World War began. From the German official handbook Beute-Maschinengewehre *(1916).*

of some 8in beneath the gun otherwise the actuating lever buried itself in the ground.

The Colt operated smoothly, and was reliable enough to encourage the US Navy to purchase about 210 of them for shipboard use – half in .236, the remainder .30 – in addition to the mounts and carriages necessary for land service. The US Army purchased at least a hundred .30 examples, even though the design was never officially approved; the militia took approximately seventy-five.

None of the Colts saw active service in the Spanish-American War, except possibly those in the hands of the US Marine Corps during the attack on Guantanamo Bay; however, the machine-guns were well proven in the Philippine insurrection, and in particular in the defence of the Peking legations during the Boxer Rebellion.

Many guns were still being used in 1917 and spent the war years as training machine-guns, though the Canadian Army successfully used small numbers in combat on the Western Front.

Maxim Automatic Machine Gun, Caliber .30, Model of 1904

This gun was invented by the American-born Hiram Maxim (1840–1916); however, its early history is related in the British section, so little influ-

Colt Automatic Machine Gun, .30 M1895	
Synonym:	'Colt Potato Digger'
Adoption date:	1898 (US Navy only)
Length:	1,036mm (40.89in)
Weight, gun only:	18.14kg (30lb)
Barrel length:	711mm (28in)
Chambering:	30 rimmed (7.62 × 59mm, '.30-40 Krag')
Rifling type:	six-groove, concentric, RH
Feed type:	250-round cloth belt
Cyclic rate of fire:	430rd/min
Front sight:	open blade
Backsight:	leaf-and-slider type
Muzzle velocity:	610m/sec (2,000ft/sec)

Maxim Automatic Machine Gun, .30 M1904	
Synonym:	'US Army Maxim'
Adoption date:	1904
Length:	1,219mm (48in)
Weight of gun:	31.07kg (68.5lb)
Weight of tripod:	36.3kg (80lb)
Barrel length:	725mm (28.54in)
Chambering:	.30, rimless (7.62 × 63mm, '.30-06')
Rifling type:	four-groove, concentric, RH
Feed type:	250-round cloth belt
Cyclic rate of fire:	600rd/min
Front sight:	open blade
Backsight:	leaf-and-slider type
Minimum backsight setting:	200yd (182m)
Maximum backsight setting:	2,400yd (2,195m)
Muzzle velocity:	861m/sec (2,825ft/sec)

ence did the USA have on its development and progress. The first US Army trial of a .45-calibre 1889 pattern 'Maxim Automatic Machine Gun' occurred in 1890, when the testing board was sufficiently impressed to recommend that additional guns be acquired for troop trials. However, money was short, and the army authorities were well satisfied with the hundreds of service Gatlings.

Nothing further happened until 1900. The Spanish-American War had shown the potential of the machine-gun, and as a result the US Army tested a .30-calibre British-pattern Maxim (its unpopular wheeled carriage was replaced by a tripod soon after submission), the M1895 Colt-Browning, and a .30-calibre strip-feed Hotchkiss.

The water-cooled Maxim was preferred to the quirky Hotchkiss and the otherwise efficient Colt, as it could deliver a greater volume of sustained fire than either of its air-cooled rivals. Consequently, though a licence to make the Maxim in the USA was negotiated, the army simply bought its first 282 'Maxim Automatic Machine Guns, Caliber .30, Model of 1904' from Vickers, Sons & Maxim in Britain. Rechambered for the .30 M1906 cartridge, the guns proved to be sturdy and dependable; some

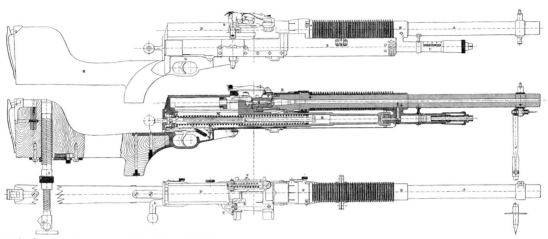

A longitudinal section of the .30-calibre M1909 Benét-Mercié machine rifle, developed by Hotchkiss. The guns used by the US Army were made in Springfield Armory, but it is suspected that many of their components came from France. From Attridge & Longstaff, The Book of the Machine Gun *(1915).*

saw active service during the Mexican border clashes in 1916, while others were used as training weapons in World War One.

Benét-Mercié Machine-Rifle, Caliber .30, Model of 1909

This was the third and last automatic weapon to be adopted by the US Army prior to 1914; it was a lightweight version of the standard Hotchkiss Mle 1908/13 described in the French section. The Benét-Mercié had been the best of the guns submitted to trials in 1908 and 1,070 guns were subsequently made in Springfield Armory and by Colt's Patent Fire Arms Manufacturing Company. The M1909 had a combined shoulder-stock/pistol-grip, a spindly butt monopod and a light bipod.

The Benét-Mercié acquired a particularly unfortunate reputation after a raid made in 1916 on Columbus, New Mexico, by the Mexican bandit Pancho Villa. Four machine-guns managed to fire 20,000 rounds in the dark of night, with only a few problems, but the deaths of American citizens in the raid provoked the Press to seek a

scapegoat. Misreading lapses of firing as jams, instead of indicating an absence of targets, and paying too much heed to claims that the feed-strips were difficult to load in the dark, the Benét-Mercié acquired the sobriquet 'Daylight Gun'.

Benét-Mercié Machine-Rifle, .30 M1909	
Synonyms:	'M1909 US Army Light Hotchkiss' and 'Daylight Gun'
Adoption date:	1909
Length:	1,187mm (46.75in)
Weight:	12.25kg (27lb)
Barrel length:	596mm (23.5in)
Chambering:	.30, rimless (7.62 × 63mm, '.30-06')
Rifling type:	four-groove, concentric, RH
Feed type:	thirty-round metal strip
Cyclic rate of fire:	600rd/min
Front sight:	open blade
Backsight:	leaf-and-slider type
Minimum backsight setting:	200yd (182m)
Maximum backsight setting:	2,400yd (2,195m)
Muzzle velocity:	850m/sec (2,788ft/sec)

PART THREE: THE WAR YEARS

12 Great Britain

Though most Britons believed that the war 'would be over by Christmas', the harder-headed elements of the army took a more pessimistic view and as early as September 1914 were ordering the manufacture of weapons to accelerate. It soon became clear that Britain, in common with every other belligerent, lacked the capacity to make war material in the quantities that would be needed. Peacetime plans for wartime production, based upon experience in colonial wars, bore no relevance to the demands made by a major European conflict.

When the fighting began in 1914, only the Royal Small Arms Factory among government-owned facilities was making small arms. Otherwise the Birmingham Small Arms Co. Ltd, the London Small Arms Co. Ltd, Webley & Scott Revolver & Arms Co. Ltd, and Vickers Ltd were principal among the very few commercially involved in this particular field. Others that had once contracted to make rifles had lost interest owing to a lack of government contracts placed since the end of the Second South African War in 1902. However, though problems were readily identified, it would take time before manufacturing capacity could keep pace with the ever-grow-

ing demand. Britain, like allies and enemies alike, was forced into some surprising compromises. Armouries and store-rooms were ransacked, and the gun trade was scoured for guns of virtually any type.

RIFLES

The Pattern 1914 Rifle

Once war had been declared, the War Department sensibly, if reluctantly, abandoned the .276in Pattern 1913 rifle. Contemplating a change of calibre and universal front-line re-equipment in the face of a major war was unacceptable, especially as no mass-production capacity to make P/1913 rifles existed. However, the new rifle had been designed specifically for series production, and was undoubtedly easier to make than the Lee-Enfield. Thus soon after war had begun it was decided to modify the .276 design to chamber the standard .303 rimmed cartridge, and to exploit the gunmaking potential of the USA.

A contract for 200,000 'Rifles, Magazine, .303-inch, Pattern 1914' was let with Winchester

A typical .303 P/1914 rifle, derived from the experimental .276 gun issued shortly before the First World War began. Courtesy of Ian Hogg.

on 24 November 1914, a few days after a similar contract had been agreed with Remington Arms–UMC. A prototype Winchester-adapted .303 rifle was accepted on 22 March 1915 and ordered into immediate mass production. Test-firing of the first Ilion-made Remington rifles took place in October, followed by final assembly of the first series-made guns in the Winchester factory in New Haven in January 1916.

The P/1914 was similar to the experimental .276 P/1913, but had an elongated horizontal finger-groove in the fore-end instead of separate diagonal finger-holds. The magazine was adapted for rimmed .303 cartridges, and the gradations on the back-sight leaf were altered. The battle-sight aperture was set for 400yd, whilst the long-range sights on the left side of the fore-end could be used at ranges as great as 2,600yd.

Three minor variants of the P/1914 rifle were introduced to British service in June 1916, suffixes being used to distinguish them. Parts could be exchanged between guns of the same make, but reliance on three manufacturers prevented interchangeability. Rifles made in the Eddystone factory in 1915–16 were designated 'Mark I (E)'; Remington products were 'Mark I (R)'; and Winchester's were 'Mark I (W)'. Individual components were marked 'EA', 'RA' and 'W' respectively.

An improved Mark I* was accepted in December 1916, with changes in the design of the bolt. Five-point stars on the bolt handle,

Rifle, Magazine, .303in, Pattern 1914, Mark 1

Synonym:	'P/14 rifle'
Adoption date:	21 June 1916
Length:	46.16in (1,172mm)
Length with bayonet attached:	63.30in (1,608mm)
Weight:	8.69lb (3.94kg), without sling
Weight with bayonet attached:	9.81lb (4.45kg)
Barrel length:	26in (660mm)
Chambering:	.303 (7.7 × 56mm), rimmed
Rifling type:	five-groove, concentric
Depth of grooves:	0.005in (0.12mm)
Width of grooves:	0.085in (2.16mm)
Pitch of rifling:	one turn in 10in (254mm), LH
Magazine type:	integral box
Magazine capacity:	five rounds
Loading system:	charger or loose rounds
Front sight:	protected blade
Backsight:	leaf-and-slider aperture type
Minimum backsight setting:	200yd (183m)
Maximum backsight setting:	1,650yd (1,509m), with special long-range sights to 2,600yd (2,377m)
Velocity:	2,525ft/sec (770m/sec)

the chamber, and the right side of the butt identified these guns, and an additional 'F' suffix in the pattern mark revealed the presence of finely adjustable backsights.

The successful acceleration of SMLE production encouraged the British in the

British soldiers pose with .303 P/14 rifles, c. 1918. This particular postcard was taken in Swansea. Some of the shoulder straps bear 'GLAMORGAN' and a 'V' for a volunteer battalion, but little else can be determined.

autumn of 1916 to curtail orders for the P/1914, which was regarded only as an interim measure. Work soon ceased in the Winchester factory in New Haven, though the Remington–UMC factory in Ilion continued assembly until early 1917.

The 'Rifle P/14 Mark I* (W) T' was adopted in April 1918 as the official British Army sniper rifle. Mounts for the P/1918 Aldis telescope sight were added on the left side of the breech and backsight protector, and the long-range sights were removed from the fore-end. About two thousand rifle/sight combinations had been assembled prior to the Armistice, but few were issued in time to take part in the fighting. Most surviving P/1914 rifles were withdrawn in 1926, to be held in reserve stocks as 'Rifles No. 3 Mark 1' (or 'Mk 1*' or 'Mk 1*(F)'), to be reissued to the Home Guard in 1940.

The Arisaka Rifles

Though sufficient rifles existed in August 1914 to equip the regular army, the rapid expansion of the forces and the unexpectedly high losses of equipment caught the authorities unprepared. The expansion of the British Army from 255,000 to 1,220,000 men in a matter of months (strength peaked at 3,838,265 in the summer of 1918) occurred before series production of .303 P/1914 rifles could begin in the USA. No country outside the British Empire used the .303 cartridge, and there was no hope of a ready supply of rifles for front-line use. The immediate needs were satisfied by withdrawing serviceable Lee-Enfield rifles – short, long, charger-loading or otherwise – from the Royal Navy and the Territorial Army. The void was filled with virtually anything that could be acquired, working on the principle that a

The 'P/1907' (Meiji 38th Year Type) Arisaka rifle, issued in surprisingly large quantities to the British armed forces. Many guns were subsequently sent to Russia, and are now rarely encountered in the United Kingdom.

Rifle, Magazine, .256-inch, Pattern 1900	
Synonyms:	'Meiji 30th Year Type rifle', and 'M1897 Arisaka'
Adoption date:	24 February 1915
Length:	50.16in (1,274mm)
Weight:	9.88lb (4.48kg), without sling
Barrel length:	30.98in (787mm)
Chambering:	6.5 × 50 semi-rimmed
Rifling type:	six-groove, concentric, RH
Magazine type:	internal box
Magazine capacity:	five rounds
Loading system:	charger or loose rounds
Front sight:	open blade
Backsight:	tangent-leaf type
Minimum backsight setting:	200m (219yd)
Maximum backsight setting:	2,000m (2,187yd)
Velocity:	2,493ft/sec (760m/sec)

Rifle, Magazine, .256-inch, Pattern 1907	
Synonyms:	'Meiji 38th Year Type rifle', and 'M1905 Arisaka'
Adoption date:	24 February 1915
Length:	50.19in (1,275mm)
Weight:	9.12lb (4.12kg), without sling
Barrel length:	31.45in (799mm)
Chambering:	6.5 × 50 semi-rimmed
Rifling type:	four- or six-groove, concentric, RH
Magazine type:	integral box
Magazine capacity:	five rounds
Loading system:	charger or loose rounds
Front sight:	open blade
Backsight:	tangent-leaf type
Minimum backsight setting:	200m (219yd)
Maximum backsight setting:	2,400m (2,625yd)
Velocity:	2,493ft/sec (760m/sec)

bolt-action of any type could arm second-rank or lines-of-communication units.

Japan was an ally, but involved only on the peripheries of the war once Tsingtao had fallen. The imperial army had recently replaced its 1897-pattern Arisaka rifles with the improved 1905 type, and held many old guns in store. Before August 1914 had run its course, at least 150,000 Arisaka rifles had been purchased. Some were old-pattern guns, rather quirkily known in Britain as the 'Pattern 1900', but many were new-type guns ('Pattern 1907'); there may even have been a few carbines. Only a few rifles seem to have been new, as virtually all those that survive also bear Japanese issue marks.

Suitably refurbished, the Arisakas were issued to the British Army in the spring of 1915. The origin of their designations remains in question; they may have been based on the date of issue in the Japanese army, or perhaps on the first tests by the Small Arms Committee. Most of the rifles were used by training battalions, but a passage from the autobiography of T.E. Lawrence (Lawrence of Arabia), *Seven Pillars of Wisdom*, suggests that at least a few reached Arabia. It is assumed they were landed by warships, part of a 20,000-gun consignment issued to the Royal Navy from 15 June 1915 to free Lee-Enfields for land service. Japanese rifles also served the Royal

Flying Corps and its 1918-vintage successor, the Royal Air Force.

The Arisakas were soon recalled, however, as the Royal Navy guns were replaced in the summer of 1917 by Canadian Ross rifles. About 128,000 assorted Japanese guns, together with quantities of ammunition, were subsequently sent from Britain to Russia, and the patterns were declared obsolete in British service in October 1921.

The Savage Rifles

Like the British, the Canadians soon discovered that they had too few rifles to mobilize efficiently. Among the many weapons acquired to free service-pattern Ross rifles for the Canadian Expeditionary Force were a few hundred lever-action 1899-pattern Savages, purchased by leading Montreal businessmen to arm local militia. It is assumed that the guns were discarded in 1916, once Ross rifles had been displaced from front-line service by the SMLE.

The guns had a full-length fore-end with a cleaning rod beneath the muzzle, military-style sights, a single barrel band, and a nosecap with a lug for a knife bayonet. The commercial .303 Savage cartridge consisted of a .308 bullet loaded in a rimmed case which differed greatly from the standard British service pattern.

The Ross Rifles

In September 1914, shortly after World War One began, the British government ordered 100,000 Mark III Ross rifles from Canada. Unfortunately, deliveries proved to be erratic and the contract was cancelled in March 1917, owing to the appropriation of the Ross Rifle Company's Quebec factory by the Canadian government; fewer than 70,000 guns had been accepted. Most of them were used for training, but 45,000 were issued to the Royal Navy in the spring of 1917 (replacing unwanted Japanese Arisakas), to

supplement 750 acquired from the USA in 1915.

The Ross was declared obsolete in British service in November 1921, but surviving guns were reissued in 1940 to the Royal Canadian Navy and auxiliary units. A few thousand were even sent to Britain for the Home Guard.

Rifle, .303, Savage, Model 1899

Adoption date:	never accepted officially
Length:	49.95in (1,269mm)
Weight:	8.75lb (3.36kg), without sling
Barrel length:	28in (711mm)
Chambering:	.303 Savage, rimmed
Rifling type:	six-groove, concentric, RH
Magazine type:	integral rotary box
Magazine capacity:	five rounds
Loading system:	loose rounds
Front sight:	open blade
Backsight:	ramp-and-leaf type
Minimum backsight setting:	200yd (183m)
Maximum backsight setting:	2,000yd (1,828m)
Velocity:	2,180ft/sec (665m/sec)

Wartime Lee-Enfields

For all the substitutes and expedients, the short Lee-Enfield Mark III was still the standard rifle and remained in volume production throughout the war. But in order to increase production, by shortening manufacturing time, the manufacturers were allowed a few 'concessions': the ineffectual long-range sights were abandoned, and BSA discarded the cut-off plate from a few Mark III rifles made in the autumn of 1915. The cut-off eventually became optional. A cocking piece with grooved flat sides was introduced in August 1916, details of finish were either abandoned or modified to accelerate production, and the 'Rifle, Short, Magazine, Lee-Enfield Mark III*' was approved on 2 January 1916.

Though no target rifle, the Lee-Enfield could still be effective at 1,000yd (900m) or more in the hands of a trained firer – and during the jumbled

The potentially dangerous straight-pull 1910-pattern Ross rifle Mk 3B, tried and found wanting in the trenches of the Western Front, but an excellent sniping weapon if kept clean. Courtesy of Ian Hogg.

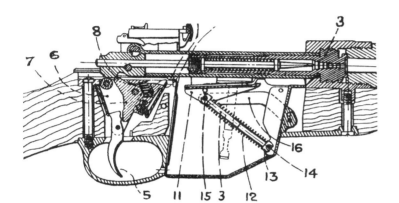

A longitudinal section of the 1910-type Ross rifle, showing the multiple locking lugs that gave the action tremendous strength.

Rifle, .303, Magazine, Ross, Mark IIIB

Synonym:	'Ross Rifle Mk IIIB'
Adoption date:	21 October 1915
Length:	50.5in (1,282mm)
Weight:	9.88lb (4.48kg), without sling
Barrel length:	30.50in (775mm)
Chambering:	.303 (7.7 × 56mm), rimmed
Rifling type:	four-groove, concentric, LH
Magazine type:	internal box
Magazine capacity:	five rounds
Loading system:	charger or loose rounds
Front sight:	adjustable blade
Backsight:	tangent aperture
Minimum backsight setting:	200yd (183m)
Maximum backsight setting:	2,000yd (1,828m)
Velocity:	2,600ft/sec (792m/sec)

fighting that characterized the early months of the war, many soldiers became so adept at picking off enemy officers at long ranges that special 'sniping schools' were soon created to hone the skills of the best shots.

The earliest sniper rifles were Lee-Enfields, often old full-length guns, fitted with fragile Galilean sights consisting of nothing but two widely separated lenses. By mid-1915, however, the value of conventional telescope sights (often German, and mounted on sporting rifles) was established beyond doubt. One of the earliest standardized designs, made by the Periscopic Prism Company, was 12in long, had a 9-degree field of view, and range drums graduated at 100–600yd (90–550m). By 1918, however, the sturdy sights made by Aldis Brothers of Birmingham were preferred; typically these had a 19mm objective lens and a range drum calibrated '1' to '6' (100–600yd).

Rifles fitted with telescope-sight mounts were identified by a 'T'-suffix in official

British soldiers pose with SMLE rifles in France, c. 1916. Close inspection of the photograph suggests that they may be from the Inns of Court Regiment, with one man from the 13th London (Princess Louise's Kensington) Regiment.

'The Musketeers': men of the Royal Field Artillery, identified by their shoulder-strap titles, pose with SMLE Mk III rifles (note the long range sights visible on the fore-ends). This postcard was sent by 'Cyril' to his son from 'France, July 1918', but bears no other identifying marks.

A British cavalryman urges his horse forward; France, 1916. Note the SMLE rifle in the saddle-scabbard.

nomenclature. Production was surprisingly large, as nearly ten thousand SMLE Marks III (T) and III* (T) were made during World War One.

The 'EY' Rifle

The rise of trench warfare in the winter of 1914/15 created a demand for rifle grenades, because trench lines were pitched – for obvious reasons – well beyond hand-grenade range. The Hale grenade had been offered to the War Office long before fighting began, but had been rejected. Hale had then placed his design on the open market, and ironically it had been adopted by Germany by August 1914 – another reason for the British infantry to demand a way to retaliate.

Quickly brought into British service as the 'Grenade, Rifle, No. 1', Hale's weapon was little more than an explosive-filled tube of serrated cast iron, fitted with a simple impact fuse and a long steel rod protruding backwards. The rod fitted so snugly into the barrel of a Lee-Enfield rifle that the gas generated by a blank cartridge could launch the grenade as far as 100yd (90m) from the muzzle. Unfortunately, experience showed that the base of the rod provided such great resistance to the rapid generation of gas that 'ring bulging' gradually occurred in the barrel; the rifle therefore lost its accuracy, and was usually relegated to training or drill routines.

The introduction in 1915 of the Mills (No. 5) hand grenade was soon followed by the 'No. 23 Hand & Rifle Grenade' – this was simply a No. 5 with the base-cap bored and threaded to accept a rifle rod. No. 23 was heavier than the Hales

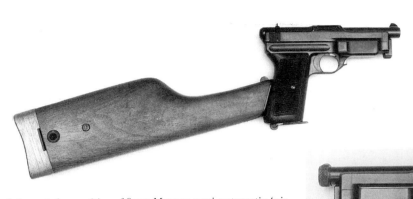

Substantial quantities of 9mm Mauser semi-automatic 'pistol carbines' were seized in 1914 from stores supplied to equip warships being made in Britain for Brazil and Chile. It is assumed that they were delayed-blowback guns of the type shown here, accompanied by distinctive holster-stocks. One of the guns shown – probably purchased prior to 1914 through commercial sources – is clearly marked 'C. ERSKINE GRAY' on the left side of the frame.
Courtesy of Henk Visser.

grenade, thus demanding a more powerful 'grenade cartridge', and this placed even more strain on the barrel. Next came a cup discharger, clamped to the muzzle of the rifle, which accepted the newly introduced No. 36 Mills grenade with a special 2in-diameter plate screwed to its base.

The grenade was inserted into the cup, to be projected about 125yd (115m) with the help of a new and even more powerful cartridge. However, this gave the rifles such severe punishment that a rash of burst barrels resulted. Binding the barrels and fore-ends with copper wire, reinforced by soldering, not only strengthened the barrels but also conferred limited protection from bursts. Rifles of this type were used with ball ammunition only in dire emergencies, but were readily identified by the wire binding. They were known as 'SMLE Mark III EY' and 'SMLE Mark III* EY', though no authentic official document has yet been found to explain 'EY'. The most plausible explanation is that the suffix represents 'EmergencY'; less likely, perhaps, is the 'soldier's tale' that they commemorate Edgar Yule (sic), the proposer of the barrel-binding. 'EY' rifles were abandoned at the

end of World War One, although the idea was revived in 1940 for the Home Guard.

Other Rifles

Like most of the combatants, the British purchased a surprising variety of weapons from the most unlikely sources. The Royal Navy alone used more than 20,000 .44-40 M1894 Winchester carbines, 4,000 .45-calibre and 4,500 7 × 57mm Remington Rolling Block rifles, and a selection of old .303 Martini-Enfield rifles and carbines obtained 'from the trade'. There were even a few .450 Martini-Henry rifles, and 970 'Lee-Enfield Sporting Rifles, .303-inch' purchased in 1915. The most interesting weapons, however, were 820 'Mauser 9mm Carbines' requisitioned from the prospective armament of warships being built in British shipyards for the navies of Brazil and Chile. It is assumed that, despite the nomenclature, these were the delayed-blowback pistols equipped with stock-holsters.

HANDGUNS

British Army officers could purchase any handgun they wished, as long as it fired regulation .455 ammunition. Once war began, however, the influx of new officers and reservists called back to the Colours soon cleared the shelves of commercial gun dealers, who thereafter found it difficult to obtain supplies from factories that were fully commited to war work. The Webley revolver became the only readily available weapon.

The Webley Revolver

A variety of Webley patterns had been approved – and even declared obsolete – since the advent in 1887 of the .442 Mark I, but obsolete weapons customarily served until they needed repairs grave enough for scrapping to be preferable. Webleys of all regulation types were still being issued when World War One began, even though the basic design had advanced to Mark V.

Approved on 5 May 1915, the Mark VI Webley revolver became the most important of the entire series, production during the war years alone exceeding 300,000. It differed from the Mark V principally in the substitution of a 6in barrel for the 4in type; in the squaring of the previous bird's head butt; and in modifications to the barrel catch. The front sight was adjustable.

Some guns will be encountered with the 'Prideaux Quick Loader', patented in 1893 and again in 1914 in an improved form. Others may be accompanied by a shoulder stock, shared with the contemporary signal pistol, and even by a bayonet promoted by W.W. Greener. Held to the revolver by a pivoting catch, this had a cast brass or white-alloy hilt and a short 'T'-section blade made from scrapped French Gras épée bayonets.

Wartime modifications to older revolvers were intended to make them as close to Mark VI standards as possible. The 'Mark I**(N)', destined for Naval Service, was a Mark I refurbished and fitted with a Mark V cylinder and a Mark IV barrel; the 'Mark II**(N)' was simply the Mark II with the same modification. The 'Pistol, Revolver, Webley, 6-inch Barrel Mark I**(N)' was similar, but had a Mark VI barrel.

The 'Mark II* (L)', a Land Service variant, was one of those entertaining nonsenses that

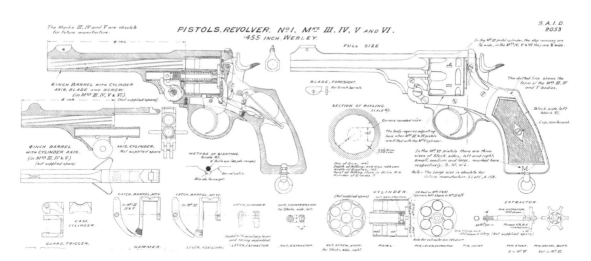

The later Webley revolvers, from British Official drawing SAID 2053.

occasionally occur in any army. It was, said the appropriate List of Changes paragraph censoriously, 'Not an Approved Nomenclature, but arrived at by virtue of a number of Mark II pistols being fitted with Mark IV hammers and having * stamped after the number on the barrel.' The 'Pistols, Revolver, 6-inch Barrel Mark V' were old Mark V pistols fitted with new and longer barrels to bring them up to Mark VI standard.

Emergency Revolvers

World War One found the British Army short of all types of weapon, handguns included. The shortages were rectified by accelerating production of Webleys, but also by purchasing Smith & Wesson New Century and Colt New Service revolvers chambered for the British .455 cartridge. Orders were even placed in Spain, two suitable revolvers being approved on 8 November 1915. Declared obsolete in 1921, the 'Pistols, Revolver, .455, Ordnance Pattern' were made in Eibar by Garate, Anitua y Cia (No. 1 Mark I) and Trocaola, Aranzabal y Cia (No. 2 Mark I). The two guns were essentially similar top-break weapons more or less based upon the Smith & Wesson designs of the early 1890s,

though the Garate pattern had a square-backed trigger-guard and a humped backstrap. Its bakelite grips ended some way above the lanyard ring. The Trocaola version had a rounded backstrap and trigger-guard, and its plain chequered grips extended to the full depth of the butt.

Webley & Scott Pistols

The Pistol 'Mark 1 No. 2' was approved for the Royal Flying Corps in April 1915, similar to the experimental RHA guns (with an adjustable drum-type backsight and a board-type shoulder stock) but clearly marked 'Mark I No. 2 1915' instead of 'Mark I 1913'.

The recoil-operated Webley was about 8.5in overall, had a 5in barrel and weighed 2lb 7oz. It fed from a seven-round detachable box magazine in the butt, and locked by displacing the barrel diagonally downwards to release the slide. Very cumbersome, though not unpleasant to shoot, the design proved unsuited to service. Production was small, apparently amounting to a little over 8,000 service weapons and 1,248 commercial examples. Claims that tens of thousands were

Pistol, Revolver, .455 Mark VI	
Synonym:	'Webley Mk VI'
Adoption date:	24 May 1915
Length:	11.25in (2,860mm)
Weight:	2.4lb (1.09kg)
Barrel length:	6in (152mm)
Chambering:	.455 rimmed
Rifling type:	seven-groove, concentric, RH
Magazine type:	six-chambered cylinder
Loading system:	loose rounds or 'quick-loader'
Front sight:	adjustable blade
Backsight:	fixed 'U'-notch
Velocity:	650ft/sec (199m/sec)

The '.455 Pistol, Ordnance Pattern, No. 2 Mk I' was purchased in Spain to alleviate handgun shortages during the First World War. This particular example, made by Garate y Anitua of Eibar, has a Sealed Pattern tag hanging from the trigger guard. Courtesy of Ian Hogg.

made arise from the serial numbers of commercial versions, which were intermixed with the other Webley auto-loaders.

The Webleys were supplemented by .455 M1911 Colts, distinguished by 'W'-prefix numbers, which were ordered in the USA in 1914–16; standard .45 Colts were issue in the Canadian Army.

It is not clear how many .455 pistols had been acquired by 1918, though the commonly accepted total is 13,150. They were apparently confined to officers, the Royal Flying Corps (later the RAF) and the navy. The .455 rimless pistol cartridge would chamber in a standard .455 revolver, developing pressures greater than the revolver proof round, so attempts were made to keep it out of the trenches.

MACHINE-GUNS

The Lewis Gun

Just prior to the outbreak of war the Belgian army had adopted a light machine-gun developed by a retired American army officer, Isaac Newton Lewis, on the basis of an unsuccessful weapon designed by Samuel McClean in the period 1906–9. The patents had been assigned to the McClean Arms & Ordnance Company of Cleveland, Ohio, but had soon passed to the Automatic Arms Company of Buffalo, New York State. Lewis was instructed to refine McClean's patents into an efficient gun. Five were exhibited at Fort Myers in 1911, but the US authorities were unenthusiastic; moreover the guns had all exhibited a very harsh action. Lewis therefore elected to try his luck in Europe, and in the summer of 1913 accepted the offer of BSA's Tool Room facilities.

Conceived as a medium machine-gun, the perfected gas-operated Lewis had a rotating pan magazine above the receiver, and relied on a turning bolt to lock an action that was more than a little odd. The striker was carried on a post, mounted on the rear of the piston; the post reciprocated in a slot in the bolt. When the trigger was pressed, the sear disengaged the piston and the latter began its forward movement under the action of the main spring. The striker post, lodged in a recess in the slot at the rear end of the bolt, bore against the curved portion of the slot. Lugs on the head of the bolt engaged grooves in the body to prevent rotation until the bolt reached the chamber.

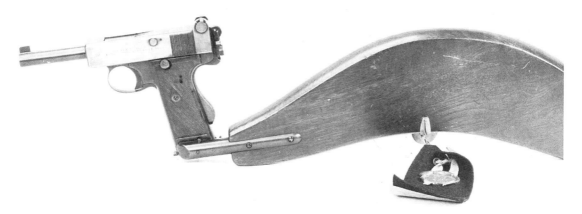

A .455 Mk I No. 2 Webley & Scott semi-automatic pistol with a Sealed Pattern tag attached to the shoulder stock. Guns of this type were used in the early stages of the First World War by personnel of the Royal Flying Corps. Courtesy of Ian Hogg.

A .303 Mk I Lewis Gun, with a canvas bag to catch ejected cartridge-cases. Courtesy of Ian Hogg.

A few Portuguese troops fought on the Western Front during the First World War. Most were issued with British equipment, including SMLE rifles and the Lewis Guns shown here. Courtesy of the Trustees of the Imperial War Museum, negative no. Q5554.

As the bolt closed, a fresh round was stripped out of the pan magazine and pushed forwards into the chamber. The striker post then travelled along the curved portion of the slot, turning the lugs into the receiver walls and locking the bolt closed. The post then finally reached the short, straight slot end, and ran forwards far enough the carry the striker onto the primer of the chambered round.

After the gun fired, gas was tapped off the barrel and led back to push the piston back; this retracted the striker and revolved the bolt lugs out of engagement with the receiver walls. A large helical spring in a prominent housing beneath the receiver, ahead of the trigger, returned the piston and bolt assembly as long as the trigger was pressed.

The Belgian Lewis Gun, that chambered 7.65mm rimless cartridges, was made for Armes Automatiques Lewis by the Birmingham Small Arms Co. Ltd. Very few had been supplied when World War One began, but when the British government cast around for machine-guns late in 1914, BSA was ready. The 'Gun, Machine, Lewis, .303-inch Mark I' was introduced in the autumn of 1915, though series production had been underway for some time. In addition to BSA's output, Lewis Guns were also made in the USA by the Savage Arms Company of Utica, New York State.

The standard British Land Service Lewis was air-cooled, but incorporated a forced-draught

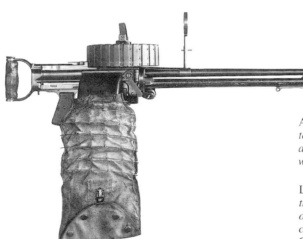

Above: *Ambitious British soldiers armed with a telescope and a Lewis Gun on an anti-aircraft tripod attempt to down a German plane in defence of their well-camouflaged artillery battery.*

Left: *The light weight and ready manoeuvrability of the Lewis Gun suited to aerial use. This is an observer's gun, intended for flexible mounts, with a cartridge-case bag and auxiliary sights.*
Courtesy of Ian Hogg.

system absent from the original Belgian prototypes. The barrel was encased in a ribbed aluminium radiator, which was itself inserted in a plain cylindrical jacket. The mouth of the jacket, which was partially open, projected in front of the muzzle. Expansion of propellant gases at the muzzle was supposed to draw in air from the rear of the radiator, along the ribs and out of the muzzle opening. However, whether the air-circulation system worked efficiently has never been satisfactorily demonstrated.

Mark I Lewis Guns were typically 50in overall, had 26in barrels with standard Enfield four-groove rifling, and weighed a little over 26lb 5oz without the magazines. Most fed from 47-round pan magazines, though a two-tier 97-round version was successfully developed for aerial use.

Because the Lewis Gun was so easy to make

(BSA alone made nearly 146,000 for the British, Belgians and Russians during the war), the fire-power of the infantry was soon increased. With the formation of specialist Machine-Gun Corps in the summer of 1915, Vickers machine-guns were withdrawn from the infantry battalions. Each Vickers Gun was replaced by four Lewis Guns, and from then on issue was broadened until, by the autumn of 1916, each of the sixteen platoons had one light machine-gun. They were each given a second gun in 1918, and four additional guns were issued to the battalion headquarters for anti-aircraft defence.

Air Service adaptations included the Lewis Gun Mark I*, introduced on 10 November 1915; this was simply a Mark I with a spade grip. The forced-draught cooling system was abandoned, and many guns were stripped down to a bare minimum. The Mark II* (converted) and the Mark III (newly made) of 13 May 1918 were variants of the Mark I* with modifications made to the gas system to increase the rate of fire to about 700rd/min. The Mark III was also often fitted with the Hazelton booster, invented by a Royal Navy officer. There were five magazines, all except the 97-round two-tier No. 5 holding forty-seven rounds. They differed in the design of the handles added to the top of the magazine to facilitate reloading in the air: thus No. 1 was the standard pattern without a handle; No. 2 had a wire loop; No. 3 had a 'T'-latch; and No. 4 had a leather strap.

The Hotchkiss Gun

When World War One began, the British Army was very short of machine-guns, and only the Erith factory of Vickers Ltd and the Royal Small Arms Factory at Enfield were involved in production. On 11 August 1914, one week after the declaration of war, merely 192 Vickers Guns were ordered, in the belief that peace would return by Christmas; another hundred guns were ordered on 10 September. However, as it became clearer that hostilities would be protracted, 1,000

were ordered on 28 September. October brought an order for 500, and then an open-ended contract was placed by the French government for fifty Vickers-pattern guns per week.

The doubling and re-doubling of work stretched Vickers' production capacity well beyond its limits, and by the anticipated delivery date for the last of 1,792 guns ordered by the British government, only 1,022 had been accepted.

Salvation came in the form of the Lewis Gun (*q.v.*), made by the Birmingham Small Arms Co. Ltd, and by the Société d'Armes Portatives Hotchkiss & Cie of Saint-Denis. The original Hotchkiss machine-gun of the 1870s was a manually operated, multi-barrel pattern similar to the Gatling, and had proved more popular as a 37mm revolver-cannon than in small-arms chamberings. Hotchkiss et Cie had eventually been approached by Adolf von Odkolek zu Augezd, whose gas-operated machine-gun design had met nothing but apathy in Austria-Hungary. Hotchkiss's management immediately saw its potential and acquired manufacturing rights, and the Odkolek gun became the Hotchkiss automatic machine-gun.

Hotchkiss machine-guns of this period all fed from distinctive metal strips. They had been tested by the French army in 1897, and introduced to service as the Mle 1900, but had then been 'improved' by government technicians to become the Mle. 1905 ('APX' or 'Puteaux') and Mle. 1907 ('Saint-Étienne'). These had been made in the government-owned small-arms factories, and purchases from the Société d'Armes Portatives Hotchkiss virtually ceased. But the Hotchkiss company had the last laugh, as neither of the 'improved' French guns was successful. Thus when World War One began, the French were as short of machine-guns as the British, and were obliged to order huge numbers of the 8mm Mle 1914 Hotchkiss to supplement the Saint-Étienne.

Hotchkiss had also made small quantities of the Fusil Mitrailleur Mle 1909 (the 1909-pattern machine-rifle), designed by Laurence Benét and Henri Mercié. This light machine-gun relied on a

A British .303 No.1 Mk 1 Hotchkiss Gun, on its minuscule tripod mount. Though restricted by its strip feed, the Hotchkiss was surprisingly reliable. Courtesy of Ian Hogg.

This coloured postcard, one of the 'Daily Mail Official War Pictures' ('Series 14, No. 110'), shows Indian soldiers with a Hotchkiss machine-gun – probably training, owing to the background. Note the feed strip projecting from the right side of the receiver and the armoured shield resting on the sandbags to the left of the bipod.

locking collar or 'fermeture nut' containing an interrupted screw of a type commonly encountered in the breech of artillery pieces. The bolt entered slots in the locking collar, and at the end of the closing stroke, the collar was rotated by a cam slot on the piston working on a projecting lug. As the collar rotated, its internal interrupted threads engaged similar threads on the outside of the bolt, and locked the action.

The feed was inverted so that the cartridges lay underneath the strip. The standard Hotchkiss feed-strip where the cartridges lay uppermost made an excellent platform upon which rain, mud or dust could be conveyed into the action: as a result, even the otherwise efficient Mle 1914 jammed frequently in bad weather. The inverted feed of the Mle 1909 minimized this particular drawback, although the strips were much more difficult to load.

It seems that Hotchkiss had substantial quantities of 'Fusils Mitrailleur' on hand in 1914, but the French government allowed the British to purchase them. As the Hotchkiss was much easier to make than a Vickers or a Maxim, a production line was installed in the Royal Small Arms Factory at Enfield.

The .303 Mk I Hotchkiss was officially adopted in Britain in the spring of 1916. The wooden butt originally had an integral pistol-grip, an oil bottle and a hinged shoulder plate. The mechanism could feed only from metal strips, and the guns were mounted on tiny 'cavalry' tripods. The Mark I was made for infantry ('Mark I No. 1') or tank use ('Mark I No. 2'), the variants being identical except for the sights and the butt fittings. No. 1 had a conventional tangent-leaf backsight on the left side of the feed cover, and a wood butt with distinctive metal strengthening plates; the No. 2 had a pistol-grip adapted to take an optional tubular extension known as the 'Shoulder Piece No. 1'. Tank guns were customarily accompanied by the simple 'Sights, Tubular, No. 2'.

A Mark I* Hotchkiss was introduced on 22 June 1916, with a modified feed mechanism capable of accepting a 'belt' in the form of articulated three-round strips. The Mark 1* came in 'No. 1' and 'No. 2' versions, the latter having a special pan to carry the folded cartridge belt, and a bag to catch spent cases.

Benét-Mercié-pattern Hotchkiss guns fed from the right and were cocked by a bolt handle protruding from the back of the receiver above the pistol-grip. They were 46in long, weighed 27lb, and had 23in barrels with five-groove Enfield rifling. The bolt handle doubled as a selector, allowing single shots or sustained fire depending on how far it was turned upwards after cocking the gun; the cyclic rate was about 500rpm.

Enfield-made Hotchkiss guns had 'E'-prefix serial numbers, the mark 'SC' above the chamber indicating that the diameter of the 'small cone' (the 'lead' or forcing cone) had been increased. Several thousand survived the war, going into store until 1939.

The 'G' Maxims

A universal shortage of machine-guns was still evident in 1915, though substantial quantities of German Maxims were being acquired as a result of territorial gains, trench raids and even minor skirmishes. The 7.92mm MG. 08, essentially similar to the Maxim .303 Mk 1, was easily converted to fire British service ammunition. Converted weapons were reissued as 'Guns, Maxim, 'G', Mk 1', the pattern ('A', 'B' or 'C') depending upon the original variant. Never formally introduced, their first 'public' mention was a declaration of obsolescence in June 1917.

Gun, Machine, Hotchkiss, .303 Mark I	
Synonym:	'British Army Hotchkiss Gun'
Adoption date:	3 March 1916
Length:	46.75in (1,187mm)
Weight:	27lb (12.24kg)
Barrel length:	23.50in (597mm)
Chambering:	.303 (7.7 × 56mm), rimmed
Rifling type:	five-groove, concentric, RH
Feed system:	thirty-round metal strip
Front sight:	open barleycorn
Backsight:	leaf-and-slider type
Minimum backsight setting:	100yd (91m)
Maximum backsight setting:	2,000yd (1,828m)
Velocity:	2,450ft/sec (747m/sec)

13 France

HANDGUNS

When World War One began, the French were so
desperately short of weapons that they ordered
substantial quantities of 7.65mm 'Ruby' pistols
from Gabilondo y Urresti of Eibar, in the spring
of 1915 giving the gunmakers an open-ended
contract to supply them with 10,000 Ruby pistols
every month. The demands were subsequently
trebled, forcing the recruitment of five additional contractors: SA Alkartasuna, Fábrica de
Armas of Guernica; Beistegui Hermanos of
Eibar; Eceolaza y Vicinai of Eibar; Hijos de
Angel Echeverria of Eibar; and Bruno Salaverria
y Cia of Eibar. Production is believed to have
totalled between 150,000 and 200,000 by
November 1918.

Echeverria-made 'Star' semi-automatic pistols
were also acquired in quantity, together with a
variety of commercial-pattern ('du Commerce')
revolvers chambering the standard 8mm service
cartridge.

RIFLES

8mm Gras conversions

Although the French authorities had approved the
adoption of box-magazine Berthier rifles for colonial
service, there had been no great hurry to replace the
venerable Mle 86/93 Lebel in the hands of the regular army. When World War One began, the sudden

*A typical patriotic postcard, dating from the early
days of the First World War period. The French
'soldier', his aim guided by 'La France', holds an
old 11mm Chassepot needle-fire gendarmerie rifle.*

Large quantities of the old 11mm Mle 74/80 Gras rifles, of the type shown here, were converted to fire standard 8mm ammunition. Known as 'M1870/80/14', they were only marginally strong enough to withstand smokeless ammunition – but lasted for many years in colonial service. Courtesy of the MoD Pattern Room Collection, Royal Ordnance plc, Nottingham.

influx of reservists and conscripts created an equally unexpected shortage of weapons. One of the easiest ways to obtain weapons chambering the 8×51mm rimmed cartridge was to re-barrel the thousands of Mle 74 M.80 Gras rifles being held in reserve.

Experiments revealed that the action was sturdy enough to handle the comparatively small increases in chamber pressure. The face of the detachable bolt head was modified to accept a different case head, and the backsight was replaced. A new wooden hand-guard ran forwards from the receiver ring beneath the barrel band, but the original mounts were retained. Few 8mm Gras conversions were fired in anger; survivors were shipped to the French African colonies or Indo-China after 1920, remaining there until the end of World War Two.

8mm Fusil d'Infanterie Mle 1874 M.80 M.14	
Synonym:	'M1874/80/14 French Gras rifle'
Adoption date:	October 1914?
Length:	1,305mm (51.38in)
Length with Mle 74 bayonet attached:	1,824mm (71.84in)
Weight:	4.08kg (9lb), without sling
Barrel length:	820mm (32.28in)
Chambering:	8×51mm, rimmed
Rifling type:	four-groove, concentric, LH
Magazine type:	none
Loading system:	single rounds
Front sight:	open blade
Backsight:	leaf-and-slider type
Minimum backsight setting:	250m (273yd)
Maximum backsight setting:	2,000m (2,182yd)
Muzzle velocity:	700m/sec (2,296ft/sec)

8mm Fusil Remington Mle 1915	
Synonym:	'M1915 French Remington Rolling Block'
Length:	1,158mm (45.6in)
Weight:	3.88kg (8.56lb), without sling
Barrel length:	765mm (30.1in)
Chambering:	8×51mm, rimmed
Rifling type:	four-groove, concentric, LH
Magazine type:	none
Loading system:	single rounds
Front sight:	open blade
Backsight:	leaf-and-slider type
Minimum backsight setting:	200m (218yd)
Maximum backsight setting:	2,400m (2,625yd)
Muzzle velocity:	700m/sec (2,295ft/sec)

Remington Rifles

The USA provided a fruitful source of weapons prior to entering into World War One in April 1917. However, although the British authorities were quick to take advantage of unused industrial capacity to order the .303 P/14, the French had no such plan; instead, they were forced to order what could be scraped together from store-rooms.

Among the pickings were 100,000 single-shot 'No. 5 Military & Sporting rolling block' rifles made by the Remington–UMC Company. The contract was largely complete by November

1918. The guns, which included a few half-stocked carbines, embodied the improved 1901-patent ejector and chambered the 8 × 51mm cartridge – though a few 7 × 57 guns with 2,000m sights were supplied from stock while changes were being made for the French cartridge.

The guns were issued to non-combatants, lines-of-communication units and the heavy artillery, though many had been withdrawn by the end of hostilities. Survivors were sent to Indo-China in the 1920s.

The M1907/15 Berthier rifle

Lengthening the Mle 92 artillery musketoon to infantry-rifle proportions provided a different response to the French army rifle shortage, even though the small-capacity clip was retained. The 07/15 rifle was essentially similar to the 1907 colonial pattern, except for its straight bolt handle and a cleaning rod let into the left side of the fore-end.

Fitted with the standard internal three-round clip-loaded magazine, Mle 07/15 guns fed from the Chargeur Mle 90 and were sighted for the Balle 1886 D. They were issued to some of the infantry units raised in the period 1916–18. The Mle 07/15 T.16, approved in 1917, had their magazines altered to accept the five-round Chargeur Mle 16. Though outwardly similar to the Mle 16 rifles, with the same sheet-metal magazine case protruding beneath the stock, they lacked the above-barrel hand-guard and were marked '1907–15' on the left side of the receiver.

Five rifles used by the French army during the First World War, drawn by J.E. Coombes for a post-1920 Bannerman catalogue. Top to bottom: the 8mm Mle 86/93 Lebel rifle; the 8mm three-shot Mle 92 Berthier musketoon; the 8mm five-shot Mle 16 Berthier rifle; the 8mm Mle 1917 RSC semi-automatic rifle; and the 7mm single-shot M1915 Remington.

8mm Fusil d'Infanterie Mle 1907/15	
Synonym:	'M1907/15 French Berthier rifle'
Length:	1,305mm (51.4in)
Weight:	3.8kg (8lb 6oz), without sling
Barrel length:	802mm (31.6in)
Chambering:	8 × 51mm, rimmed
Rifling type:	four-groove, concentric, LH
Magazine type:	internal single-column box
Magazine capacity:	three rounds
Loading system:	clip
Front sight:	open blade
Backsight:	leaf-and-slider type
Minimum backsight setting:	250m (273yd)
Maximum backsight setting:	2,400m (2,636yd)
Muzzle velocity:	700m/sec (2,296ft/sec)

The M1916 Berthier Rifle

French infantrymen soon realized that the three-cartridge clips of the Mle 07/15 rifles and Mle 92 short rifles placed them at a distinct disadvantage when the Germans had Mausers with five-round charger-loaded magazines. Their complaints were loud and long, and were eventually heard late in 1915, when a new rifle with a larger magazine and a five-cartridge clip was developed. The 1916-pattern Berthier rifle soon became the standard French infantry weapon, more than a million and a half being made by the government small-arms factories and Remington–UMC prior to the Armistice.

The rifle was little more than an Mle 07/15 adapted to accept a five-round clip, with a hand-guard running from the receiver ring beneath the barrel band, and a pivoting cover protecting the spent-clip aperture (though the spent clip remained in the magazine unless the firer had deliberately pulled the cover downwards). The backsight leaves were originally graduated for the Balle 1886 D, though most were altered when the sight-line was raised in the 1920s, and will display an additional 'A' mark.

8mm Fusil d'Infanterie Mle 16	
Synonym:	'M1916 French Berthier rifle'
Length:	1,305mm (51.4in)
Weight:	4.17kg (9lb 3oz), without sling
Barrel length:	802mm (31.6in)
Chambering:	8 × 51mm, rimmed
Rifling type:	four-groove, concentric, LH
Magazine type:	integral single-column box
Magazine capacity:	five rounds
Loading system:	clip
Front sight:	open blade
Backsight:	leaf-and-slider type
Minimum backsight setting:	250m (273yd)
Maximum backsight setting:	2,400m (2,625yd)
Muzzle velocity:	700m/sec (2,296ft/sec)

The action of the M1916 Berthier rifle, showing the magazine and the bolt handle turned downward against the stock. Courtesy of Ian Hogg.

The 8mm M1916 Berthier rifle was distinguished by its five-round magazine, which, unlike the earlier three-round M07/15 type, protruded beneath the stock ahead of the trigger. The Berthier was elegant, but lightly made. Courtesy of Ian Hogg.

French soldiers carrying Mle 86/93 Lebel rifles march down Rue Royale, Paris, to celebrate 14 July 1916 – Bastille Day. Sent from France by John A. Weston to Millport, Isle of Cumbrae, Scotland, the postcard is dated 17 August 1916.

The M1892/16 Berthier Short Rifle

Development of the five-shot M1916 rifle inspired the introduction of a comparable short rifle or Mousqueton to equip artillerymen, engineers and mounted units. The Mle 92/16 was little more than a newly made Mle 92 with the magazine altered to accommodate the Chargeur Mle 16. A sling ring was fixed to the left side of the barrel band, and a barred sling recess was cut into the left side of the butt. The earliest guns lacked the otherwise customary over-barrel hand-guard. A clearing-rod channel was cut into the left side of the fore-end, and the backsight leaves were originally graduated for the 8mm Balle 1886 D.

Other Rifles

French records indicate that sizable quantities of 1899-pattern Remington-Lee carbines were purchased in the USA, chambering the British rimmed .303 cartridge (7.7 × 56mm). They were 1,015mm

8mm Mousqueton d'Artillerie Mle 1892/16	
Synonyms:	'M1892/16 French Berthier short rifle', and 'M1916 Berthier carbine'
French Length:	945mm (37.2in)
Weight:	3.23kg (7lb 2oz), without sling
Barrel length:	445mm (17.85in)
Chambering:	8 × 51mm, rimmed
Rifling type:	four-groove, concentric, LH
Magazine type:	integral single-column box
Magazine capacity:	five rounds
Loading system:	clip
Front sight:	open blade
Backsight:	leaf-and-slider type
Minimum backsight setting:	250m (273yd)
Maximum backsight setting:	2,000m (2,187yd)
Muzzle velocity:	637m/sec (2,090ft/sec)

long, weighed about 3.35kg, and had backsight leaves graduated to 1,500yd. A hand-guard ran forwards from the receiver ring to the barrel band.

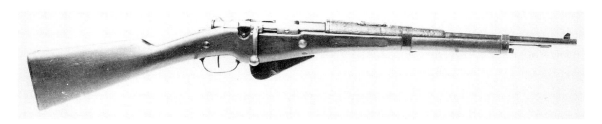

The Berthier Mousqueton or 'short rifle' Mle 92/16. This had the five-round magazine, but was otherwise similar to its three-shot predecessor. Courtesy of Ian Hogg.

French and British soldiers fraternise during a lull in the fighting on the Western Front in 1917. The Tommy second from the right holds an SMLE (probably a Mk III) with a P/1907 sword bayonet attached; the Frenchman to his right – from the 94th infantry regiment – holds a Berthier Mle 92/16 musketoon. The field gun is an obsolete 155mm Mle 1877 pressed into emergency service.

A typical wartime expedient. A French soldier fires a standard Mle 86/93 Lebel rifle through a wood-lined port in a sandbag wall. Note the improvised horse-shoe-clamp elevator and the periscope sight. By courtesy of the Trustees of the Imperial War Museum, negative no. Q69982.

There were also a few old British .303 Lee-Metford rifles, apparently purchased in 1914 from dealers' stocks. However, their distribution seems to have been meagre.

The Meunier Rifle

The French had been amassing considerable, if leisurely, experience of semi-automatic rifles since 1890, but the onset of war dramatically increased the need to find an efficient design. The A6, developed by the Section Technique d'Artillerie (STA) under the chairmanship of Colonel Meunier, had been provisionally adopted in 1910 after successfully undergoing field trials. Construction of a production line began in Tulle in 1913, but the increasing likelihood of war delayed progress and only pre-production samples had been made by August 1914.

The recoil-operated A6, the culmination of a

series of experimental models, relied on rotating lugs on the bolt head to lock the breech. Guides for a Mauser-style charger were milled in the receiver, the horizontal bolt handle had a distinctive hollow head, and a radial safety lever lay on the right side of the trigger-guard. The one-piece stock had a small, sharply pointed pistol-grip, with ventilation slots in the fore-end between the barrel band and the special nosecap. A short hand-guard ran under the band.

Small-scale assembly began in 1916, owing to unexpected problems with the prototype RSC rifles. About 750 A6 rifles were subsequently issued to selected marksmen, but owing to shortages of the special 7mm ammunition, by the spring of 1918 they had all been replaced by the Mle 1917.

7mm Fusil Automatique A6

Synonym:	'French Meunier automatic rifle'
Length:	1,293mm (50.9in)
Weight:	4.03kg (8lb 14oz), without sling
Barrel length:	720mm (28.35in)
Chambering:	7 × 59mm, rimless
Rifling type:	four-groove, concentric, LH
Magazine type:	internal, staggered-column box magazine
Magazine capacity:	six rounds
Loading system:	charger or loose rounds
Front sight:	open blade
Backsight:	leaf-and-slider type
Minimum backsight setting:	250m (273yd)?
Maximum backsight setting:	2,300m (2,515yd)
Muzzle velocity:	795m/sec (2,610ft/sec)

The M1917 RSC Rifle

Designed by Ribeyrolles, Sutter and Chauchat, this was created as soon as it was realized that the Fusil A6 (Meunier) was too complicated to mass-produce satisfactorily. Experiments that began in 1915 with prototypes adapted from Mle 86/93 Lebel rifles showed great promise, allowing the RSC rifle to be provisionally adopted in May 1916. An assembly line was readied in Saint-Étienne, but the difficulties of making a promising prototype into series-production reality slowed progress so greatly that limited assembly of the 7mm Fusil A6 began as an expedient.

The first batches of RSC rifles, assembled early in 1917, were issued on a scale of sixteen to each company of the line infantry regiments. Sufficient guns were available by the end of the year for general issue to begin, though they were usually given to squad leaders and the best marksmen.

Gas tapped from the underside of the barrel struck a piston, driving back the operating slide (exposed on the right side of the breech) to rotate the multiple interrupted-screw lugs on the separate bolt head out of engagement with the receiver. A stubby retracting handle projected from the bolt; a safety button lay on the right side of the receiver between the trigger guard and the magazine; and a manual hold-open lever was added after the first few guns had been assembled. A distinctive rounded magazine case projected beneath the receiver.

The band and nosecap resembled those of the Mle 1916 Berthier bolt-action rifle, allowing the standard epee bayonet to be used. The hand-

The gas-operated 8mm Mle 1917 'RSC' semi-automatic rifle was issued in surprisingly large numbers towards the end of the First World War, though its shorter successor, the Mle 1918, had scarcely reached production when the fighting ended. Courtesy of Ian Hogg.

guard ran from the front of the backsight base, over the top of the band to approximately half-way to the nosecap.

Rigorous service showed the Mle 1917 rifle to be surprisingly efficient, even though the projecting rim and unsatisfactory body-shape of the 8mm French service cartridge promoted jamming. The exposure of the operating rod on the right side of the fore-end was also less than ideal. Ultimately the gun was judged to be too long, too heavy, and not very handy, and by the time fighting stopped, it had been superseded by the 1918 pattern described below. However, only 1917-type RSC rifles had seen active service.

Short, 1917-pattern 'Mousquetons' had a modified nosecap moved back around the gas-port assembly, and minor improvements in the action. However, only a few guns of this type had been made when the M1918 was substituted.

8mm Fusil Automatique Mle 1917

Synonyms:	'RSC M1917', and 'M1917 French Saint-Étienne automatic rifle'
Length:	1,328mm (52.3in)
Weight:	5.19kg (11b 7oz), without sling
Barrel length:	800mm (31.5in)
Chambering:	8 × 51mm, rimmed
Rifling type:	four-groove, concentric, LH
Magazine type:	integral staggered-column box
Magazine capacity:	five rounds
Loading system:	charger or loose rounds
Front sight:	open blade
Backsight:	leaf-and-slider type
Minimum backsight setting:	250m (273yd)?
Maximum backsight setting:	2,000m (21,870yd)
Muzzle velocity:	700m/sec (2,296ft/sec)

The M1918 RSC rifle

The 'Mousqueton' of the Mle 1917 RSC rifle was so obviously a more practical size that it became the model for the improved RSC design, the Mle

1918. Shorter and lighter, the Mle 1918 was otherwise essentially similar. The hand-guard ran from the front of the receiver to the nosecap; a lever on the right side of the receiver held the action open after the last case had been ejected; and a tubular sleeve prevented debris entering the charging-handle slot. Production began in the late summer, but by the Armistice no guns had been issued, and only a few thousand of them were made in 1919 before the project was abandoned. Some were issued for service in Morocco in the early 1920s, but the introduction of a 7.5mm rimless cartridge in 1929 rendered them obsolescent.

8mm Fusil Automatique Mle 1918

Synonyms:	'RSC M1918', and 'M1918 French Saint-Étienne automatic rifle'
Length:	1,099mm (43.25in)
Weight:	4.73kg (10lb 7oz), without sling
Barrel length:	580mm (22.85in)
Chambering:	8 × 51mm, rimmed
Rifling type:	four-groove, concentric, LH
Magazine type:	integral staggered-column box
Magazine capacity:	five rounds
Loading system:	charger or loose rounds
Front sight:	open blade
Backsight:	leaf-and-slider type
Minimum backsight setting:	250m (273yd)?
Maximum backsight setting:	2,000m (2,187yd)
Muzzle velocity:	655m/sec (2,150ft/sec)

MACHINE-GUNS

The French Army reduced the purchase of Hotchkiss machine-guns in the early 1900s, and, as related in Part Two, set about developing designs of their own to avoid paying licensing fees. Unfortunately neither the Puteaux (APX) nor the Saint-Étienne pattern was particularly successful, and on the outbreak of war the Société Française d'Armes Portative Hotchkiss & Cie was asked to provide standard 8mm M1914 machine-guns on an open-ended contract.

The tripod-mounted Hotchkiss became the standard French medium machine-gun, the equivalent of the Maxim or Vickers. It was gas-operated, and fed with metal strips containing twenty-five cartridges pushed into retaining clips, though three-round strips could be linked together to produce a 249-round 'belt'.

Characteristic of the Hotchkiss were the five large brass fins around the barrel, immediately ahead of the chamber, which were intended to keep the gun cool by presenting a large surface area to the atmosphere. In service, they tended to harbour oil and dirt which, as the barrel heated, generated enough hazy smoke to obscure the line of sight. Yet the Hotchkiss was simple, reliable, and easy to operate and maintain. Some guns even survived long enough to see action in 1939.

A few guns were chambered for special 11mm Gras cartridges loaded with incendiary bullets, principally to attack the artillery-observation balloons that regularly flew at a height of 1,000ft (300m) a few hundred yards behind German front-line trenches – a powerful round was needed to propel the bullet across No Man's Land with sufficient power to down a balloon. The cumbersome 11mm Hotchkiss was discarded at the end of the war, but not before a few had seen service aboard French warplanes.

8mm Mitrailleuse Hotchkiss Mle 1914	
Synonym:	'M1914 French Hotchkiss machine-gun'
Length:	1,310mm (51.57in)
Weight:	23.50kg (51.80lb)
Weight of mount (Mle 1916 tripod):	24kg (52.9lb)
Barrel length:	785mm (30.90in)
Chambering:	8 × 51mm, rimmed
Rifling type:	four-groove, concentric, LH
Feed type:	metal strip
Strip capacity:	24 (fixed) or 249 (articulated) rounds
Fire selector:	none, automatic fire only
Cyclic rate:	600rd/min
Front sight:	open blade
Backsight:	tangent-leaf type
Minimum backsight setting:	200m (219yd)?
Maximum backsight setting:	2,000m (2,187yd)
Muzzle velocity:	700m/sec (2,296ft/sec)

An M1914 Hotchkiss machine-gun manned by Frenchmen of the 21st infantry regiment support British soldiers on the Western Front, 1916. Note the Mle 92 Berthier musketoon slung over the shoulder of the man nearest the camera.

A typical 1914-pattern 8mm Hotchkiss machine-gun on its tripod. Note that there are only five large-diameter cooling fins on the barrel, which distinguishes the M1914 from some of the earlier Hotchkiss guns. Courtesy of Ian Hogg.

A French machine-gun crew with an 8mm Mle 1907 Saint-Étienne keep a vigilant watch over No Man's Land, Western Front, 1915. Courtesy of Ian Hogg.

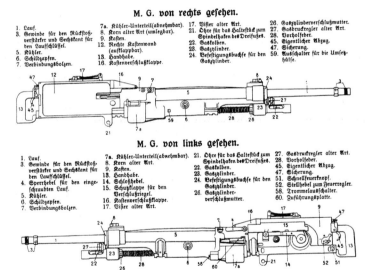

Drawings of the Saint-Étienne machine-gun, from the German official handbook Beute-Maschinengewehre *(1916).*

The M1914 Colt Machine-gun

Supplied from the USA, this was widely used in the air in the early part of World War One. It had a finned barrel (the barrel of original 1895-guns had been plain), and was often fitted with an oscillating segmental weight to damp the vibration caused by the actuating lever as the gun fired. Others were fitted with special semi-circular sheet-steel shields to prevent the radial arm damaging the delicate structure of the warplanes.

The M1915 Chauchat Light Machine-gun

The triumvirate of Chauchat, Sutter and Ribeyrolles developed the RSC semi-automatic rifle which proved successful; however, it was also responsible for what was unquestionably the worst military weapon of the war: a light machine-gun known as the 'Chauchat', 'CSRG' or 'Gladiator'.

The weapon owed its origins to the 'Fusil-Mitrailleuse Chauchat' developed in 1903–7 by

The infamous 8mm M1915 Chauchat machine rifle
– recognizable by its unique semi-circular magazine
– was a quirky design made worse by poor
manufacturing standards. Prone to breaking down,
it was heartily disliked by the troops.
Courtesy of Ian Hogg.

Captain Chauchat of the Commission Technique de Versailles (CTV); this was a long-recoil design developed specifically for the use of cyclist formations. It had been refined in the Ateliers de Puteaux to produce the Fusil-Mitrailleuse APX Mle 1910, though development work was still being carried out in 1914.

The French realized that the Chauchat/APX was ideally suited to the new tactical doctrine of 'walking fire'. Infantrymen would spring from their trenches, each man armed with an automatic weapon and (apparently) an unlimited supply of loaded magazines. With the gun held at waist level with the aid of a shoulder sling, the line would advance, spraying the German trenches with bullets as they went – a withering, continuous fire that no enemy could possibly withstand. All the doctrine needed was the automatic weapon, and in this lay the inspiration for the CSRG.

Satisfactory operation depended on the barrel and the breech recoiling, locked together, about 3in (75mm) across the frame; the bolt was unlocked and held back as the parts halted, allowing the barrel to run forwards into battery. The empty case was extracted and mechanically ejected before the bolt could be released to run forwards, collect a fresh round from the semicircular magazine, lock with the barrel, and then fire.

Simplicity was the essence of the design, but there is little doubt that many of the problems

arose from recruiting an untried weapons-maker: Établissements de Cycles 'Gladiator', famous pre-war for bicycles and cycling accessories. It was assumed that experience with steel tubing would be an asset, but even though some of the components were supplied by gunmakers Société Anonyme 'Sidarme' of Saint-Étienne, work did not proceed smoothly. In addition, the unsuitable shape of the sharply tapered French 8mm cartridge, with its rounded base and prominent rim, was no great help.

More significantly, the Chauchat was made of inferior materials, and its long-recoil action was a magnet for dust and grit. The moving parts wore much more rapidly than had been expected, the feed was erratic, and extraction gave constant trouble – it was noteworthy if a twenty-round magazine was fired without a stoppage. When stoppages did occur, the gun invariably required dismantling to clear them. Nevertheless, the Chauchat was the only light automatic suited to French walking-fire tactics available in 1915, and it was ordered straight into series production despite its many defects. In practice, of course, the walking-fire concept collapsed under deficiencies of its own, and any chance of success was nullified when participants were obliged to stop in order to unjam their machine-guns. The Chauchat was impressed as an emergency trench weapon, and 'walking fire' was quietly forgotten.

Many guns served the Belgian Army in World War One, some being rechambered for the 7.65 ×

53mm rimless cartridge, and a modified version (worse even than the original) was adopted by the US Army in 1918. Survivors of the European conflict reappeared in the Spanish Civil War, World War Two, and even in Vietnam.

The Madsen Machine-gun

Small quantities of these, chambered for the 8mm Balle 1886 D, were used by the French in 1914–15. They had a reputation for jamming, owing to the unsuitable shape of the cartridge case, and were rapidly superseded by the CSRG and the Lewis Gun.

The Darne Machine-gun

Although a handful of Mle 1909 Hotchkiss 'machine rifles' were used by observers in the early days of World War One, most French aircraft were armed with Vickers, Colt or Lewis machine-

guns. The Lewis was made under licence by the Darne company of Saint-Étienne, previously known only as shotgun makers. Experience with the Lewis (which was notoriously time-consuming to make) led the Darne brothers to conclude that little was to be gained expending time and energy on immaculately finished products which, in the harsh reality of aerial combat, often had a service life measured in minutes.

Work began on a cheap, simple and easily produced weapon, and it succeeded so well that approval for service was gained in 1918. Unfortunately the war ended before the Mle 1918 reached the front line in quantity, and success in the hands of the French and others was delayed until the 1920s.

Adopted at the end of the First World War as an aircraft gun, but too late to see service, the belt-fed Darne was potentially an excellent design. This is a postwar light machine-gun adaptation. Courtesy of Ian Hogg.

8mm Mitrailleuse 'Chauchat' Mle 1915

Synonyms:	'CSRG' (Chauchat, Sutter, Ribeyrolle, Gladiator); 'Gladiator'; 'Chauchard'
Adoption date:	July 1915
Length:	1,143mm (45in)
Weight:	9.07kg (20.38lb)
Barrel length:	469mm (18.5in)
Chambering:	8 × 51mm, rimmed
Rifling type:	four-groove, concentric, RH
Feed type:	detachable box magazine
Magazine capacity:	twenty-five rounds
Fire selector:	none, automatic only
Cyclic rate:	250rd/min
Front sight:	blade
Backsight:	tangent leaf
Minimum backsight setting:	200m (219yd)
Maximum backsight setting:	2,000m (2,187yd)

8mm Mitrailleuse d'Aviation Darne, Mle 1918

Synonym:	'M1918 French Darne machine-gun'
Approval date:	August 1918
Length:	937mm (36.9in)
Weight:	7kg (15.44lb)
Barrel length:	660mm (25.98in)
Chambering:	8 × 51mm, rimmed
Rifling type:	four-groove, concentric, RH
Feed type:	cloth belt
Belt capacity:	250 rounds
Fire selector:	none, automatic only
Cyclic rate:	850rd/min
Front sight:	fixed post
Backsight:	ring
Muzzle velocity:	700m/sec (2,300ft/sec)

14 Belgium & Italy

Belgium

The greater part of Belgium – including all its arms factories – was overrun by the German army in the first few weeks of the war and remained under German control until the summer of 1918. Though the Belgian army continued to fight on the northern section of the Western Front until the Armistice, very little weapons development could be undertaken. Individual units customarily used French or British equipment, depending on their location. An attempt was made to resume production of the 1889-type Mauser rifles, 8,000 being made in the USA in 1915 by Hopkins & Allen of Norwich, Connecticut; manufacturing facilities were also acquired in Britain, but it is believed that only a few guns were ever completed. M1889 rifles with British origins will be marked simply ETAT BELGE and BIRMINGHAM.

A Model 1889 sniper rifle (*pour Tireur d'Élite*) was introduced in 1916 in small numbers, though it was little more than a standard infantry rifle with an offset mount for a suitable telescope sight on the left side of the receiver to allow charger-loading. Winchester optical sights were preferred, but alternatives were permissible.

This postcard shows Belgian soldiers with Maxim machine-guns defending their homeland against the Germans, August/September 1914. Note that guns of this type were often hauled by dogs. Courtesy of Ian Hogg.

The 7.65mm M1915 Beretta semi-automatic pistol, a simple blowback design, was accepted by the Italian army in large quantities. The distinctive slide, cut away to reveal the top surface of the barrel, was a Beretta trademark for many years.

Italy

HANDGUNS

The M1915 Beretta Pistol

The first Beretta semi-automatic pistol was a wartime project, and its quality fell below the manufacturer's peacetime standards. The M1915 was a 7.65mm blowback with the slide cut away at the sides behind a narrow bridge over the barrel, which was a separate unit pinned to the frame. Extracted cases were ejected simply by striking the tip of the firing pin, which moved forwards in the breech-block during the recoil stroke owing to the resistance of the internal hammer, and a separate ejection port was cut in the solid-topped portion of the slide. Guns were also chambered for the 9mm Glisenti and 9mm Short cartridges, but not until fighting had ended.

Some guns have been reported with a prominent safety catch on the left side of the frame, which could also engage recesses in the slide to hold the action open. A few even have a second catch on the frame, under the rear end of the slide, but its origins are unclear.

7.65mm Pistola automatica Beretta Modello 1915	
Synonym:	'M1915 Italian Beretta pistol'
Adoption date:	1915
Length:	150mm (5.90in)
Weight:	570g (20oz), empty
Barrel length:	84mm (3.3in)
Chambering:	7.65mm Browning
Rifling type:	six-groove, concentric, RH
Magazine type:	single-column detachable box in butt
Magazine capacity:	eight rounds
Loading system:	single cartridges
Front sight:	open blade
Back sight:	fixed 'V'-notch
Muzzle velocity:	266m/sec (875ft/sec)

This longitudinal section of the 1915-pattern Beretta pistol emphasises its simplicity. Courtesy of Pietro Beretta SpA, Gardone Val Trompia.

Many surviving 10.35mm Vetterli-Vitali rifles were converted for the standard 6.5mm M1891-95 cartridge. The resulting 'M70/87/15' transformations (readily identifiable by the protruding box magazine) were only just strong enough to withstand the pressures generated by the smokeless ammunition, but were largely relegated to lines-of-communication and colonial forces. Courtesy of Ian Hogg.

RIFLES

The 6.5mm Vetterli Conversions

The conversion of obsolescent M1870/87 Vetterli-Vitali rifles was authorized in about 1916, partly to offset losses of M1891 Mannlicher-Carcano guns, and partly to arm newly raised units. The original barrel was bored out, a rifled liner was inserted, the sights were changed, and a clip-loading Mannlicher magazine was substituted for the old Vitali box.

Positioning the lugs at the back of the bolt, where they locked into the receiver bridge, ensured that the Vetterli breech was only just

strong enough to withstand the pressures generated by 6.5mm cartridges loaded with smokeless propellant. The rifles were relegated to artillerymen, lines-of-communication units, and home defence formations wherever possible, though large numbers were still arming colonial infantrymen in North Africa in 1941.

M1870/87 TS short rifles and M1870/87 cavalry carbines were also converted in large numbers, together with a few Carabinieri weapons. Their history parallels that of the rifles; however, most were discarded after 1918.

MACHINE-GUNS

The M1914 FIAT-Revelli Machine-gun

Another of the many designs that flowed from the prolific brain of Italian army officer Abiel Bethel Revelli (1864–1930), this water-cooled, recoil-operated gun appeared in 1908. The essence of its action was a swinging wedge-lock, though the 'lock' was so brief that the FIAT-Revelli machine-gun is usually classed as a delayed blowback.

When the Revelli design appeared, the Italian army was testing the Perino pattern against the Maxim and showed very little interest in anything new. Testers were taking their time, however, and when the Italians declared war with Austria-Hungary in 1915, no decision about the Perino had been taken. FIAT had created a production line for the Revelli machine-gun, apparently hopeful of attracting export orders, and were able to offer an instant alternative.

6.5mm Fucile di Fanteria Mo. 1870-87-15	
Synonym:	'M1870/15 Italian Vetterli rifle'
Length:	1,345mm (52.95in)
Weight:	4.63kg (10.19lb), without sling
Barrel length:	860mm (33.86in)
Chambering:	6.5 × 52mm, rimless
Rifling type:	four-groove, concentric, RH
Magazine type:	single-row protruding box
Magazine capacity:	six rounds
Loading system:	reversible clip
Front sight:	open blade
Backsight:	quadrant type
Minimum backsight setting:	500m (546yd)
Maximum backsight setting:	2,000m (2,187yd)
Muzzle velocity:	730m/sec (2,395ft/sec)

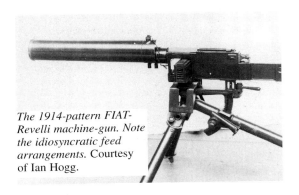

The 1914-pattern FIAT-Revelli machine-gun. Note the idiosyncratic feed arrangements. Courtesy of Ian Hogg.

6.5mm Mitriaglice FIAT Modello 1914

Synonym:	'M1914 Italian FIAT-Revelli machine-gun'
Adoption date:	1915
Length:	1,180mm (46.5in)
Weight:	17kg (37.5lb)
Barrel length:	643mm (25.75in)
Chambering:	6.5 × 52mm, rimless
Rifling type:	four-groove, concentric, RH
Feed type:	compartmented strip-feed box
Feed capacity:	fifty rounds
Selector:	none, automatic fire only
Cyclic rate:	400rd/min
Front sight:	open blade
Backsight:	leaf-and-slider type
Muzzle velocity:	645m/sec (2,100ft/sec)

The principal idiosyncracy of the FIAT-Revelli was its feed: a metal cage with ten compartments, each capable of holding five cartridges. The cage was fed into the gun and the first compartment emptied from the bottom, round by round, after which the cage shifted across to the next compartment, and so on until the final compartment was emptied and the empty cage was ejected from the other side. Though needlessly complicated, the cage mechanism worked surprisingly well and was easily loaded with loose cartridges. The spray of an oil pump lubricated each cartridge automatically as it entered the chamber, easing extraction and ejection problems.

The M1914 Revelli machine-gun was made during World War One by Fabbrica Italiana Automobili Torino ('FIAT'), by Metallurgica

Bresciana gia Tempini SA ('MBT'), and by Società Italiana Ernesto Breda of Brescia. Lightweight versions with slotted half-length barrel casings were adapted for aerial combat.

The M1914 Colt Machine-gun

This was simply a variant of the American M1895 'Potato Digger' machine-gun chambering the standard Italian 6.5mm rifle cartridge, small quantities being purchased from the USA in 1915 to alleviate shortages of automatic weapons. Dimensions and data are similar to those of the original Colt-made gun (q.v.), excepting that the muzzle velocity was 655m/sec (2,150ft/sec).

Machine-gun Shortages

Shortages of machine-guns during the opening stages of the war were partly solved by purchasing 8mm Saint-Étienne and M1914 Hotchkiss guns from France, though many captured Austro-Hungarian Schwarzlose machine-guns were pressed back into service against their erstwhile owners. A selection of Lewis and (allegedly) Darne guns had been acquired to equip Italian aircraft by 1918.

The Villar Perosa Machine-gun

Most of the fighting between Italian and Austro-Hungarian forces took place in the north of Italy along the border with the Austro-Hungarian empire. As a large segment of the border lay in the Venetian and Carnatic Alps – far farther south in 1915 than it is today – both armies employed specialist mountain units. The Italian Alpini demanded compact, lightweight, fast-firing automatic weapons suited to their particular tactics.

The concept of the light machine-gun as a squad weapon lay several years in the future, and so the weapon that resulted was unique. It had been patented in Italy by Abiel Revelli prior to

The twin-barrelled 9mm Villar-Perosa, designed as an ultra-light machine-gun, was accompanied by a bipod mount and even an armoured shield. Effective enough in its intended role, it made a better submachine-gun when adapted by Beretta after World War One had ended. Courtesy of Ian Hogg.

9mm Pistola Mitriaglice Villar-Perosa Modello 1915	
Synonym:	'Villar Perosa machine-gun'; 'RIV machine-gun'; 'OVP machine-gun'
Length:	533mm (21in)
Weight:	6.52kg (14.38lb), empty
Barrel length:	318mm (12.5in)
Chambering:	9 × 19mm Glisenti, rimless
Rifling type:	six-groove, concentric, RH
Feed type:	detachable box magazines
Magazine capacity:	twenty-five rounds apiece
Operating system:	delayed blowback, automatic fire only
Cyclic rate:	1,200rd/min
Front sight:	open barleycorn
Backsight:	leaf-and-slider type
Muzzle velocity:	365m/sec (1,200ft/sec)

The 6.5mm M1918 SIA machine-gun was introduced during World War One in a ground role. This aircraft gun lacks the customary spade grips and back-plate trigger assembly. Aberdeen Proving Ground photograph A51033 (1948), courtesy of Ian Hogg.

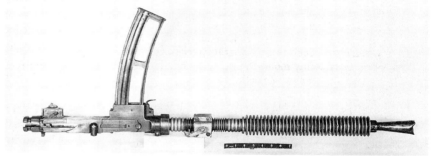

the war, on 8 April 1914, and perfected in 1915. Rights had been assigned to Officine Villar Perosa ('OVP') of Pinerola, though it was also made by FIAT in Turin and by the Canadian General Electric Company of Montreal.

Taking its name from the original manufacturer, the Villar Perosa consisted of two guns mounted side by side on a light platform slung from a strap around the gunner's shoulders. The guns took the simplest form imaginable: a tubular receiver containing a cylindrical bolt, a short barrel, and a top-mounted magazine loaded with 9mm pistol cartridges. A lug on the bolt rode in a curved track in the receiver, marginally delaying the opening stroke – though the point of this was more to prevent the firing pin going forwards until the bolt had revolved

into its closed position. The lightweight bolts promoted a stupendous fire rate of 1,200rd/min per barrel, and so gunners were customarily attended by two men carrying loaded magazines.

For all its oddities, the Villar Perosa was ideally suited to alpine warfare; it was also mounted in naval craft and aircraft, and was subjected to infantry-weapon trials, but it was less successful in less specialized roles. Surviving guns were withdrawn at the end of the war, dismantled into separate units, and fitted into wooden stocks to make a highly effective submachine gun known as the 'Moschetto Automatica Beretta Modello 1918'. However, few 'MAB' reached the Front before the fighting ceased, and their reputation rests largely on postwar exploitation.

15 Russia

On 1 January 1914, the military inventory stood at 3.427 million M1891 rifles – but by October, more than five million men had been mobilized, and the rifle reserve fell woefully short of needs. In December, therefore, the Chief of Staff ordered the acquisition of any weapon that could be pressed into service. This was subsequently restricted by the war minister to weapons chambering the regulation 7.62 × 54mm rimmed cartridge – but not before large numbers of 6.5mm Japanese Arisakas and a collection of obsolescent French guns had been purchased.

RIFLES

The Arisaka Rifles

The Russians obtained 600,000 6.5mm Arisaka rifles in the period 1914 to 1915, nearly all of them old Meiji 30th Year Type guns stored since improved patterns had been issued in 1907–9; but the Japanese also disposed of 35,400 7 × 57mm 38th Year Type rifles, held since the Mexican revolution of 1911 had interrupted deliveries.

About 128,000 30th Year and 38th Year Type

A parade of machine-guns captured by the German army in the early stages of the war on the Eastern Front. A 7.62mm 1895-pattern Colt is nearest the camera. There are several Russian Maxims, on Sokolov mounts, and two retaken German-type Maxims on sled mounts.

rifles were subsequently supplied from Britain in 1916–17, many being withdrawn from the Royal Navy in favour of Ross rifles displaced from the trenches. Most of these guns already had British and Japanese markings.

The Mosin-Nagant Rifles

Polivanov replaced Sukhomlinov as the war minister in the summer of 1915, and immediately placed orders for standard 1891-pattern rifles in the United States of America. Contracts for 1.5 million and 1.8 million guns were agreed with Remington–UMC and the New England Westinghouse Corporation in 1915. Deliveries by 1 January 1917 amounted to only 131,440 Remington–UMC and 225,260 Westinghouse Mosin-Nagants.

The shortfall was partly offset by the greatly improved performance of the Russian ordnance factories, which, by 1 October 1917, had completed 3.286 million Mosin-Nagants (with full-length infantry guns predominating) since 1 July 1914. The October Revolution brought the Bolsheviks control of the country, and on 15 December 1917 an armistice was concluded with Germany. Russia had finally opted out; supplies of weapons from the remaining Allies ceased, and civil war had soon stopped much of the production in the state arms factories.

The M1915 Winchester Rifle

An order for 300,000 M1895 lever-action rifles (known as 'obr. 1915g' in Russia) was placed with the Winchester Repeating Arms Company in the summer of 1915. They followed the standard commercial pattern, but chambered the rimmed Russian rifle cartridges and were sighted accordingly. Charger guides were mounted above the receiver, and a hand-guard ran from the receiver ring to the band.

The October Revolution caused deliveries to cease in 1917. Winchester recorded the despatch of 293,816 7.62mm rifles, though the Russians subsequently claimed to have received 299,000. A few thousand 1895-type rifles may have been acquired in other chamberings, but this was probably misinformation, due simply to poor record-keeping. Nine thousand survivors were sold in 1936, at a profit, to the Spanish Republican government.

The M1915 Winchester rifle, chambered for the standard Russian 7.62 × 54 rimmed cartridge, was purchased to alleviate the shortage of rifles evident almost as soon as fighting started in 1914. The breech was locked by a vertically sliding block, visible in the detail view above the pivoted trigger assembly, and there are charger guides above the receiver. Courtesy of the MoD Pattern Room Collection, Royal Ordnance plc, Nottingham.

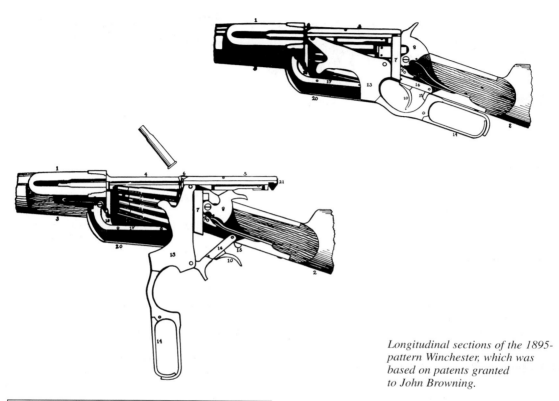

Longitudinal sections of the 1895-pattern Winchester, which was based on patents granted to John Browning.

7.62mm Vintovka Vinchestya, obr. 1915g

Synonym:	'M1915 Russian Winchester'
Length:	1,160mm (45.67in)
Weight:	4.11kg (9.06lb), without sling
Barrel length:	712mm (28in)
Chambering:	7.62 × 54mm, rimmed
Rifling type:	four-groove, concentric, RH
Magazine type:	single-row integral box
Magazine capacity:	five rounds
Loading system:	charger or loose rounds
Front sight:	open blade
Backsight:	leaf-and-slider type
Minimum backsight setting:	400 arshin (280m, 306yd)
Maximum backsight setting:	2,700 arshin (1,920m, 2,100yd)
Muzzle velocity:	820m/sec (2,690ft/sec)

The Federov Avtomat

Vladimir Federov and Vasily Degtyarev were obliged to suspend work on their promising semi-automatic rifle in 1914, in order to attend to more pressing demands; however, once the supply and repair of service-pattern rifles had been organized, they were permitted to recommence development work.

The perfected design, colloquially known as the 'Avtomat', was made by the imperial ordnance factory in Sestroretsk. Little more than an improved version of the 1913-type rifle, chambered for the Japanese 6.5mm cartridge in an attempt to reduce weight, it embodied the short-recoil action and locking system of its predecessor. The Avtomat could be distinguished by a detachable box magazine, a rudimentary forward hand grip, and an abbreviated

The 1916-pattern Federov Avtomat, one of the most successful 'assault rifles' to be made during the First World War. From a painting by John Walter.

sheet-metal fore-end. The first guns had plain-body magazines and three sighting notches in the backsight slider; there were no charger guides or mechanical hold-open catches.

Enough guns had been made by October 1916 to equip a company of the 189th Ismail'skiy infantry regiment, but work proceeded exceptionally slowly and teething troubles persisted throughout the spring of 1917, long after the design had been refined. The October Revolution stopped progress until the Bolshevik authorities, realizing that the Avtomat had great potential, ordered work to begin again. However, though the first batch of rifles was supposed to have been delivered from Sestroretsk by 1 February 1919, only two hundred post-Revolutionary guns had been made by February 1920.

6.5mm Avtomaticheskaya vintovka V. Federova obr. 1916g

Synonym:	'M1916 Russian automatic rifle', 'FederovAvtomat'
Length:	975mm (38.4in)
Weight:	4.42kg (9.75), without magazine and sling
Barrel length:	520mm (20.45in)
Chambering:	6.5 × 50mm, semi-rim
Rifling type:	six-groove, polygonal, RH
Magazine type:	detachable box
Magazine capacity:	twenty-five rounds
Loading system:	loose rounds
Front sight:	open barleycorn
Backsight:	leaf-and-slider type
Minimum backsight setting:	200 arshin (142m, 155yd)
Maximum backsight setting:	2,000 arshin (1,422m, 1,550yd)
Muzzle velocity:	705m/sec (2,310ft/sec)

16 The United States of America

HANDGUNS

The .45 M1911 Pistol

When the USA declared war on the Central Powers in April 1917, about 98,500 .45 M1911 Colt-Browning pistols had been made, 76,000 serving the army and the remainder with the US Navy and Marine Corps. As early as November 1916 the War Department had been seeking to expand the manufacturing base in the event of the USA entering hostilities, and had sought drawings and manufacturing details from Colt's Patent Fire Arms Mfg Co. But by the spring of 1917 things were still only under discussion, together with negotiations to make Colt and Smith & Wesson revolvers chambered for the rimless M1911 .45 cartridge.

When war began, Colt estimated that 6,000 pistols could be produced monthly by the end of 1917, and that the weekly output of revolvers could reach 600 before April had run its course. Contracts for 500,000 pistols and 100,000 revolvers were let with Colt, and Smith & Wesson received another for 100,000 revolvers.

Production of this magnitude might have sufficed had not the US Army, for reasons best known to itself, increased the issue of handguns, in particular to the infantry. By December 1917, a decision had been taken to offer a contract for 150,000 M1911 pistols to Remington Arms–UMC. Drawings prepared by Colt were not sufficiently detailed to allow production until remedial action had been taken, and so, in the summer of 1918, additional orders were given to The National Cash Register Company of Dayton,

Ohio; the North American Arms Company of Quebec, Canada; the Savage Arms Company of Utica, New York; Caron Brothers of Montreal, Canada; the Burroughs Adding Machine Company of Detroit, Michigan; the Winchester Repeating Arms of New Haven, Connecticut; and the Lanston Monotype Company of Philadelphia, Pennsylvania. The new contractors set to work preparing production lines for the M1911 pistol – but the Armistice came before any guns had been made in quantity, other than 375,404 made by Colt and Remington–UMC.

US Revolver, .45in, M1917

Synonym:	'Colt New Service' Revolver, Model 1909'
Length:	10.75in (273mm)
Weight:	2.5lb (1134g)
Barrel length:	5.5in (140mm)
Chambering:	.45 ACP, rimless
Rifling type:	six-groove, concentric, LH
Magazine type:	rotating cylinder
Magazine capacity:	six rounds
Loading system:	clips of three cartridges
Front sight:	open blade
Backsight:	fixed open notch
Muzzle velocity:	860ft/sec (262m/sec)

The M1917 Revolvers

These were adaptations of the two standard large-calibre models of their respective manufacturers: the 'New Service' made by Colt's Patent Fire Arms Mfg Co., and the 'Hand Ejector' made by Smith & Wesson. A total of 268,351 revolvers

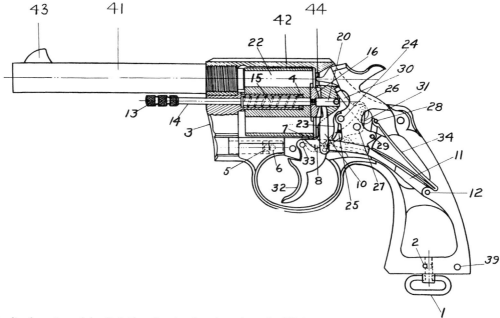

A longitudinal section of the Colt New Service Revolver, from the US Army manual. Courtesy of Ian Hogg.

was produced. Modifications were confined largely to new cylinders, shortened to leave sufficient clearance at the rear to admit the spring-steel clip that snapped into the extraction grooves of three cartridges. Two three-round clips could then be dropped into the cylinder. Clips were needed to hold the rimless cartridges in the cylinders, and to provide bearing surfaces for the ejecting mechanism.

Smith & Wesson bored chambers with a slight step, which allowed cartridges to be inserted singly (the case mouth abutted the shoulder in the chamber), but collective ejection was impossible unless the clips were used.

RIFLES

The M1917 Enfield Rifle

In April 1917, the US Army inventory contained 600,000 1903-pattern Springfield rifles and about 160,000 obsolescent Krag-Jørgensen rifles. But faced with bold plans for a five-million-man field army, it was obvious to the War Department that rifle production conducted at the leisurely peace-time pace would not suffice.

The M1903 rifle had been made in Springfield Armory and Rock Island Arsenal, but the latter

US Revolver, .45in, M1917	
Synonym:	'Smith & Wesson Mark 2 Hand Ejector Revolver, Second Model'
Length:	10.78in (274mm)
Weight:	2.25lb (1,020g)
Barrel length:	5.5in (140mm)
Chambering:	.45 ACP, rimless
Rifling type:	six-groove, concentric, RH
Magazine type:	rotating cylinder
Magazine capacity:	six rounds
Loading system:	clips of three cartridges
Front sight:	open blade
Backsight:	fixed open notch
Muzzle velocity:	860ft/sec (262m/sec)

Chambered for the .30-06 cartridge, the M1917 Enfield rifle was a minor adaptation of the British .303 P/14, lacking the long-range sights on the side of the stock. Courtesy of Ian Hogg.

had ceased production at the end of 1916 and work in Springfield was proceeding very slowly. Much of the skilled workforce had moved elsewhere, and there seemed little likelihood of accelerating production as rapidly as the authorities had hoped. One possible option was to entrust the manufacture of the M1903 to privately owned gunmakers, but this was abandoned when it was realized that it would take years to prepare the thousands of tools, jigs and gauges required. Salvation took an unexpected form: the Winchester Repeating Arms Company and Remington–UMC were just delivering the last of the .303 P/1914 rifles ordered by Britain in 1914, and the massive production lines threatened to stand idle.

Early in May 1917 the US Army Ordnance Department elected to modify the Enfield rifle to fire regulation .30 M1906 ball ammunition, simultaneously ensuring that the output of the three factories, unlike the British guns, would be fully interchangeable. Prototype rifles were successfully tested on 12 July, and full-scale production was authorized, even though final standardization was delayed for another month.

By 9 November 1918, 312,878 M1903 Springfield rifles had been made in the Springfield and Rock Island factories, and 2,193,429 M1917 Enfields had come from the Winchester and Remington plants. About twenty thousand Ross rifles had been purchased from Canada for training purposes, together with 280,049 Mosin-Nagant rifles acquired from the incomplete Russian contracts broken by the October Revolution.

It is worth remarking that the price paid by the US Government for the M1917 rifle was $26. The British had paid $42 for each 'Pattern 1914' made in the same factories – although they were, of course, also paying for the machinery itself.

US Rifle, Caliber .30, M1917	
Synonyms:	'American Enfield rifle', and 'Enfield M17'
Adoption date:	12 August 1917
Length:	46.3in (1,164mm)
Weight:	9lb (4.08kg)
Barrel length:	26in (660mm)
Chambering:	.30in M1906, rimless
Rifling type:	five grooves, concentric, RH
Magazine type:	integral box
Magazine capacity:	five rounds
Loading system:	loose rounds or chargers
Front sight:	open barleycorn
Backsight:	leaf-and-slider type
Minimum backsight setting:	200yd (182m)
Maximum backsight setting:	1,600yd (1,463m)
Muzzle velocity:	2,750ft/sec (838m/sec)

MACHINE-GUNS

The M1915 Vickers Machine-gun

The course of the war in Europe soon showed that the machine-gun was vital in combat, and, belatedly, the US Ordnance Department reviewed its limited stocks of obsolescent weapons. Several promising guns had been considered in 1910–14, but none had been accepted, and few could be spared after 1914 apart from the British .303 Vickers Gun (q.v.). First tested by the US Army in 1913, this was adopted as the '.30 Machine Gun M1915' after encouraging trials had been undertaken in April 1916. A production licence was acquired by Colt's Patent Fire Arms Mfg Co., and 125 guns chambering the .30 M1906 cartridge were ordered.

Towards the end of 1916, with the situation in Europe worsening daily, the Secretary of War order a commission to review the machine-gun situation; a report made in December reaffirmed adoption of the Vickers Gun, and an additional 4,000 were ordered from Colt. The commission had also examined the Lewis Gun, but the trials guns had been hastily converted from British .303 to US .30-06 chambering, and time had not been spared to adapt the action for changes in chamber pressures and associated characteristics. The .30 Lewis Guns worked violently and extracted so poorly that the testers were unimpressed. However, if the guns could be improved, it was arranged that they could be tested in additional trials in May 1917, and the promoters were informed accordingly.

The M1917 Lewis Machine-gun

When the USA entered World War One in April 1917, the army had 670 Benét-Mercié machine rifles, 282 1904-pattern Maxims, 353 Lewis guns chambering the British .303 cartridge, and 148 M1895 'Potato Digger' Colts; and 4,125 Colt-made Vickers Guns had been ordered.

Excepting Colt, only two gunmaking companies were making machine-guns: the Savage Arms Company was coming to the end of a 12,500 Lewis Gun order for Britain, and Marlin-Rockwell was making Colt M1895 guns under licence for the Russian government.

The first supplementary US Army orders went to Savage in April 1917, requesting 1,300 .30 Lewis guns (which had been perfected since the disastrous trials of 1916); and then to Marlin, for 2,500 1895-pattern Colts intended for training. Agreement was also reached with the French to provide the first US troops to arrive in France with 8mm M1914 Hotchkiss and M1915 Chauchat machine-guns.

Machine-Gun, Vickers, Caliber .30, Model of 1915

Synonym:	'US Vickers Gun'
Adoption date:	summer 1916?
Length:	45.5in (1,155mm)
Weight:	40lb (18.1kg)
Barrel length:	28.5in (723mm)
Chambering:	30 (7.62 × 63mm), rimless
Rifling type:	four-groove, concentric, RH
Feed type:	belt
Belt capacity:	250 rounds
Rate of fire:	500rd/min
Front sight:	open blade
Backsight:	leaf-and-slider type
Minimum backsight setting:	200yd (182m)
Maximum backsight setting:	2,400yd (2,195m)
Muzzle velocity:	2,850ft/sec (858m/sec)

Machine-Gun, Lewis, Caliber .30, Model of 1917

Synonym:	'US Army Lewis Gun'
Length:	51.75in (1,314mm)
Weight:	25.25lb (11.45kg)
Barrel length:	26.26in (667mm)
Chambering:	.30 (7.62 × 63mm), rimless
Rifling type:	four-groove, concentric, RH
Magazine type:	detachable pan
Magazine capacity:	forty-seven rounds
Rate of fire:	500rd/min
Front sight:	open blade
Backsight:	leaf-and-slider type
Minimum backsight setting:	200yd (182m)
Maximum backsight setting:	2,400yd (2,195m)
Muzzle velocity:	2,830ft/sec (862m/sec)

The M1917 Browning Machine-gun

May 1917 was occupied with the testing of machine-guns, recommended by the commission convened in 1916. The show was stolen by the recoil-operated water-cooled gun designed by John M. Browning on the basis of patents dating back to 1901; ironically, a prototype had been rejected only a few months previously. The performance of the carefully made, belt-fed Browning was sensational: 20,000 rounds were fired at a rate of 600 per minute without a failure, then 20,000 more. Browning then produced a second gun, which was fired continuously until all available ammunition was expended, firing 28,920 shots in a little more than 48 minutes. By the end of the test period, one of the Brownings had fired 396,000 rounds and was still in good working order.

As the Browning was simpler, easier to make, and cheaper than its Vickers or Hotchkiss rivals, it was ordered straight into mass-production. A 15,000-gun contract was let with the Remington–UMC. Colt was given responsibility for preparing the master drawings, delaying the grant of its own 10,000-gun order until October 1917, and finally, in January 1918, 20,000 Browings were ordered from the New England Westinghouse Company. When the Armistice was declared on 11 November 1918, Colt had made about 600 guns, Remington–UMC had contributed 12,000, and Westinghouse had completed 30,150. Assembly continued into 1919 to raise the final total to 68,839.

Service experience revealed the Browning to be an excellent design, and it had soon replaced the Vickers Gun in front-line service. In one of the first 'trials by combat', four M1917 machine-guns fired 52,000 rounds in the mud of the Western Front with only one stoppage. A weakness was eventually discovered in the bottom of the receiver, and this was corrected by simply welding a reinforcing plate onto surviving guns in the 1920s.

Machine-Gun, Browning, Caliber .30, Model of 1917	
Synonym:	'US Army Browning'
Length:	37.5in (952mm)
Weight, gun only:	32.62lb(14.97kg), without water
Weight of tripod:	45.5lb (20.64kg)
Barrel length:	24in (610mm)
Chambering:	.30 (7.62 × 63mm), rimless
Rifling type:	four-groove, concentric, RH
Loading system:	250-round fabric belt
Selector:	none, automatic only
Cyclic rate:	450–600rd/min
Front sight:	open blade
Backsight:	leaf-and-slider type
Minimum backsight setting:	200yd (182m)
Maximum backsight setting:	2,400yd (2,195m)
Muzzle velocity:	2,800ft/sec (853m/sec)

The water-cooled .30 M1917 Browning, introduced in haste, proved to be the best of the First World War machine-guns: simple, sturdy and very reliable. Courtesy of Ian Hogg.

The Marlin Machine-guns

These were variants of the old Browning-patent Colt 'Potato Digger' (M1895) made by the Marlin Firearms Company of New Haven, Connecticut (Marlin Firearms Corporation from 8 December 1915, Marlin-Rockwell Corporation from the autumn of 1916). The 1914-pattern guns, which had finned barrels, were licensed from Colt's Patent Fire Arms Mfg Co., so 12,000 could be supplied to Russia. The order was placed from Britain in the expectation that they could be delivered in 1916. The US Navy purchased 1,605 'Heavy Barrel Colt Machine Guns, Mark V' (serving alongside 400 M1895 Colts converted for the .30 M1906 cartridge) and, eventually, when the US Army entered the war, 2,500 of essentially similar weapons were acquired for training. A few were even used successfully on the Western Front by the Canadian Army before being replaced by Vickers Guns, and others, fitted with cartridge-case catchers, were pressed into service on US warplanes.

In 1916, at the request of the US Navy, Marlin replaced the original radial actuating lever of the M1914 with a straight-line piston system and a new cocking mechanism designed by Carl Swebilius. This resulted in the M1916 aircraft machine-gun. Though many of the parts remained interchangeable with the 1914-pattern ground gun, constant modifications were required to slow the opening of the breech, minimize casehead separations, and reduce the number of extractors broken by the violence of the straight-line action. The M1916 was replaced by the modified M1917 in July 1917, new-type guns being found with mechanical or hydraulic trigger motors above the receiver.

An M1917 ground gun was developed experimentally, with a new pistol-grip incorporating a safety lever, a lightweight receiver and barrel, and a modified gas system. An 1896-type Krag rifle backsight was offset to the left of the breech. There was also an M1918 tank machine-gun, easily identified by its fluted aluminium radiator.

Acquisitions of Marlin machine-guns amounted to 4,105 original 1914-pattern guns, about 38,000 M1916 (scarce) and M1917 (common) aircraft guns, and 2,646 M1918 tank guns. However, by the Armistice only 13,235 M1917 aircraft guns had been delivered, a few hundred being converted into M1918 tank guns before fighting ceased, and it is clear that much of the assembly work continued into 1919.

Another view of the M1917 Browning.

Machine-Gun, Marlin, Caliber .30, Model of 1914	
Synonyms:	'Colt-Marlin machine-gun'
Length:	40in (1,016mm)
Weight:	22.5lb (10.1kg)
Barrel length:	28in (711mm)
Chambering:	.30 (7.62 × 63mm), rimless
Rifling type:	four-groove, concentric, RH
Loading system:	250-round fabric belt
Rate of fire:	600rd/min
Front sight:	open blade
Backsight:	leaf-and-slider type
Minimum backsight setting:	200yd (182m)
Maximum backsight setting:	2,400yd (2,195m)
Muzzle velocity:	2,800ft/sec (853m/sec)

The Pedersen Device

When the USA entered the war, the French immediately viewed them as potential reinforcements for the French sectors of the front line. One of the first reactions was to flood the USA with French 'advisers' keen to inculcate the French view of tactics in the US Army. This caused trouble, and among the greatest problems were attempts to train the American infantrymen in the French 'walking fire' theory. The lack of suitable weapons in the American armoury inspired development of the 'Pedersen Device'.

Developed by John Pedersen with the assistance of Remington engineer Oliver Loomis, working prototypes for the French Lebel, Russian Mosin and US Springfield rifles were readied in 1917. Adapting the M1903 Springfield rifle needed little more than a minor alteration in the cut-off to lock the Pedersen Device in place, the addition of an auxiliary sear in the trigger mechanism, and the cutting of an ejection port through the left side of the receiver. A modified rifle, the Pedersen Device and a magazine for forty 30 M1918 cartridges together weighed merely 10.3lb. The cartridge consisted of a straight-sided case loaded with an 80-grain bullet developing a muzzle velocity of 1,300ft/sec (396m/sec), and was claimed to have an effective range of 350yd (320m). The firer had only to substitute the Pedersen Device for the standard bolt and insert the magazine to transform the M1903 Mark 1 (as the altered rifle was known) into a low-powered semi-automatic. The Device was little more than a blowback pistol, with a 'slide' behind the receiver bridge and a short barrel extending forwards into the chamber.

Tests undertaken in 1918 in the presence of General Pershing convinced the US Army that the new secret weapon, its identity camouflaged as the '.30 Automatic Pistol, Model of 1918', promised great things. An order for 100,000 was given to Remington, to be made in the Bridgeport factory, and was almost immediately extended to 500,000. However, the war ended before any could be delivered.

About 65,000 Pedersen Devices had been made by 1919, and 101,780 rifles were converted in Springfield Armory in 1919–20. Reappraisal then centred on the weaknesses of the system instead of its strengths, and Devices were scrapped in the early 1930s – though the M1903 Mark 1 rifles served until they were worn out. They could be identified by the ejection port in the receiver.

The .30 Browning Automatic Rifle

An alternative to the Pedersen Device, viewing 'walking fire' somewhat differently, was taken by John Browning. On the day that Browning first demonstrated his water-cooled medium machine-gun to the Machine-Gun Board, civilian observers and

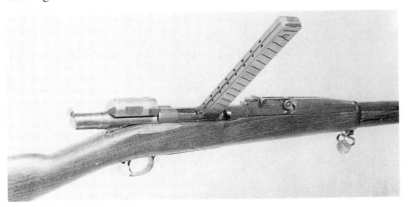

Designed by John Pedersen, the 'US Automatic Pistol, .30, M1918' (the 'Pedersen Device') was really little more than a replacement bolt assembly that transformed the standard .30-06 M1903 rifle into a sub-machine-gun. The only alteration required was an ejection port cut through the left side of the rifle receiver, but the Pedersen Device promised rather more than it delivered and was abandoned before reaching service. Courtesy of Ian Hogg.

The .30 M1918 Browning Automatic Rifle ('BAR'). Courtesy of Ian Hogg.

The BAR, which weighed about 16lb in its original guise, was light enough to be handled by one man – as long as he was reasonably strong.

interested journalists – 27 February 1917 – an automatic rifle prototype was produced. Just like the machine-gun, the rifle passed a flawless test and, after a formal trial, was ordered into series production.

Browning completed development work in collaboration with Colt's Patent Fire Arms Mfg Co., and the Winchester Repeating Arms Company was asked to refine the project for mass-production. The first gas-operated, air-cooled 'Browning Machine Rifle' was completed in February 1918; by Armistice Day, Colt, Winchester, Marlin-Rockwell and an assortment of sub-contractors had assembled 52,000, though only a few thousand ever reached the Western Front. The Brownings first saw action on 3 September 1918. Work continued into 1919, the final total amounting to 102,155; many were subsequently converted to M1918A1 standards, principally by adding a bipod and altering the butt.

The Browning was officially regarded as a semi-automatic support weapon, issued to a few selected men in each squad, with its automatic-fire capability held in reserve. In practice, however, the selector was always set for rapid fire – partly to prevent fumbling for the catch when it mattered most, but also because the cyclic rate was slow enough for an experienced man to fire short bursts or even single shots.

**Machine Rifle, Browning, Caliber .30,
Model of 1918**

Synonyms:	'Browning Automatic Rifle' ('BAR'), and 'Colt Monitor' (postwar commercial/ police version)
Length:	47.05in (1,194mm)
Weight:	16lb (7.26kg) empty, without sling
Barrel length:	24in (610mm)
Chambering:	.30 (7.62 × 63mm), rimless
Rifling type:	four-groove, concentric, RH
Magazine type:	detachable staggered-row box
Magazine capacity:	twenty rounds
Loading system:	loose rounds
Selector:	radial lever on the receiver
Cyclic rate:	about 550rd/min
Front sight:	open blade
Backsight:	pivoting leaf type, with 'battle peep'
Minimum backsight setting:	300yd (274m)
Maximum backsight setting:	2,000yd (1,820m)
Muzzle velocity:	2,805ft/sec (85m/sec)

The Chauchat Machine-gun

Negotiations with the French government gained the US Army 9,592 air-cooled, strip-fed M1914 Hotchkiss medium machine-guns in exchange for the money and raw materials necessary to make new weapons. The Hotchkiss was solid and reliable, as long as the feed strips were kept in good condition, and earned undying fame as the first machine-gun to be used in combat by the American Expeditionary Force (AEF). However, it was gradually replaced by the M1917 Browning.

If the Hotchkiss represented the acceptable face of the arrangement with the French, the CSRG or 8mm Chauchat Machine Rifle was the disaster: simple and comparatively easily made by poorly equipped factories, but possessing a multitude of serious faults. The US Army

acquired 12,864 of the standard 1915-pattern French Chauchats, characterized by their extraordinary semicircular magazine, and then requested a version chambering the .30 M1906 round – a catastrophic error, as the American cartridge was not only much more powerful than the French 8mm pattern, but had different contours. Case sides that were almost parallel did not suit the Chauchat action, which was violent enough with the sharply tapered French cases.

Although 25,000 '.30 M1918 Chauchat Automatic Rifles' were ordered (and, oddly, paid for prior to delivery), so many casehead separations and parts breakages ensued that men virtually refused to fire them. Only about 2,200 guns were issued for training purposes, survivors being scrapped, unmourned, as soon after the Armistice as possible.

**Machine Rifle, Chauchat, Caliber .30,
Model of 1918**

Synonym:	'US Army Chauchat'
Length:	45in (1,143mm)
Weight:	20lb (9.07kg) empty, without sling
Barrel length:	18.5in (469mm)
Chambering:	.30 (7.62 × 63mm), rimless
Rifling type:	four-groove, concentric, RH
Magazine type:	rectangular detachable box
Magazine capacity:	sixteen rounds
Loading system:	loose rounds
Cyclic rate of fire:	300rd/min
Front sight:	open blade
Backsight:	leaf-and-slider type
Minimum backsight setting:	200yd (183m)
Maximum backsight setting:	2,000yd (1,830m)
Muzzle velocity:	2,700ft/sec (822m/sec)

The Berthier Light Machine-gun

In contrast to the Chauchat, the French-designed .30 Berthier Machine Rifle – rejected in 1916 by the British, unwilling to disrupt production of

Carrying SMLE Mk III rifles, with P/1907 sword bayonets fixed, British occupation troops parade through Köln in 1919.

well tried weapons – passed eminently satisfactory trials in the summer of 1917 and was immediately adopted as the 'Model of 1917'.

Unfortunately for Berthier, the inefficiency of the United States Machine-Gun Company prevented progress with a 7,000 gun order (5,000 for the army and 2,000 for the navy). The success of the 1918-pattern Browning Automatic Rifle then so eclipsed the Berthier that the contract was cancelled. Although prototypes of the M1917 worked impressively and would have been unimaginably superior to the Chauchat, the army disliked the top-mounted box magazine. The success of the Browning, which fed from a conventional box beneath the receiver, ensured that top-mounted magazines were unofficially banned from US service.

Bibliography

Ball, Robert W.D., *Mauser Military Rifles of the World* (Krause Publications, Inc., Iola, Wisconsin; 1996).

Banks, Arthur: *A Military Atlas of the First World War* (Heinemann Educational Books Ltd, London; 1975).

Barthorp, Michael: *The Anglo-Boer Wars ('The British and the Afrikaners, 1815-1902')* (Blandford Press, Poole, Dorset; 1987).

Bayly, Dr Christopher ['General Editor']: *Atlas of the British Empire ('A New Perspective on the British Empire from 1500 to the Present')* (The Hamlyn Publishing Group Ltd/Amazon Ltd, London; 1989).

Belfield, Eversley: *The Boer War. Concise Campaigns series* (Leo Cooper Ltd, London; 1974).

Bolotin, David N.: *Soviet Small Arms and Ammunition.* (Finnish Arms Museum Foundation, Hyvinkää, and Handgun Press, Glenview, Illinois; 1996).

British Official Publications: *Hand Book for Officers Under Instruction at the School of Musketry, Hythe.* (HMSO, London; 1863, 1868, 1877 and 1880 editions).
— *Instructions for Armourers ('in the care, repair, browning, etc., of small-arms, machine guns, "parapet" carriages...')* (HMSO, London; 1912).
— *Text Book of Small Arms* (HMSO, London; 1894, 1904 and 1909 editions).
— *Treatise on Military Small Arms and Ammunition ('With the Theory and Motion of a Rifle Bullet. A Text-book for the Army').* (HMSO, London; 1884 and 1888. The 1888 edition was reprinted by Arms & Armour Press, London; 1971).

Brophy, [Lieutenant-Colonel] William S,: *Krag Rifles.* (The Gun Room Press, Highland Park, New Jersey; 1980).
— *The Springfield 1903 Rifles.* (Stackpole Books, Mechanicsburg, Pennsylvania; 1985).

Bruce, Gordon, and Reinhart, Christian (editors): *Webley Revolvers ('Revised from W.C.*

Dowell's *The Webley Story')* (Stocker-Schmidt, Dietikon-Zurich, Switzerland; 1988).

Dowell, William Chipchase: *The Webley Story ('A History of Webley Pistols and Revolvers and the Development of the Pistol Cartridge').* (The Skyrac Press, Kirkgate, Leeds; 1962).

Fuller, Claud E,.: *The Breech-Loader in the Service, 1816-1917.* (N. Flayderman & Co., New Milford, Connecticur; 1965).

Greener, William Wellington: *The Gun and Its Development. Ninth edition. London; 1910* (Reprinted by Arms & Armour Press, London; 1973).
— *Modern Breech Loaders* (Cassell, Petter & Galpin, London; 1871. Reprinted by Greenhill Books, London; 1985).

Haythornthwaite, Philip J.: *The Boer War* (Arms & Armour Press, London; 1987).
— *Victorian Colonial Wars* (Arms & Armour Press, London; 1988).

Hicks, James E.: *French Military Weapons, 1717–1938* (N. Flayderman & Co., New Milford, Connecticut; 1964).

Hobart, F.W.A.: *Pictorial History of the Machine Gun* (Ian Allan Ltd, Shepperton; 1971).

Hogg, Ian V., and Weeks, John S.: *Military Small Arms of the 20th Century ('A comprehensive illustrated encyclopedia of the world's small-calibre firearms')* (Krause Publicastions, Inc., Iola, Wisconsin; seventh edition, 2000).

Honeycutt, Fred L., Jr: *Military Rifles of Japan* (Julin Books, Lake Park, Florida; fourth edition, 1989).

Keegan, John: *The First World War* (Hutchinson, London, 1998; paperback edition, Pimlico, 1999).

Liddell-Hart [Captain] Sir Basil H.: *History of the First World War* (Cassell & Co., London; 1970).

Lloyd, Alan: *The War in the Trenches* (The British at War series. Granada Publishing, London; 1976).

Macdonald, Lyn: *Somme* (Michael Joseph Ltd, London; 1986).

— *The Roses of No Man's Land* (Michael Joseph Ltd, London; 1984).

— *They Called it Passchendaele* (*'The story of the Third Battle of Ypres and of the men who fought in it'*) (Michael Joseph Ltd, London; 1978).

— *1914* (Michael Joseph Ltd, London; 1987).

Markham, George: *Guns of the Empire* (*'Firearms of the British Soldier, 1837-1987'*) (Arms & Armour Press, London; 1990).

— *Japanese Infantry Weapons of World War Two.* (Arms & Armour Press, London; 1976).

Marquiset, Roger, and Lorain , Pierre: *Armes à Feu Françaises Modèles Réglmentarires.* (Published privately in several volumes; 1969–72).

Martin, [Colonel] Jean: *Armes à Feu de l'Armée Française* (Editions Crepin-Leblond, Paris; 1974).

Middlebrook, Martin: *The First Day on the Somme* (Allen Lane, The Penguin Press, London; 1971).

— *The Kaiser's Battle* (*'21 March 1918: the first day of the German Spring Offensive'*) (Allen Lane, The Penguin Press, London; 1978).

Myszkowski, Eugene: *The Remington-Lee Rifle* (Excalibur Publications, Latham, New York; 1994).

Pakenham, Thomas: *The Boer War* (Weidenfeld & Nicholson, London; 1979).

Pitt, Barrie: *1918. The Last Act.* (Cassell & Co., London; 1962).

Poyer, Joe, and Riesch, Craig: *The .45-70 Springfield* (North Cape Publications, Tustin, California; 1991).

Reynolds, Major E.G.B.: *The Lee-Enfield Rifle* (Herbert Jenkins Ltd, London; 1960).

Rogers, Colonel H.C.B., OBE: *Weapons of the British Soldier. The Imperial Services Library, volume V* (Seeley Service & Co. Ltd, London; 1960).

Simone, Gianfranco, Belogi, Ruggero, and Grimaldi, Alessio: *Il 91 (The 1891-pattern Mannlicher-Carcano rifle).* (Editrice Ravizza, Milan; 1970).

Skennerton, Ian: *A Treatise on the Snider* (*'The British Soldier's Firearm, 1866–c.1880'*). (Published by the author, Margate, Queensland, Australia; 1977).

— *Lists of Changes in British War Material* (*'in relation to edged weapons, firearms and associated ammunition and accoutrements'*). In three volumes: *1860-86, 1886-1900* and *1900–10* (Published by the author, Margate, Queensland, Australia; 1976-9).

— *The British Service Lee* (*'Lee-Metford and Lee-Enfield Rifles and Carbines, 1880-1980'*). (Published by the author, Margate, Queensland, Australia, in association with Arms & Armour Press, London; 1982).

Taylerson, A.W.F.: *The Revolver, 1865–1888* (Herbert Jenkins Ltd, London; 1966).

— *The Revolver, 1888–1914* (Barrie & Jenkins, London; 1970).

— with Andrews, R.A.N., and Frith, J.: *The Revolver, 1818–1865* (Herbert Jenkins Ltd, London; 1968).

Temple, B.A., and Skennerton, I.D.: *A Treatise on the British Military Martini* (*'The Martini-Henry, 1869–c.1900'*) (Published privately by B.A. Temple, Burbank, Australia, and in Britain by Arms & Armour Press, London; 1983).

— *A Treatise on the British Military Martini* (*'The .40 and .303 Martinis, 1880–c.1920'*) (Published privately by B.A. Temple, Burbank, Australia, and in Britain by Greenhill Books, London; 1989).

Wahl, Paul, and Toppel, Donald R.: *The Gatling Gun* (Arco Publishing Company, New York; 1965).

Walter, John [editor]: *Guns of the First World War* (*'Rifles, handguns and ammunition, from the Text Book of Small Arms, 1909'*). Greenhill Books, London; 1988.

— *Rifles of the World* (*'The Definitive Illustrated Guide to the World's Centerfire and Rimfire Rifles'*) Krause (Publications, Inc., Iola, Wisconsin; second edition, 1998).

— *The German Rifle* (*'A comprehensive illustrated history of the standard bolt-action designs, 1871–1945'*) (Arms & Armour Press, London; 1979).

Williamson, Harold F.: Winchester. *The Gun that Won the West* (A.S. Barnes & Company, South Brunswick and New York, and Thomas Yoseloff Ltd, London; 1952).

Young, Brigadier Peter, DSO MC MA [with Brigadier Michael Calvert]: *A Dictionary of Battles (1816–1976)* (New English Library, London; 1977).

Index